Re-Imagining Community and Civil Society in Latin America and the Caribbean

Latin American and Caribbean communities and civil societies are undergoing a rapid process of transformation. Instead of pervasive social atomization, political apathy, and hollowed-out democracies, which have become the norm in some parts of the world, this region is witnessing an emerging collaboration between community, civil society, and government that is revitalizing democracy.

This book argues that a key explanation lies in the powerful and positive relationship between community and civil society that exists in the region. The ideas of community and civil society tend to be studied separately, as analytically distinct concepts, however this volume seeks to explore their potential to work together. A unique contribution of the work is the space for dialogue it creates between the social sciences and the humanities. Many of the studies included in the volume are based on primary fieldwork and place-based case studies. Others relate literature, music and film to important theoretical works, providing a new direction in interdisciplinary studies, and highlighting the role that the arts play in community revival and broader processes of social change.

This is a truly multidisciplinary book, bridging established notions of civil society and community through an authentically interdisciplinary approach to the topic.

Gordana Yovanovich is a professor and graduate coordinator for the Latin American and Caribbean Studies program at the University of Guelph, Canada.

Roberta Rice is an assistant professor in political science at the University of Calgary, Canada.

Routledge Studies in Latin American Politics

Re-Imagining Community and Civil Society in Latin America and the Caribbean

Edited by Gordana Yovanovich
and Roberta Rice

Routledge
Taylor & Francis Group

NEW YORK AND LONDON

First published 2017
by Routledge
711 Third Avenue, New York, NY 10017

and by Routledge
2 Park Square, Milton Park, Abingdon, Oxon OX14 4RN

First issued in paperback 2018

Routledge is an imprint of the Taylor & Francis Group, an informa business

Library of Congress Cataloging-in-Publication Data
Names: Yovanovich, Gordana, 1956– | Rice, Roberta, editor.
Title: Re-imagining community and civil society in Latin America and the Caribbean / edited by Gordana Yovanovich and Roberta Rice.
Description: New York, NY : Routledge, 2016. | Series: Routledge studies in Latin American politics ; 13 | Includes bibliographical references and index.
Identifiers: LCCN 2016007463 | ISBN 9781138693371 (hbk)
Subjects: LCSH: Community development–Latin America. | Civil society–Latin America. | Social change–Latin America. | Community development–Caribbean Area. | Civil society–Caribbean Area. | Social change–Caribbean Area. | Communities in literature. | Civil society in literature.
Classification: LCC HN110.5.Z9 C634 2016 |
DDC 307.1/4098611–dc23
LC record available at https://lccn.loc.gov/2016007463

ISBN 13: 978-1-138-59968-0 (pbk)
ISBN 13: 978-1-138-69337-1 (hbk)

Typeset in Sabon
by Wearset Ltd, Boldon, Tyne and Wear

The initial stage of our collaborative interdisciplinary project was supported by the College of Arts at the University of Guelph. We thank the College and all the colleagues who have participated. We were a community of researchers.

GY and RR

Contents

Part I
Concepts

1 Re-Imagining Community and Civil Society

Gordana Yovanovich and Roberta Rice

Following the violent period of the 1970s and 1980s, community and civil society in Latin America and the Caribbean have proven that they can be remarkably resilient and adaptive. They have taken on a wide range of forms, expressions, and activities depending on the sociopolitical context. Since the 1990s, the region's historically fragile civil societies have been bolstered externally by transnational nongovernmental organizations (NGOs) and nurtured internally by community activists as well as by left-leaning governments. To date, the theoretical discussion regarding community has taken place mainly in the context of liberal societies of the United Kingdom and the United States. North American and European scholars have spoken of the 'crisis of community' since the late 1970s owing to massive urbanization, global migration, neighborhood violence, and accelerated advances in technology and general processes of globalization. For example, *The Future of Community: Reports of a Death Greatly Exaggerated* (2008) by Clements et al. suggests that communities in England were deliberately destroyed by governments and other centers of power because communities are or can be places of political resistance.

Intentionally or due to circumstances, community has been shaken in all parts of the Western world. Nevertheless, the 'crisis of community' has not been felt everywhere equally. Regardless of tremendous violence and political turmoil in the 1970s and 1980s, Latin America and the Caribbean did not experience a serious crisis in belonging, despite high levels of economic and political insecurity. There is no doubt that a great deal of willingness to trust was lost in this period, as well as that the feeling of solidarity is less spontaneous today, but the loss was compensated by gains which came through communication and consciousness-raising. It is extremely significant that political and private events have been discussed. This change, we argue, has taken place because communities, which originally served as the basis for civil and political engagement, have been working together with civil societies. Together they have attempted to heal the social fabric, repair state–society relations, and heed the demands of disadvantaged and marginalized groups. In this course, international NGOs and the process of *conscientization* (Freire, 1970) or consciousness-raising have played an important part.

The notion or the phenomenon of *conscientization,* introduced and developed by Brazilian education theorist Paolo Freire in his book *Pedagogy of the Oppressed,* has been important worldwide, but his theories on the role of the oppressed have entered the realm of popular education throughout Latin America. The book, first published in Portuguese in 1968, was translated and re-published in English in 1970, and has been considered one of the foundational texts of critical pedagogy worldwide. As he presents education as a means of consciously shaping an active individual and collectively creating community, Freire calls this process *conscientization,* a term first coined in this book. He evokes the idea of engagement on behalf of the individual, explaining that an individual must have an analytical approach to absorbing information and formulating solutions to social problems. In this case, the learner or the individual is not a passive listener who records information but rather a critical thinker who is changed through complex dialogical processes (Freire, 1970). And, as Bordenave (1977) explains, the *conscientization* of citizens has become the key for participation and social change.

The topics of community and civil society tend to be studied separately, as analytically distinct concepts. The aim of this volume is to study the interrelationship between the two concepts through an interdisciplinary lens. If community and civil society are approached from the point of view of *conscientization,* they have the potential to work together in the pursuit of positive social change, and for this reason, they should be viewed together. In this approach literature has a significant role to play, particularly in how literature narrates civil society and associational life, and in how literature helps us understand the constraints of community, how it leads us to imagine its contours and goals, and how it shows its challenges and confrontations. Works of fiction appeal to the senses in ways that abstract theories and political generalizations cannot (Keren, 2015; Zuckert, 1995). As postcolonial studies have shown, films, novels, and other aesthetic forms provide effective ways to see the world through the eyes of others and they deepen our understanding of otherwise incomprehensible, complex sociopolitical phenomena. They also disseminate ideas regarding civil society and play a role in community revival, thus broadening processes of social change.

Civil society is seen here as the nongovernmental space between the government and the people, while community is understood as a place of cultural sharing, belonging, trust solidarity, mutual support and communication. The chapters on civil society work towards an understanding of the features, forms, and norms of more organized forms of association, whereas the chapters on community examine less structured common cultural practices, congealing functions of collective memory and other aspects of community in light of the changes stirred by globalization. Many of the studies included in the volume rely on primary fieldwork and place-based case studies, while others relate literature, music and film to theoretical works in the social sciences. Works of artistic groups, intellectual associations, and social and political movements map and mediate power relations, and expand the disciplinary boundaries. The humanities, thus, include civic elements—leading the imagination towards what Robert Putnam (1993) would call *civic communities*. In the context of post-1980 Latin America and the Caribbean, this means heterogeneity of associational life.

Recreating Community in Latin America and the Caribbean

In both academic research and the public imagination, there has been a tendency "to romanticize about the quality of life within communities" (Blackshaw, 2010). Since the community is romantic by definition (Oxhorn, Chapter 2) and "an ideal model of an imaginary way of life" (Blackshaw, 2010, 138), its romanticizing, imaginative and emotional dimensions have been perceived as a conflict-prone weakness. However, as Gerard Delanty (2010, 64) explains, "The point about community is not its ability [or inability] to overcome conflicts, but [its ability] to promote values of trust, commitment and solidarity." Since the same values are important in the development of a civil society, the visceral qualities associated with community can serve as a driving force in keeping a community and a civil society alive, while the respect for rules and order emphasized by civil society may control excessive emotive spontaneity associated with community, fostering thus a better "human situation" (Bauman, 2004).

In his opening essay, Philip Oxhorn debates if the notions of community and civil society should be analytically separated, or if the two can be reimagined in a complementary fashion. He suggests that the problematic relationship between civil society and community can be overcome by forming a *thin societal consensus*, and by *social construction of citizenship*. As Robert Nisbet wrote, "in many spheres of thought, the ties of community—real or imagined, traditional or contrived—come to form an image of the good society" (1966, 47). In the process of democratization in Latin America, the goal of civil societies has been to "collectively resist subordination to the state, at the same time demand[ing] inclusion into national political structures" (Oxhorn, 1995, 251–252), but also to maintain the ideal of a general good; as Venezuelan psychology scholar Maritza Montero believes, in a community, members cooperate and show solidarity for the sake of the general good (1998, 212).

It is interesting that the notion of community outside Latin America has been discussed mainly by sociologists, while in Latin America the topic is explored primarily by psychology scholars. Thus, in 1999, Chilean professor of community psychology and clinical psychology, Mariane Krause Jacob wrote that community is associated with three concepts: belonging to, identification with, and interrelation or interdependence. Belonging is *'sentirse parte de'* [to feel yourself as a part of] as well as *'identificado con'* [identified with] a group (Krause, 1999, 55). This group is connected by a vision of the world, an interpretation of daily life: *"una vision del mundo, una interpretación de la vida cotidiana"* (56). As for Delanty, for Krause also communication plays an important role in the creation of community; this common culture—or group—is constructed and re-constructed permanently through communication: *"esta cultura común es construida y reconstruida permanentemente a través de la comunicación"* (56). The notion of interrelation or interdependence, we will see in this volume, also plays an important part in the formation and maintenance of a community.

In her study *"Comunidad, individuo y libertad. El debate filosófico-político sobre una triada (pos)moderna"* (2011), political scientist Georgina Flores Mercedes, another Latin American woman–academic hailing from Mexico, argues that in Latin American culture, community is highly valued because of its belief in *reciprocidad* [reciprocity], which is seen by local groups as *"ayuda mutua"* [mutual aid] not only *"de individuo a individuo y de familia a familia sino también intercomunitariamente"* [from an individual to an individual and from a family to a family but among communities as well]. In the urban environment, she points out, *"la reciprocidad se entiende como solidaridad"* [reciprocity is understood as solidarity/reciprocity is synonymous with solidarity] (Flores Mercado, 2011, 18). The individual participates actively as he or she is *"un elector autónomo de fines, es decir que tiene la capacidad innata de escoger objetivos"* [an independent selector of ends, that is to say, he or she has innate ability to choose his or her goals] (25). As a political scientist, Flores Mercado values the idea of a social contract and believes that Liberalism protects the individual from *"comunidades autoritarias o totalitarismos estatales"* [authoritarian communities or state totalitarianism] (2011, 26). For her, *"la relación explícita que existe entre el individuo y la comunidad es por medio del contrato social … [y] el contrato social implica una elección por las partes contratantes y por lo tanto el ejercicio de la libertad individual"* [The explicit relationship which exists between the individual and the community is that of a social contract … [and] the social contract implies election or choice on the contractor's part and thus the individual freedom] (Flores Mercado, 2011). The Mexican scholar derives many of these ideas from Tony Blackshaw and Michael Taylor, while also quoting works by Emitai Etzioni (1995) and Will Kymlicka (1996), who advocate communitarian ideas in which the group is defined by a common good, despite the individual limitations. To give her work further depth, Flores Mercado quotes Piotr Kropotkin who advocated in the 19th century that solidarity and collective effort are the motor of history (*El apoyo mutuo*, 2009).

Community, as the Oxford dictionary tells us, derives from Latin *communitas* and is divided into *com-unus* or 'together as one' (us against them, as when facing an enemy) and *com-munis* or 'mutual indebtedness.' The notion of community as *com-unus* has been important for marginalized groups for whom community is defined by boundaries on the outside and by the spirit of survival and the strength of cultural heritage on the inside—as this collection will show. Community as mutual support has become less important in the developed world because the economic situation allows independence. However, community as reciprocal appreciation, respect and belonging, or *com-munis*, has been expressed as a need by European and North American sociologists. As Delanty believes, in the developed world, "community is more likely to be expressed in an active search to achieve belonging than in preserving boundaries" (Delanty, 2010, 154).

The question of belonging has become exigent not only because urbanization, massive migration, and advancement of technology have removed us from belonging to traditional communities and their values, but, because since the 1970s, Dave Clements argues in "Faking Civil Society" governments have had "divisive community agendas" (18). According to this British scholar, modern politics has not been promoting "real solidarity" but "coercive participation" in which governments establish their control. Such politics has isolated the individual and has been killing the spirit of association, leading to what Melanie Phillips calls "a spiritual sickness" (Philips, 2005).

In his article "Bowling Alone: America's Declining Social Capital" (1995) and his book *Bowling Alone: The Collapse and Revival of American Community* (2000), Robert Putnam explains how TV has contributed to a "collapse" in communal, group and collective living, and how it has destroyed the feeling of belonging. The disappearance of face-to-face connections, Putnam explains, has led to a general feeling of alienation and unhappiness, a state more individuals experience than this American political scientist ever imagined. Malcolm Gladwell's book *Outliers: The Story of Success* (2008) suggests that not only has watching the TV destroyed the face-to-face connection and weakened the social bonds, but modern media has spread the North American myth regarding the importance of individualism. In his book Gladwell attempts to dispel the notion that success depends solely on our smarts, ambition, hustle and hard work. In his 2008 interview with Donahue he calls the North American ideology of individualism "the biggest misconception."

Before Putnam and Gladwell, in his discussion of the question of community in the United States, Robert Nisbet named the idea of progress and the centralization of the state as other factors which have adversely impacted the community. However, in *The Quest for Community* ([1953] 1969) Nisbet points out that community is "a fusion of feeling and thought, of tradition and commitment, of membership and volition" (Nisbet, 1966, 47–48) implying that feeling, spirituality, spontaneity and nostalgia associated with the notion of community are not incompatible with thought, rules and order associated with civil society. Therefore, collective spirit associated with community may be difficult—but not impossible—to revive in the North, just as thought and order can be brought into violent or disorganized communities in the South. In fact, it will be shown that *concientización* and education have already made significant changes in this direction in Latin America and the Caribbean.

In the process of education, since the 1990s, heterogeneity is favored over singularity, and the relationship of the individual to community is no longer that of fitting and obedience, but is advanced as active participation, negotiation and communication. As Gerard Delanty highlights communication as the mode of building communities, he explains that now "personal self-fulfillment and individualized expressions can be highly compatible with collective participation" (2010, 120). Rejecting "fake" government policies, Dave Clements argues that there is the potential of politics to transform communities for the better, but this can be achieved only by "cultivating a sense of ourselves as robust and truly active citizens able to work together to that end" (Clements, 2008, 22). His position is echoed by Alastair Donald who also argues against a greater amount of regulation. He states that "in order to build communities successfully, human beings must be seen as central positive actors" (Donald, 2008, 35) putting emphasis on human beings as social agents, not on political and philosophical concepts such as democracy and humanity.

The *voluntaristic* position of active engagement and the notion of the 'active' citizen in an 'active' community advanced by mostly British and U.S. sociologists has been contested by Zygmunt Bauman, who disagrees with the notion that modern fragmentation and insecurity can be overcome without major social changes, especially if there is no leadership for such undertaking. The Polish-born scholar of European community shares Jean-François Lyotard's position that the loss of credibility in the *grand récits* such as Christianity, Revolution, or the Hegelian Absolute Spirit has left communities without a fuel, figuratively speaking. The idea of the 'active' participation raises the volunteer's self-esteem (Williams, 2008, 2), but whether it has enough power to move communities forward remains to be seen. Bauman agrees that active participation leads to formation of short-lived "cloakroom communities," as he calls them, which provide "shelter" (Bauman, 2004, 6) and fulfill one of the important requirements of community. But as projects end, the community of active participants ends as well. This, however, does not have to be the case if small communities, working together with civil societies, link themselves to governments. The cases in Latin America seem to be hopeful, and the experiment has yet to be fully developed.

If literature alongside newspapers played an important role in the imagining of community as nation in the 19th century (Anderson, 1982), literature can continue to play an important role in the reimagining of community today. Caribbean writer and critic, Celia Britton, holds onto this notion, arguing that "novels propose their own *models* of community, and while some of these are fairly traditional, others offer a radically different conception" (Britton, 2008, 4). She agrees with Martinican writer, Édouard Glissant, that individuals who belong to a community have to be "autonomous subjects, able to overcome their alienation and instigate social change" (Britton, 2008, 40). She argues further that "happiness derives from psychological strength" and "the individual's ability to endure hardship and recover from despair and madness" (Britton, 2008, 57). In order to achieve this, what is needed above all are "role-models" which literature has the capacity to create. She also suggests "newly formed communities would be defined in terms of their goals rather than their antecedents" (Britton, 2008, 6). Given the past role of literature in the creation of community, particularly in the 19th century, this collection of essays looks at literature again to provide the imagination and educate the reader in modern recreation of communities. Music and film also play an educational function in the creation of a new consciousness or a new worldview in which the individual and the community mutually help each other.

Rethinking Civil Society in the Latin American and Caribbean Context

Civil society occupies the interesting analytical terrain between public and private life. In an expansive project on the topic, Edwards (2011, 4) defined civil society as "the sphere of uncoerced human association between the individual and the state, in which people undertake collective action for normative and substantive purposes, relatively independent of government and the market." The concept of civil society contains both descriptive and normative elements. It describes and envisions a complex and dynamic consortium of nongovernmental organizations (NGOs) which tend to be non-violent, self-organizing, self-reflective, and in a permanent state of tension with each other and with the state institutions that provide the context within which their activities take place (Keane, 1998; Oxhorn & Ducatenzeiler, 1998; Rosenblum & Post, 2001). Political scientists, in particular, have long debated the relationship between civil society and democracy. According to Robert Putnam (1993), there is a strong correlation between the development of effective democratic governance and the existence of a robust associational life in society. A strong civil society is said to nourish democracy from both the demand and the supply side. From the demand side, a well-organized civil society is able to act collectively to achieve its shared goals and to serve as a check on state power. From the supply side, civil society organizations are suggested to enhance democratic institutions by providing an important venue for the learning of democratic habits. The so-called third wave of democracy that swept the Global South, beginning in the mid-1970s, brought with it renewed attention to the role of civil society in building and sustaining democracy in the developing world context (Hagopian & Mainwaring, 2005; Huntington, 1991). Latin America and the Caribbean, which experienced the most extensive and protracted democratization process, have provided fertile ground for examining the relationship between civil society and democracy.

The literature on the democratic transitions of the 1980s and 1990s assumed that democratization and institutional politics would lead to civil society demobilization as social movement struggles were subsumed or displaced by formal institutions (O'Donnell & Schmitter, 1986; Oxhorn,

1994). Social mobilization was expected to increase at the early stages of the democratization process, and then decrease as the political dynamic shifted toward electoral contestation as political parties rose to the forefront of social struggles. In other words, electoral politics were thought to pull activists out of civic arenas and into partisan activities. By the late 1990s and early 2000s, however, Latin America and the Caribbean witnessed a dramatic upsurge in protest activities in response to globalization that culminated in civil society coups which toppled successive national governments in a handful of countries and prompted a region-wide shift to more socially progressive governments (Hershberg & Rosen, 2006; Johnston & Almeida, 2006; Silva, 2009). Rather than flattening communities and civil society, globalization has provoked/caused massive new protest campaigns and associational forms. The debate in the literature has now shifted to address the potential contributions of these new forms and expressions of civil society to the quality and functioning of democracy.

Neoliberal economic reforms have had a dramatic impact on patterns of collective action in Latin America and the Caribbean. Traditional social actors, such as trade union movements, have experienced a substantial decline in their capacity to organize and mobilize politically in the free market context (Kurtz, 2004; Roberts, 1998). The new structural conditions that impede class-based collective action and identities include a reduction in trade union membership, greater informalization of the workforce, and the resultant loss of the centrality of the capital–labor cleavage as the axis of popular mobilization. Nevertheless, while the political and economic strength of organized labor in the region may have evaporated, new forms of social mobilization have emerged to take its place in some countries. Indigenous peoples, in particular, have been at the forefront of popular protests in recent years. Today's major protest events tend to emphasize newly politicized identities, such as ethnic, regional, civic or sectoral identities (Rice, 2012). A key ingredient in the capacity of indigenous communities to mobilize in the current context is their reliance on social capital. Social capital refers to "features of social organization, such as trust, norms, and networks that can improve the efficiency of society by facilitating coordinated actions" (Putnam, 1993, 167). The social capital that is generated by networks of friends, kin and acquaintances is important in helping individuals throughout the world meet their basic needs as well as forming the basis for community organizations that make up civil society (Willis, 2005). The harmful impacts of market reforms in conjunction with the opportunities provided by democratization and pre-existing associational networks have prompted new social actors to enter the civic arena.

To advance our understanding of the multifaceted relationship between community and civil society, especially as they relate to the quality of life and the processes of democratization in Latin America and the Caribbean, this volume adopts an interdisciplinary approach. As such, our work is situated within the aesthetic turn in the social sciences (Keren, 2015; Zuckert, 1995). Scholars seeking to understand incredibly complex social and political

realities have increasingly looked to novels, visual arts, films and other aesthetic representations as new forms of inquiry that may complement and
enrich our analyses. According to Zuckert:

> the questions that led political scientists to look to works of art for
> enlightenment concern the aspects of human life that are most difficult,
> if not impossible, to study and observe externally or objectively—the
> attitudes, emotions, and opinions that shape and are shaped by
> people's circumstances, especially their political circumstances.
>
> (1995, 189)

At the very least, fiction allows us to see the world from another point of
view. The novels and films analyzed in this volume, alongside the more
conventional social scientific studies, augment our understanding of what
appears to be a contingent and unpredictable relationship between civil
society and community. An interdisciplinary perspective enables us to re-
examine anew the concepts of community and civil society at the turn of
the millennium.

The findings of our contributors challenge accepted notions of civil
society in a number of important ways. First, our authors recognize the
heterogeneity of civil society and call for an expanded notion of the
concept. The literature on civil society suggests that associational life is on
the decline—citizens are either showing signs of civic malaise or their capacity to organize and mobilize has been undercut by free market reforms
and social atomization (Kurtz, 2004; Putnam, 2000; Roberts, 1998).
Instead, our case studies point to the rise of new actors (e.g., indigenous
peoples and social entrepreneurs) and new types of associations and forms
of engagement that cross state–society lines and even national borders. In
other words, civil society is more diverse and flexible than traditionally
assumed. Second, the case studies in this volume question the rigid divide
between civil society and the state that has been posited by much of the
literature. Based on liberal norms and expectations, social actors are
viewed as either inside or outside of the polity (Davis, 1999; Tilly, 1978).
In contrast, civil society groups in Latin America have captured spaces
within the state, through top-down as well as bottom-up processes. Third,
our contributors challenge the conventional wisdom that strong and
vibrant civil societies are marked by positive social norms such as high
levels of interpersonal trust, tolerance, and cooperation (Almond & Verba,
1963; Edwards, 2011). In Latin America, relatively strong civil societies
have emerged despite striking levels of poverty and inequality and recent
histories of authoritarianism (Dagnino, 2011; Oxhorn, 2011).

Organization of the Book

The book is organized into four parts. Part I (Chapters 1 and 2) establishes
the conceptual framework of the study. Part II (Chapters 3, 4, 5, 6, and 7)

is dedicated to the study of community. It details the shifting dynamics of Latin American and Caribbean communities under the influences of internationalization and globalization. Part III (Chapters 8, 9, 10, 11, and 12) is dedicated to the study of civil society. It addresses the changing nature of civic participation in the region's democracies. For an appreciation of how fiction contributes to social science inquiries, we suggest that the chapters on community and civil society be read in pairs (e.g., Chapter 3 with Chapter 8, Chapter 4 with Chapter 9, etc.). Part IV (Chapter 13) concludes the volume by re-evaluating community and civil society in Latin America and the Caribbean in light of the findings of our contributors. We call for greater dialogue between the humanities and social sciences.

In the conceptual chapter of this volume (Chapter 2), Philip Oxhorn takes to task the dominant assumption that a high level of interpersonal trust is a prerequisite for the emergence of civil society. The idea in the literature is that civil society should be strong (in terms of the density of associational life in society) as well as civil (in terms of exhibiting positive values and achievements). These characteristics are said to nurture strong democracies. According to Oxhorn, civil society is inherently conflictual in nature. This is particularly the case for societies scarred by high levels of inequality and social exclusion, such as those found in Latin America and the Caribbean. In such circumstances, conflict may be necessary to push for the greater recognition of individual and collective rights. The role of civil society, however, is to mediate conflicts to ensure their non-violent resolution. Violent encounters tend to occur in settings where civil society is weak. Based on his analysis of state reforms intended to strengthen civil society in Bolivia and Brazil, Oxhorn finds that institutional experiments that promote citizenship as agency (as opposed to citizenship as consumption) can result in a profound transformation of civil society. Furthermore, he argues that civil society is the only mechanism capable of mediating conflict in a way that is supportive of democratic inclusion.

The first essay on community (Chapter 3), entitled "Modernized Honor Culture and Community" by Gordana Yovanovich, is based on the study of Gabriel García Márquez's 1980 novel *Chronicle of Death Foretold* or *Crónica de una muerte anunciada*. Yovanovich's analysis sheds light on the ineffectiveness of patriarchal honor structures in the modern world. *Chronicle of Death Foretold* shows the oppressive nature of a traditional community created by its geographical location and Spanish or Hispanic honor culture. For the main female character in the novel, Angela Vicario, community, with its net of constraints, prescriptions and proscriptions, is, as Bauman says, a "nightmare: a vision of hell or prison" (2004, 61). In this short work, with the fragmented narrative line, parody of detective genre, and the use of a magical realist worldview, García Márquez activates the reader to participate in the recreation of the honor culture which is similar to that of classical Rome. In the reimagination of a new relationship between the individual and the community, and in the activation of the individual, women play a major role, but this role is not one of open communication, despite the fact that the main character in the novel writes a thousand letters. Her letters are never opened by the man who returned her to her parents on the day of their wedding because she was not a virgin, but she has earned his trust with her dedication and love, a concept which is now synonymous with the notion of honor. In the reimagined community, love and sexuality of women and men are "the fire in the bones" (Barton, 2001) which moves the community and creates a good society.

In Chapter 4, "Reframing the Archive and Expanding Collective Memory in order to Bridge the Divide between Community and Civil Society," Pablo Ramirez discusses Yxta Maya Murray's *The Conquest* (2003), which illustrates how the Chicana/o community utilizes the archive in order to engage collective memory. Ramirez argues that the text's approach to the archive represents a significant shift for the Chicana/o community. Because archives have traditionally helped in the formation of a national history and the consolidation of political territory, collective memory and the archive therefore represent two opposite approaches to the past that borderland Chicanas and Chicanos often find difficulty in reconciling. *The Conquest*, however, helps the reader imagine a different relation to the past, one that bridges the divide between the archive and collective memory, as well as orality and textuality, by embracing what historian Susan Crane calls "historical consciousness," which represents a middle ground between history (memory that resides in abstract frameworks like chronology) and collective memory (lived experiences). This historical consciousness is established through a borderlands approach to an ethics of reading in which the act of reinterpretation can allow the Chicana/o community to appropriate the archive for their own political ends.

In Chapter 5, "Memory and Temporary Communities in Laura Restrepo's *The Dark Bride/La novia oscura*," authors Maca Suazo and Lisa Bellstedt explore how different types of communities are formed. They argue that while the communities in the novel are fictitious, they characterize communities that have existed in Colombia's history. They are communities formed around places of work, and are temporary because they last as long as companies find the work profitable. Suazo and Bellstedt explain the formation of communities among workers at the foreign-owned petroleum plant, and among the prostitutes in La Catunga neighborhood. They discuss the relationships between the three main characters in the novel, and point to the oppression their community faces at the hands of the Colombian government, the Tropical Oil Company, and Colombia's military forces. Suazo and Bellstedt conclude that while communities are built on the bases of similar experience, they do not exist for long, given that solidarity between workers and prostitutes is threatened by centers of power which do not favor group activities. The novel takes us inside the emotional life of the community and shows many of the challenges that marginalized communities face.

In Chapter 6, "Community and Learning: The Process of *Conscientiza-tion* among Nicaraguan Peasants through Song," Mery Perez discusses the transformation of a small community of peasants located in the southeast area of Lake Nicaragua prior to the Nicaraguan revolution. In her discussion of the community, Perez expands the idea of *conscientization* introduced by Paolo Freire (1970) by referring to the work of U.S. scholar Etienne Wenger (2000) who used Freire's notion to create the idea of *community of practice* and *social learning*. Perez explains how the small Nicaraguan community is turned into a community of practice with the arrival of Ernesto Cardenal, a Nicaraguan poet nominated for the 2005 Nobel Prize in literature, a Liberation Theology priest, and Nicaragua's minister of culture from 1979 to 1987 at the time when Pope Paul II visited Nicaragua and publicly chastised him for his disagreement with the Catholic church. Cardenal started with faith-sharing, reading of the Bible, and participation in music-playing which led community members to become aware of their social reality. The music of *Misa Campesina* or the Peasant Mass, written by Nicaraguan musician, composer and singer Carlos Mejía Godoy, incorporated local musical instruments and familiar song form in its reinterpretation of readings from the Bible. This played an effective role in the education of peasants and in changing the community from the inside out.

In Chapter 7, "Community and the State: Piecing Together Differences in Alejandro Brugués' *Juan of the Dead*," Miharu Miyasaka and Patrick Horrigan discuss why the horror film genre was used, given that the genre was not common in Cuba's post-1959 'realist' cinema, as monsters had nearly vanished from the national audiovisual imagination. In Brugués' 2011 film there is a confrontation between 'cultural zombies,' the majority of individuals who have been made sleepwalkers by the powerful Cuban state, and 'zombie ghouls' or outsiders who attack local zombies. The confrontation awakens the individual, but it also shows that survival is dependent upon individuals' abilities to draw together, be it as business associates, family members, or through friendship. Miyasaka and Horrigan relate the content of the film to the experience of Alejandro Brugués and his community of filmmakers who had to negotiate with the Cuban state, as well as to use familiar Hollywood film genres to appeal to an international audience in order to realize their artistic production. Without being antagonistic to the state, the filmmakers develop serious negotiation strategies, and succeed because they act as a community. Similarly, in the film, the characters in *Juan of the Dead* embrace a mindset of inclusiveness and negotiation. The paper explores notions of community and the power of individual and collective action, showing how the two groups were able to overcome their obstacles, as they engaged in community-building and strategic negotiation.

In Chapter 8, the first essay on civil society, entitled "Intercultural Democracy and Civil Society Participation in the New, Decolonized Bolivia," Roberta Rice examines indigenous and participatory governance innovation in Bolivia under the country's first indigenous head of state. In this case, civil society actors captured state power through a social movement–party led by President Evo Morales. Rice argues that the incorporation of civil society actors into the structures of the state has produced a more meaningful form of democracy, one that is custom fitted to Bolivia's indigenous-majority population. Instead of undermining representative democracy, the introduction of elements of direct, participatory, and communitarian democracy has broadened and deepened Bolivian democracy by making it more inclusive and the government more responsive and representative. The chapter also reveals some of the challenges of reconciling the government's programs and policies with indigenous peoples' demands and expectations for change. Nevertheless, the extension of the political sphere towards civil society, which has blurred the lines between the state and society, is suggested to have improved state–society relations. Both Rice (Chapter 8) and Yovanovich (Chapter 3) shine a light on the devastating impacts of colonial values and practices on the lives of vulnerable community members and the efforts to uproot racism and patriarchy in the region.

In Chapter 9, "Conceptualizing Transnational Civil Society in Guatemala," Candace Johnson demonstrates the incredibly complex nature of civil society in post-conflict Guatemala and its reliance on domestic and international nongovernmental organizations (NGOs) to function. In countries such as Guatemala, where the state is largely absent from indigenous citizens' lives, NGOs assume the role of interest intermediary between the state and society. They serve both state-like and societal functions. Guatemalan civil society has emerged on the basis of this externally-generated social capital. The unique transnational configuration of civil society in Guatemala is completely overlooked by analysts who are preoccupied with territorial-based, grassroots expressions of associational life. Based on conventional metrics, Guatemalan civil society is practically non-existent. Johnson argues that important developments are missed when the multiscalar dynamics of civil society resistance and engagement are not taken into account. Her analysis reveals how and why civil society looks different in different contexts. In a broadly similar dynamic to the work of Ramirez (Chapter 4), Johnson shows the necessity for local communities and civil societies to work with the established order and international organizations in today's globalized world. This borderland reality enriches the individual and empowers groups, be they Latina/o communities in the United States or indigenous communities in Guatemala.

In Chapter 10, "Collective Banks and Counter-Acts," Caroline Shenaz Hossein shows how, in the cases of Jamaica and Guyana, Afro-Caribbean women from marginalized communities are working to build civil society from within by organizing and managing informal banking cooperatives. These self-help initiatives cater expressly to those who are excluded from the state and the market. The 'banker ladies' pool the resources of the urban poor so as to enable residents to meet their basic needs and improve their life chances. They do so by drawing on historically and culturally rooted saving and lending practices that can be traced back to slave times. In the context of extreme political and economic exclusion, the social economy may serve to increase solidarity among some of society's most vulnerable members. Her work illustrates how civil society can take hold even in the most unlikely of places, provided that there are agents of social change present. She pushes us to consider cultural forms of social capital and to adopt a historically specific approach to understanding civil society. The chapters by Hossein (Chapter 10) and by Suazo and Bellstedt (Chapter 5) show that solidarity is an essential element in both community and civil society-building. They also demonstrate that hardship increases solidarity among marginalized individuals, and suggest that although communities of the marginalized are often short-lived and temporary, they are a means of survival while they last, particularly for women.

In Chapter 11, "War on Civil Society in Vargas Llosa's *The War of the End of the World*," Olga Nedvyga analyzes where in Latin America that civil society can be found and what social forces block its development. She studies Vargas Llosa's novel from the point of view of Hegel's distinction between state and civil society and the German philosopher's promotion of a more inclusive state in which reason and passions and interests of civil society are integrated. The Peruvian novelist retells the story of the War of Canudos in late 19th-century Brazil, the country's deadliest civil war, which saw the state pitted against society. The conflict resulted in the annihilation of a self-governed commune in northeastern Brazil that was founded by religious leader and preacher, Antônio Conselheiro. Nedvyga shows that the state's granting of citizenship rights only to those in support of the governing regime resulted in the eventual targeting of the Canudos commune which was perceived as a threat to the consolidation of the modern Brazilian state. The commune, as an enclosed, self-sufficient space removed from regional and national politics, is depicted by Vargas Llosa in his novel as a doomed form of civil society organization in the face of direct and violent interventions on the part of the state. Based on Vargas Llosa's account, many contemporary problems in Latin America are rooted in the region's confrontational state–society relations. The chapters by Nedvya (Chapter 11) and Perez (Chapter 6) discuss similar religious communities led by strong leaders. However, depending on the leader's relationship to the state or large institutions such as the church, the communities experience different destinies. In the Brazilian case, the isolation of the small religious community leads to stagnation and ultimate destruction. In the Nicaraguan case, a different interpretation of the Bible distances Ernesto Cardenal from the Pope, but the community not only survives but is enriched and becomes a part of the state.

In Chapter 12, " 'Radical' Participatory Democracy Institutions in Venezuela and Ecuador," Pascal Lupien questions whether top-down inclusion by the region's progressive governments strengthens or undermines authentic expressions of civil society. Local participatory mechanisms, such as Venezuela's community councils and Ecuador's citizens' assemblies, allow citizens to participate in the democratic process through institutions that are both connected to, yet somewhat autonomous from, the state. The author finds that the inherent contradiction between autonomy and inclusion that is embedded in state-sanctioned channels of participation can produce a measure of empowerment and cooptation. In other words, institutions for participatory democracy in Venezuela and Ecuador provide for the devolution of decision-making powers to citizens at the same time that they circumscribe civil society's capacity to organize and mobilize for change outside of approved channels. Lupien argues that such an institutional configuration, while divergent from the dominant liberal conception of democracy, may be more appropriate to this particular time and place. The chapter also suggests that civil society may be more versatile than is conventionally assumed. Lupien's study, alongside that of Miyasaka and Horrigan (Chapter 7), casts considerable doubt on the assertion that there is a strict divide between the state and civil society. In these cases, national governments have promoted community and civil society engagement by engineering participatory spaces within the state.

References

Almond, Gabriel A., & Sidney Verba. 1963. *The civic culture: political attitudes and democracy in five nations*. Princeton: Princeton University Press.

Anderson, Benedict. 1991. *Imagined communities: reflections on the origin and spread of nationalism*. London and New York: Verso.

Bauman, Zygmunt. 2004. In B. Vecchi (Ed.). *Identity: conversations with Benedetto Vecchi*. Cambridge: Polity Press.

Blackshaw, Tony. 2010. *Key concepts in community studies*. London: Sage Publications.

Bordenave, J. (1977). "Communication Theory and Rural Development: A Brief overview." In A. Gumucio Dagron & T. Tufte (Eds.). (2006). *Communication for social change anthology: historical and contemporary readings*. (133–141). South Orange, NJ: Communication for Social Change Consortium.

Britton, Celia. 2008. *The sense of community in French Caribbean fiction*. Liverpool: Liverpool University Press.

Clements, Dave, Donald, Alastair, Martin Earnshaw, & Austin Williams. 2008. *The future of community: reports of a death greatly exaggerated*. London: Pluto Press.

Cohen, Anthony P.1985. *The symbolic construction of community*. London: Tavistock Publications.

Dagnino, Evelina. 2011. "Civil Society in Latin America." In M. Edwards (Ed.) *The Oxford handbook of civil society*. New York: Oxford University Press.

Davis, Diane E. 1999. "The Power of Distance: Re-theorizing Social Movements in Latin America." *Theory and Society* 28(4), 585–638.

Delanty, Gerard. 2010. *Community*. New York: Routledge.

Edwards, Michael. 2011. "Conclusion: Civil Society as a Necessary and Necessarily Contested Idea." In M. Edwards (Ed.) *The Oxford handbook of civil society*. New York: Oxford University Press.

Edwards, Michael. 2011. "Introduction: Civil Society and the Geometry of Human Relations." In M. Edwards (Ed.) *The Oxford handbook of civil society*. New York: Oxford University Press.

Flores Mercado, Georgina. 2011. *Comunidad, individuo y libertad*. TRAMAS 34, UAM-X México, 15–46.

Freire, Paolo. 1993. *Pedagogy of the oppressed*. New York: Continuum.

Gladwell, Malcom. 2008. *Outliers: the story of success*. New York: Little, Brown and Company.

Hagopian, Frances, & Scott Mainwaring (Eds.). 2005. *The third wave of democratization in Latin America*. Cambridge: Cambridge University Press.

Hershberg, Eric, & Fred Rosen (Eds.). 2006. *Latin America after neoliberalism: turning the tide in the twenty-first century?* New York: The New Press.

Huntington, Samuel P. 1991. *The third wave: democratization in the late twentieth century*. Norman: University of Oklahoma Press.

Johnston, Hank, & Paul Almeida (Eds.). 2006. *Latin American social movements: globalization, democratization, and transnational networks*. Lanham, MD: Rowman and Littlefield.

Keane, John. 1998. *Civil society: old images, new visions*. Stanford: Stanford University Press.

Keren, Michael. 2015. *Politics and literature at the turn of the millennium*. Calgary: University of Calgary Press.

Krause Jacob, Mariane. 1999. "Hacia una Redefinición del Concepto de Comunidad-Cuatro Ejes para un Análisis Crítico y una Propuesta." *Revista de Psicología de la Universidad de Chile*, Vol. X, No. 2, 49–60.

Kurtz, Marcus J. 2004. "The Dilemmas of Democracy in the Open Economy: Lessons from Latin America." *World Politics* 56(2), 262–302.

Montero, Maritza. 1994. *Psicología social comunitaria: teoría, método y experiencia*. Universidad de Guadalajara.

Nisbet, Robert A. 1966. *The sociological tradition*. New York: Basic Books Publishers.

O'Donnell, Guillermo, & Philippe C. Schmitter. 1986. *Transitions from authoritarian rule: tentative conclusions about uncertain democracies*. Baltimore: Johns Hopkins University Press.

Oxhorn, Philip. 1994. "Where Did All the Protesters Go? Popular Mobilization and the Transition to Democracy in Chile." *Latin American Perspectives* 21(3), 49–68.

Oxhorn, Philip. 1995. "From Controlled Inclusion to Coerced Marginalization: The Struggle for Civil Society in Latin America." In J. Hall (Ed.) *Civil society: theory, history and comparison* (250–77). Cambridge: Polity Press.

Oxhorn, Philip & Graciela Ducatenzeiler (Eds.). 1998. *What kind of democracy? What kind of market? Latin America in the age of neoliberalism*. Pittsburgh: Pennsylvania State University.

Oxhorn, Philip. 2011. *Sustaining civil society: economic change, democracy and the social construction of citizenship in Latin America*. University Park: The Pennsylvania State University Press.

Putnam, Robert D. 1993. *Making democracy work: civic traditions in modern Italy*. Princeton: Princetown University Press.

Putnam, Robert D. 2000. *Bowling alone: the collapse and revival of American community*. New York: Simon & Schuster.

Rice, Roberta. 2012. *The new politics of protest: indigenous mobilization in Latin America's neoliberal era*. Tucson: University of Arizona Press.

Roberts, Kenneth M. 1998. *Deepening democracy? The modern left and social movements in Chile and Peru.* Stanford: Stanford University Press.

Rosenblum, Nancy L., & Robert C. Post (Eds.). 2001. *Civil society and government.* New Jersey: Princeton University Press.

Rosman, Silvia Nora. 2003. *Being in common: nation, subject, and community in Latin American literature and culture.* Lewisburg: Bucknell University Press; London: Associated University Press.

Silva, Eduardo. 2009. *Challenging neoliberalism in Latin America.* New York: Cambridge University Press.

Smith, Dennis. 1999. *Zygmunt Bauman, prophet of post modernity.* Cambridge: Polity Press.

Taylor, Michael. 1982. *Community, anarchy and liberty.* Cambridge: Cambridge University Press.

Tilly, Charles. 1978. *From mobilization to revolution.* Reading: Addison-Wesley.

Wenger, Etienne. 2000. "Communities of practice and social learning systems." *Organization,* 7(2), 225–246.

Willis, Katie. 2005. *Theories and practices of development.* New York: Routledge.

Zuckert, Catherine. 1995. "Why Political Scientists want to Study Literature." *PS: Political Science and Politics* 28(2), 189–190.

2 Civil Society from the Inside Out

Community, Organization and the Challenge of Political Influence[1]

Philip Oxhorn

There is a tendency, in both academic research and the public imagination, to romanticize about the quality of life within communities. Frequently, communities are portrayed as models for peaceful, conflict-free social relations. This is true particularly when such communities are poor or otherwise marginalized, such as indigenous people, where the quality of interpersonal relations seems to become the last recourse for groups otherwise lacking in resources and political influence, harking back to earlier times before the advent of colonialism or the impoverishment associated with market economies. This is ironic because it implicitly suggests that under what are often the worst of circumstances, people can put aside normal human foibles, thrive on diversity, reach consensus without significant contention, and offer alternatives that will serve as new ideals for the organization of the very societies which have dispossessed them of power and influence.

The experience of a soup kitchen in a Chilean slum during the dictatorship of Augusto Pinochet in the mid-1980s provides sad example of this irony.[2] The soup kitchen was one of the oldest in Santiago, having emerged in the depths of the economic collapse in the early 1980s. It was located in one of the most organized shantytowns, with a high level of participation in the social protests that began in 1983. Over the years, in addition to successfully feeding the families of its members, the soup kitchen organized a variety of complimentary activities for its members, and it was an important actor in the larger shantytown community. Much of the soup kitchen's success was directly attributable to "Olga," the elderly widow who founded the soup kitchen and became a prominent community leader.

More generally, the shantytown enjoyed a strong sense of community that was reinforced by a number of factors, including the participation of different organizations like the soup kitchen in numerous public events intended to promote a veritable celebration of the shantytown's collective identity. A shared history of collective struggle, starting with the land seizure that founded the shantytown in the 1950s and continuing on through the social protests of the mid-1980s, the ubiquitous experience of repression in the midst of poverty, and a common 'enemy' in the form of the military regime all seemed to unite the community vis-à-vis external threats. Dominated by the Communist Party (PC), which had organized the land seizure in 1957, the shantytown even benefitted from a shared world view regarding social justice and the absence of significant political alternatives. In other words, as a shantytown characterized by a high level of social organization, shared experiences dating back decades, clear common interests, and a high level of socioeconomic and political homogeneity, it provided a fertile foundation for a strong sense of 'community' that was encapsulated in and deliberately nurtured by organizations like the soup kitchen.

Despite this, any sense of community was actually quite fragile. Political tensions between the PC and other opposition parties began to mount with the winding down of the protests in the second half of 1986, resulting in the increasing political marginalization of the PC. In this context, when a donation from Europe was received by the soup kitchen, the sense of 'community' quickly began to dissolve, as people both inside and outside of the organization began to question how the money was used. The lack of transparency in how the money was spent only added to people's suspicions since it was assumed something was being covered up, even though most objective observers familiar with the situation found no evidence of wrongdoing. This, in turn, ultimately led to the soup kitchen's demise and the ostracization of Olga by the same 'community' that she had worked so hard to strengthen.[3] Instead of further strengthening both the organization and the community which it served, the unexpected economic windfall caused the community to, in effect, turn on itself. What went wrong?

This chapter will argue that while the foundation for the inclusionary, democratic ideals typified by a romantic view of community can be found in many contexts, there is an inevitable tension between such ideals, on the one hand, and sources of conflict within communities, including the inevitable inequalities associated with grassroots participatory experiences more generally, and the danger of antagonistic relations with 'other' communities. To resolve this tension, the ideal of community must be analytically separated from the concept of civil society. While the two are often seen as synonymous, their relationship can be quite problematic in practice. In particular, a strong sense of community is neither a necessary nor sufficient condition for the existence of civil society. Strong communities under some circumstances can actually subvert the possibility of a strong civil society. Conversely, through the emergence of autonomous organizations and an explicit recognition of the centrality of conflict in social relations, rather than its denial, civil society's strength ultimately reflects how successfully this tension is resolved. This, in turn, determines the capacity of any modern society to achieve the ideals of 'community.'

The chapter is organized as follows: after providing a conceptual discussion of what civil society is, the dynamics that determine the relationship between civil society and community are analyzed. A third section then discusses how the problematic relationship between civil society and communities can be overcome in terms of what I refer to as a *thin societal consensus* and the way in which both civil society and communities contribute to the *social construction of citizenship*. This is then applied to case studies of participatory reforms in Bolivia and Brazil. The implications of this for democracy are discussed in the concluding section.

Defining Civil Society: A Collectivist Perspective

While most would agree that civil society can play a vital role in democratization processes, there is still no consensus on what that role is, whether it is necessarily a positive one, or even what civil society actually consists of. Yet alternative perspectives have important implications for understanding the potential of civil society to contribute to democratization. This is particularly true when trying to understand civil society in Latin America, where both civil society and democracy have been historically fragile. Although few would deny this historic fragility, there are important disagreements regarding why this has been the case, with significant implications for understanding the prospects of democracy and civil society in the region. It is therefore essential that an appropriate conceptualization of civil society be adopted.

For the purposes of this chapter, civil society is defined as:

> the social fabric formed by a multiplicity of self-constituted territorially- and functionally-based units which peacefully coexist and collectively resist subordination to the state, at the same time that they demand inclusion into national political structures.
>
> (Oxhorn, 1995a, 251–252)

This definition reflects a collectivist approach that emphasizes the importance of organization and power relations. In particular, strong civil societies reflect the capacity of disadvantaged and marginalized groups to organize themselves. It is through this autonomous organization that groups can define and defend their collective interests and priorities in competition with other actors within civil society, as well as in interactions between civil society organizations and the state.[4] This, in turn, implies that civil society has an important role to play in promoting more inclusionary democracies (Habermas, 1992) by demanding respect for both individual and collective rights (a point I will emphasize when discussing the social construction of citizenship below), and that the weakness of civil society in Latin America is one reason for the region's notorious historical problems of inequality and socioeconomic exclusion.

It is important to emphasize that while poverty and exclusion themselves can be important obstacles to the emergence of strong civil societies, it would be a mistake to assume that they are insurmountable. This is why a collectivist perspective is essential for understanding civil society's potential. Organization and collective action, by taking advantage of the sheer numbers of people who are disadvantaged and their shared interests, are the principal resources that potentially are at the disposal of poor, marginalized groups in order to seek redress for their exclusion. For example, organized labor's demands contributed to the emergence of welfare states and democracy in both North and Latin America (Rueschemeyer et al., 1992), much in the same way that the emergence of women's movements across the globe have, since the 1960s, led to the adoption of a myriad of policies promoting greater gender equality. Without sufficient pressure for change from society itself, at best reforms will be partial, creating new forms of inequality, and conditional at the discretion of those elites benefitting most from the existing structure of society—a point I will return to when discussing citizenship.

At the heart of this perspective is the inevitability of conflict in modern societies. Societies are too complex and involve such a myriad of alternatives and issues that it would be naïve to assume otherwise. People have multiple identities and interests, and the strength of civil society mirrors this complexity in its own rich mix of organizations, which are both functionally based (e.g., trade unions) and territorially based (e.g., neighborhood councils). Whereas modernization theory lauded this multiplicity by implying it led to cross-cutting cleaves, consensus and the minimization, if not elimination, of conflict as a key driver of politics (Lipset, 1960), the collectivist perspective on civil society being espoused here emphasizes the continued importance of conflict, particularly in societies marked by high levels of inequality and social exclusion. The social fabric that defines strong civil societies needs to be diverse to capture the complexities of exclusion and ensure that those who are marginalized or disadvantaged have a role to play in deciding political outcomes. If 'modern' societies thus appear to be non-conflictual, it is because of the role civil society plays in mediating conflict in relatively peaceful ways, not because conflict is absent. "History" never ends (cf. Fukuyama, 1989), but constantly evolves as new issues enter public debate and/or new groups organize and become politically active.

Similarly, if conflict is inevitable, its consequences are not. This is in part because civil society is an important mechanism for non-violent conflict resolution. By any definition, violence should be seen as antithetical to the norms underpinning civil society. It is a direct threat to the autonomy of competing groups, including their very existence, whether it be promoted by the state or from within society. Whatever the adjective 'civil' implies when referring to civil society, at a minimum it refers to the recognized right of others to coexist—a point I will return to below. Conversely, weak civil societies leave few alternatives to tacitly tolerating subordination (i.e., submission) or civil war, as societies move toward polarization between those who benefit from the status quo and those who are subjected to it—the so-called 'haves' and 'have-nots.'[5] Revolutionary struggles and civil war are extreme examples of this. In such cases, organized societal actors can be quite strong, particularly in the case of successful revolutionary struggles. But this is distinct from the kinds of organizations associated with civil society. In addition to resorting to violence, such groups have as their goal the capture of the state. Such political hegemony is antithetical to the conceptualization of civil society used here, since it deliberately denies the possibility of competition among different actors for political power and, at least in all examples to date, is associated with the subordination of society by the state.

The fact that civil society organizations are self-constituted and enjoy a certain level of autonomy vis-à-vis other actors, particularly the state, implies that these organizations effectively represent their members. It is this representational dimension that gives these organizations legitimacy not only for their respective members, but also for other actors. This, in turn, means organizations can be effective interlocutors for important segments of a country's population in relations with other civil society actors in the state. Their roots in society and connections with their members are a form of power that is difficult to ignore as the organization grows in size and/or mobilizational capacity. Conversely, other actors can expect that the decisions made by the organization's leadership on behalf of its members will be respected by their members, which means that negotiations with such organizations are not only worth pursuing, but essential for maintaining social peace. Weak organizations or organizations that exist in name only cannot fill this role as interlocutor, undermining civil society's capacity to mediate conflict. This was the challenge the soup kitchen discussed above ultimately was unable to meet, despite an impressive track record of providing needed goods and services to its community.

The specific example of the soup kitchen and the inherently conflictual nature of civil society provide an important perspective on the role of 'trust' in civil society. In the case of the soup kitchen, people ultimately did not trust Olga—even though one might have expected the opposite, given her record of community service. In the case of civil society more generally, it would seem naïve to assume that high levels of trust would exist between groups, recognizing that they are likely to disagree on significant issues. This is important, because if trust is necessary for a strong civil society, as many have argued (e.g., Almond & Verba, 1963), then many developing countries cannot even aspire to having a strong civil society, given very low levels of inter-personal trust, particularly in Latin America (Lagos, 1997). The roots of this are less cultural than practical. Years of authoritarian rule and repression have taught people that too much 'trust' can be a dangerous thing.[6] In the context of high levels of inequality, the contradictory interests of different actors are all the more apparent, making trust problematic even in the context of political democracy and markedly reduced political repression.

Rather than rule out the possibility of a strong civil society, a collectivist approach suggests that when trust is absent or, as in the case of the soup kitchen, fragile and ephemeral, civil society is most needed. This because the organizations that compose civil society can be an effective mechanism for limiting the consequences of distrust internally, and for mediating relations among various social sectors that do not trust one another. As demonstrated by the example of the soup kitchen, growing levels of distrust belied what appeared to be a strong organization; the soup kitchen could not successfully mediate conflict once it surfaced within the organization. Other actors, similarly, were unable to help, despite the fact that such external assistance, especially from the Catholic Church, served as an important facilitator for the growth of civil society under the Pinochet dictatorship by providing a variety of forms of assistance, including training on conflict mediation (Oxhorn, 1995b).

Ironically, the lack of trust might even provide the best incentive to involve oneself in the creation of strong civil society organizations. If people are not confident that the decisions made by others will reflect their interests, then they have much to gain by organizing to demand their inclusion in decision-making processes. This is why workers began to organize in the late 19th and early 20th century, and the same could be said for most other civil society organizations representing disadvantaged and marginalized groups. Conversely, a high level of trust in the decisions of others implies that participation would not lead to different outcomes, which obviously would lessen the imperative for committing time and other resources to building civil society organizations. As Dankwart Rustow (1970, 362) points out with reference to democratic transitions, "A people who were not in conflict about some rather fundamental matter would have little need to devise democracy's elaborate rules for conflict resolution." The same is perhaps even truer for civil society organizations.

Before discussing community, it is important to examine an alternative *liberal perspective* on civil society. Drawing its inspiration from the work of philosophers John Locke and Alexis de Tocqueville,[7] the liberal perspective is increasingly dominant in the literature. 'Liberal' societies, principally the United Kingdom and the United States, come to represent the ideal of civil society (Seligman, 1992), in much the same way that these two cases represent the ideal for modernization theories. In sharp contrast with the collectivist perspective, civil society is defined in terms of individual rights and obligations. Rational individuals who decide to live together to further private, individual interests create civil society. Individual freedom is valued above all, and this requires the rule of law and respect for private property. Membership in any group becomes a function of interest maximization. Groups and group identities lose any sense of intrinsic value, while the exclusive focus on the individual has meant the concomitant marginalization of perspectives focusing more on collectivities and group identities, not to mention collective rights. Voluntarism and the absence of coercion, in turn, historically have justified unequal status by restricting citizenship rights for those who are defined as incompetent or dependent (such as women, youths, illiterates, indigenous people, the poor, and the working class).

Although it is never very clear how liberal, individualist values become predominant, particularly the high levels of interpersonal trust which are seen as pivotal in order for people to organize and form vibrant civil societies, at a minimum, their presence at the level of society is seen as a prerequisite for civil society's emergence (Almond & Verba, 1963; Fukuyama, 2001; Gellner, 1991; Shils, 1991). Because of the lack of any intrinsic value attributed to group and organizational identities stemming from the focus on individuals, an appropriate political culture in effect becomes synonymous with civil society itself; its absence is seen as precluding civil society's emergence, while an appropriate political culture presumes its existence.

This focus on the normative dimension of civil society has important analytical consequences. The requisites for a highly organized, vibrant civil society are actually quite high. This is because the liberal perspective deliberately posits a *thick* notion of the consensual basis for civil society's emergence. Conflict is assumed away because there are no fundamental disagreements among citizens living in what are seen as 'modern' societies. Moreover, this thick consensus is equated with a narrow set of Western values and unique cultural experiences. For societies that do not share (or necessarily want to share) those values and have been victimized by that history, such as most Latin American and African countries, or non-Western indigenous cultures emphasizing the collective nature of rights, such a conception of civil society is extremely alienating (Hann, 1996). In fact, disputes over competing norms and worldviews that challenge the individualism and other values associated with liberal societies are seen as anachronistic, more relevant for pre-modern times than the urban industrial societies that emerged as the epitome of 'development' in the West.

This thick notion of societal consensus is obviously consistent with the historical fact that strong civil societies, as identified by the collectivist perspective, have been relatively rare and have been most closely associated with the development of Western (and now democratic) countries. Viewed this way, civil society would be expected to remain more aspirational than real in most contexts. Yet the alleged reasons for this are antithetical to a collectivist perspective and deny the centrality of conflict for understanding modern politics and civil society's role. In other words, the problem is not that the 'bar' for entering what is a rather exclusive club is so high, but the way in which that bar is set. Conflict, which is essential to understanding the role civil society plays from a collectivist perspective, is simply assumed to be non-existent in contexts marked by strong civil societies. This is not only irrelevant for much of the world, it is ahistorical in its understanding of how Western countries themselves developed modern welfare states and consolidated democratic regimes.

Communities and Civil Society: The Ambiguous Link

Ironically, the ideal of a thick social consensus is central to how 'community' is generally understood. While the nature of the values associated with any particular community will be open-ended compared to the liberal ideals associated with predominant understandings of civil society, only a 'community' could hope to enjoy the kind of deep bonds that would unite its members and potentially eliminate conflict from everyday social and political life. Whether communities are defined geographically, culturally, socially, linguistically, religiously, racially, and/or ethnically, high levels of trust, shared experiences and beliefs, the implicit level of homogeneity would serve as the foundation for thick social consensus. The irony is that those communities which are most likely to live up to this ideal—indigenous, religious, ethnic, and linguistic communities, to name just the most obvious—are also the same kinds of communities that liberal theorists tend to view as anachronistic and increasingly less important in 'modern' societies. Only when members of such ascriptive groups disassociate themselves with those identities will they be able to consider themselves as members of multiple communities, reinforcing the cross-cutting cleavages that define modern civil society. This reflects the ways in which the liberal perspective denies any intrinsic value for identities, despite the fact that they are a primary source of social movement—hence civil society—strength in Western societies (Cohen, 1985; Melucci, 1989; Oxhorn, 1995b). From a liberal perspective, civil society seems to have almost an inverse relationship with community, in that the stronger communities are, the less likely it will be that civil society at a normative level can emerge.

The reality, however, is more ambiguous. As is the case with a liberal perspective on civil society, the general conclusions regarding community and civil society at first glance appear to hold some validity; some of the most violent conflicts in the world today are communal in nature, from Iraq to Sudan. Nevertheless, the reasons for this from a liberal perspective are mistaken. Communities with exceptionally strong bonds among their members can be either building blocks for civil society, or obstacles to its growth. Recent experiences with indigenous movements (Van Cott, 2005; Yashar, 2005) and religious groups associated with both the progressive Catholic Church and more conservative Christian Evangelical movements in Latin America, parts of Asia and Africa (Lehmann & Iqtidar, 2012; Lehmann, 1990; Oxhorn, 1995b) show the contribution 'communities' can make to democratization processes. The role communities will play in relation to civil society will depend on several factors, particularly the mechanisms for achieving consensus within the community and the consequences this has for the community's relations with other social actors and the state.

As the example of the soup kitchen highlights, no community is inherently conflict-free. The bonds that unite them can be ephemeral, belying any strong sense of shared or common interest. Moreover, members of communities are not equal, no matter how egalitarian the structure is intended to be. Natural abilities, including leadership skills and the ability to express oneself clearly, mean that some members will inevitably have more influence than others (Mansbridge, 1980). This, in turn, can reflect how 'communities' address (or fail to address) differences amongst their members along race, gender, and social class lines, to name but the most obvious (Burdick, 1992). Focusing on one identity, ignoring sources of friction and discrimination felt by members, and/or assuming sources of difference are unproblematic, means that communities can be almost unbelievably narrow in their outlook and activities. Any semblance of unity and consensus is then artificial, as people feel excluded from the community despite there being no obvious obstacle to their participation.[8]

One mechanism for maintaining such artificial consensus is to accentuate conflicts with other communities, reinforcing community bonds in order to resist the threat that outsiders are seen to represent. Manipulated by self-serving elites in pursuit of political power, this exacerbates the fragmentation of larger societies as a whole and the parochialism that is inevitably a by-product of an exclusively local focus. Rather than build strong civil societies, such dynamics have turned communities against one another and the state, feeding the kinds of communal conflicts that lead to violence, if not civil war. The recent experience of ethnic violence in Kenya during its 2007 presidential elections, not to mention the bloodshed in the former Yugoslavia and Rwanda's genocides, are only the most extreme examples of this.

While such violence is sometimes viewed as the consequence of a civil society that has become too strong (Berman, 1997; Foley & Edwards, 1996), the real problem is civil society's weakness (Oxhorn, 2006). Strong societies, as evidenced by the strength of their organizations, including possibly their capacity to engage in armed struggle, are necessarily not civil societies. This is because civil society mediates conflict rather than deliberately accentuates it. It is the lack of the mediating structures that civil society entails, both within and among communities, which generates these destructive dynamics. In other words, they epitomize—often with dramatic consequences—the failure of civil society. In such circumstances, societies tend to polarize and, in the worst cases, the ascriptive community identities that could, under appropriate circumstances, serve as the building blocks of strong civil societies, threaten to tear apart the larger societies in which they are found.

A good example of this conceptual problem is found in Sherri Berman's (1997) discussion of the collapse of Weimar Germany and the rise of Hitler. As she demonstrates, it was the ability of the National Socialist German Workers' Party (NSDAP) to use the organizations of civil society to ultimately win electoral power. Yet it was the weakness of those organizations and their inability to represent the interests of their members that was responsible for the ability of the NSDAP to do this. The vacuum created by what was effectively the collapse of civil society meant that an organizational space was left behind for a totalizing party to fill, which the NSDAP was particularly adept in doing. In this example, as well as many others, the thick consensus associated with communities becomes the project of key political actors on a national scale, making compromise increasingly impossible and forcefully limiting the participation of competing communities at the national level, if not eliminating them altogether.

Ultimately, community and civil society are not only distinct concepts, but they are also potentially complementary ones. The normally high levels of trust found among community members and their shared history and experiences have much to offer in the quest for inclusive democratic government. But trust is not the same as agreement, and shared histories and experiences are open to differing interpretations, even as they can serve as a foundation for fruitful dialogue. Although the existence of civil societies is not dependent on these or other attributes of communities, their presence can definitely facilitate the emergence of the kinds of autonomous organizations that could collectively form a strong civil society. Civil society then becomes a mechanism for mediating conflict and ensuring the interests and priorities of the people who different organizations represent are taken into account. In this sense, 'community' is a pre-political manifestation of collective identity, and communities require organization to enter the political realm. The political importance of specific communities will be determined by the kind of organization adopted, and the organizations composing civil society represent one way for communities to achieve this.

Finally, it is important to note that organizations that are not based on community are also central to understanding civil society's potential. Functional organizations such as labor movements play a critical role in representing and defending the rights of marginal groups, historically having contributed to the expansion of rights and the modern welfare state (Rueschemeyer et al., 1992). Functional organizations—defined in terms of what they seek to achieve independently of their geographical basis—have similarly played an important role in advancing the interests of groups when community-based organizations prove insufficient, and may even be obstacles. This is clear in the case of women. While women generally play important roles in community organizations, the constraints imposed on their activity by patriarchy and traditional gender roles has invariably led them to create separate women's organizations to advance gender equality more broadly. Functional organizations can also facilitate the growth of movements based on communal identities, in effect blurring the distinction between functional and territorially based organizations. In Bolivia, for example, organized labor played a central role in the rise of the indigenous movements that would transform citizenship in Bolivia with the election of Evo Morales in 2005. This was the first time that Bolivia had an indigenous president, despite the fact that a majority of the population was indigenous. Among other things, Morales oversaw the implementation of a new constitution, formally declaring that Bolivia was now a plurinational state in order to resolve the problem of contested sovereignty for indigenous peoples.[9]

Civil Society, Community and the Social Construction of Citizenship[10]

The immediate effect of this ambiguous relationship between community and civil society can be understood in terms of what it means to be a 'citizen' in a given society. More specifically, the conflicts that civil society helps mediate are reflected in the *social construction of citizenship*. As Tilly, (1996, 9) notes, historically, it was the "struggle and bargaining between expanding states and their subjects [that] created citizenship where it had not previously existed." Even today, when there is perhaps greater agreement than ever before on the normative content of democratic citizenship rights, there is still no consensus for implementing many specific rights of citizenship. In most new democracies, conflicts over basic citizenship rights were central yet unresolved issues in the transition process. The failure of democratic institutions to address these shortcomings after the transition is often the principal source of their fragility. The pressures for expanding citizenship rights that emerge (or fail to emerge) from within civil society, and how those pressures are dealt with by the state, are central to any causal theory of citizenship. In other words, citizenship reflects which groups participate in their social construction and how. In this way, the strength of civil society is mirrored in the scope and depth of citizenship rights.

In sharp contrast to the thick social consensus associated with the liberal perspective on civil society, the starting point for understanding the social construction of citizenship is a *thin* or minimal social consensus. Such a consensus has two components. First, relevant actors in a given society recognize that they are members of a geographically defined unit associated with some sense of 'public good,' even if there are sharp disagreements over what that public good entails. Such acceptance may be normative (e.g., a shared national identity) or the result of a lack of alternatives (e.g., secession is not feasible due to external resistance or viable due to a lack of resources). Second, the right of other social actors to compete for political influence in the definition of that public good without threat of violence is accepted. This may be for normative reasons, or because the inability of any one actor to dominate the others means violence will only end in stalemate.

Once again, at first glance, the outcome may appear consistent with a liberal perspective. But the reasons are fundamentally distinct. They are related to continued conflict, the lack of consensus and the impossibility of succeeding through violent means rather than any rejection of violence. In other words, actors—including the state—perceive that they have no alternative than to 'agree to disagree.' As noted above, the resultant lack of trust then can become a principal motivating factor for continued involvement in civil society, if only to help ensure that group interests are respected.

In many ways, the ambiguous relationship between community and civil society is epitomized by the situation of indigenous peoples around the world when examined through the lens of a thin societal consensus. Indigenous peoples account for just 5% of the world's population, but they comprise approximately 15% of the world's poor (IFAD, 2013). This general problem is particularly acute in Latin America, where colonial legacies and racism have contributed to the socioeconomic and political marginalization of indigenous people literally for centuries, despite some important recent gains. In many ways, indigenous communities often are seen as exemplifying the ideal of community, given their strong collective identity based on a shared history and language. In terms of 'community,' we often romanticize the nature of life in indigenous communities, forgetting that the poverty of such communities is a reflection of colonial legacies that relegate indigenous peoples to the least hospitable areas of a nation's territory, at the same time assuming a level of cultural homogeneity that ignores sometimes deep differences among indigenous groups (Oxhorn, 2001). From the perspective of a thin consensus defining the scope of civil society, the ambiguity is even greater. The nature of contested sovereignty stemming from the colonial conquest means that the nature of the public good and its relation to indigenous people is also contested. Colonial legacies, racism, and poverty imply a level of coercion that belies a strong consensus on the right of indigenous people to compete for political influence, at the same time that it also makes it particularly difficult for indigenous people to organize themselves autonomously. The result is a certain paradox: without self-constituted collective organizations, indigenous peoples can neither negotiate a solution to the problem of contested sovereignty, nor can they effectively work to overcome the racism and history of exclusion in a way that produces the shared thin social consensus and avoids radicalization.

The concept of a thin societal consensus highlights another important distinction between collectivist and liberal perspectives. Rights are inevitably an outcome of collective struggle. Indeed, it is the reluctance of elites to grant rights in the first instance that requires collective action to pressure them into doing so (Oxhorn, 2003). Whether it be civil rights such as the right to organize and express dissent, the right to vote or cultural, social and economic rights, their existence both on paper and in practice is linked intrinsically to the capacity of disadvantaged groups to effectively demand them. Moreover, the collective nature of these struggles belies the incompatibility of collective rights with other rights associated with citizenship. This is because the rights, once won, often apply to ascriptive categories of citizens, such as workers, women, the elderly, youth, and so on. From a collectivist perspective, the dichotomy between Western, individual rights and non-Western collective rights is a false one. It is a contingent relationship, reflecting national social structures and the social construction of citizenship in distinct contexts.

The process of state–civil society interaction leads to different models of citizenship. The dominant citizenship model in Latin America was *citizenship as cooptation*. It was closely associated with industrialization and urbanization, starting early in the 20th century in a number of countries.

The cornerstone of citizenship as cooptation was a unique process of *controlled inclusion* (Oxhorn, 2003). Controlled inclusion consisted of top–down processes of political and social inclusion in which citizenship rights were segmented, partial and, ultimately, precarious. Rather than substantially alter structures of inequality, it both reflected and reinforced them. Controlled inclusion was a state project intended to mediate the threat posed by organized subordinate classes through their selective and partial incorporation, severely restricting the scope and autonomy of civil society through policies of state corporatism, clientelism, and populist appeals that were made possible by the resources placed at the disposal of political elites as a by-product of rapid economic growth.

Ultimately, controlled inclusion belied the existence of strong civil societies; only select segments of society were allowed to organize and the autonomy of those organizations was seriously compromised. Important social rights of citizenship were often granted in lieu of meaningful political rights, while the authoritarian nature of the regime by definition implied that respect for basic civil rights was precarious at best.

The model of citizenship as cooptation generally began to break down in the 1970s and 1980s. This reflected the limits of the region's import substitution development model and the debt crisis of the early 1980s. It was also reflected in the fact that citizenship as cooptation co-existed with a competing citizenship model, *citizenship as agency*. Citizenship as agency reflects the active role that multiple actors, particularly those representing disadvantaged groups, must play in the social construction of citizenship for democratic governance to realize its full potential. It is synonymous with strong civil societies in Western Europe, where advanced social welfare states can be seen as one of this model of citizenship's principal achievements. Given Latin America's historical extremes of inequality and exclusion, the Left typically championed the ideal of citizenship as agency. When a citizenship as agency model threatened to predominate, military coups were often the result.

Today, the dichotomy of citizenship as agency and citizenship as cooptation has lost its centrality to a new model of citizenship: *citizenship as consumption*. Citizens are best understood as *consumers*, spending their votes and often-limited economic resources to access what normally would be considered minimal rights of democratic citizenship.

Citizenship as consumption is closely related to a market-centered mode of political incorporation and social integration, *neopluralism*. The political criteria for inclusion associated with controlled inclusion (social control and loyalty) are replaced by economic ones. While closely associated with neoliberal economic policies, it is not reducible to any specific set of economic policies or correlated with any particular level of economic liberalization.

The pluralist aspect of neopluralism reflects a normative belief that the best balance of interests and values within a given polity is produced by some form (however limited) of free competition among individuals in the rational pursuit of their self-interest. Ultimate political authority is determined through a free market of votes. Individual freedom is valued above all, and this requires respect for private property and (ideally, at least) the rule of law.

What distinguishes neopluralism from the more traditional pluralist model associated with democracy in the United States is its marked authoritarianism. While it is important that the people who govern are elected, once elected, they have few checks on their power. They frequently bypass and deliberately undermine representative democratic institutions (O'Donnell, 1994). Moreover, unelected power holders, particularly the military and "de facto powers" including dominant economic interests, exercise control over key state decisions (Garretón, 2003).

The logic of neopluralism permeates entire political systems in a variety of ways. Market-based incentives come to play a defining role in collective action. An individual's personal economic resources largely determine the extent and nature of her political and social inclusion. One's economic resources also directly affect the quality of education, health care and even the legal protection a person enjoys. Just as the state is assigned a minimal role in ensuring the smooth functioning of the market in the economic realm, the state largely abdicates its role in providing incentives to mobilize. The public and private goods formally available at the state level to those mobilized in earlier periods, as well as the coercive incentives for the hierarchical organization of economic interests under state corporatism, no longer exist or have been significantly reduced. Group identities and collective interests lose any intrinsic value, yet these are a primary potential source of power for subaltern groups.

Confronting the Limits of Citizenship as Consumption: Participatory State Reforms in Bolivia and Brazil

The limits of citizenship as consumption reflect the fact that it is both a cause and effect of weak civil societies. Political leaders have on various occasions attempted to address this problem through innovative state reforms intended to strengthen civil society by establishing mechanisms for greater state–civil society interaction. Two of the most important examples of this are the *Ley de Participación Popular* (LPP) in Bolivia and Porto Alegre's experiment with participatory budgeting (PB) in Brazil. While the latter was a success in terms of establishing a citizenship as agency model, the Bolivian experience has been much more problematic.

Bolivia's Popular Participation Law

The LPP epitomizes a deliberate attempt to strengthen civil society by establishing institutional mechanisms for achieving citizenship as agency. Through a radical decentralization of the Bolivian state in 1994, Bolivia's political landscape was completely reorganized around 311 municipal governments, the majority of which were not only new, but were erected precisely in those areas where the state had been most noticeably absent.[11] Municipal governments were given responsibility for administering health, education, and infrastructure services, among other areas of social investment. Under a new revenue sharing scheme, *co-participation*, the state would double the percentage of its revenues that it shared with municipal governments to 20%. The result was a windfall for the new city governments and many of the old ones as well. For the 42% of Bolivians who lived in rural areas, mostly members of indigenous communities, the state had dramatically 'arrived'—and with unprecedented amounts of money to be spent locally.

An elected city council and mayor governed each municipality. To ensure that the new resources would actually benefit the community, over 16,000 *Organizaciones Territoriales de Base* (OTB) were legally recognized by mid-1997 (Galindo Soza, 1998, 241). The OTBs were considered the authentic representatives of the interests of Bolivian civil society, and many were the traditional organizations through which indigenous communities had historically governed themselves. The OTBs would establish community priorities through local participatory planning exercises associated with the elaboration of a *Programa Operativo Anual* (POA) in each municipality. The OTBs would also select members for a new institution that would represent community interests at the level of the city government: *Comités de Vigilancia* (CV). The CVs would articulate and represent community priorities in POA processes. They would also exercise oversight on that portion of municipal budgets financed through co-participation.

The LPP ultimately sought to ensure governmental accountability and transparency by creating a hybrid form of democracy, incorporating Western traditions of representative democracy with local, indigenous traditions of community self-government—"individual liberty with communitarian symbiosis" (Secretaría Nacional de Participación Popular, 1997, 10). In one fell swoop, the LPP offered institutional solutions for addressing many of the problems plaguing Bolivia, from a weak state to the development of a multi-ethnic society. Despite some notable local successes, the LPP failed to live up to its expectations for generating greater citizenship as agency.[12] Several factors help explain this failure.

First, the LPP was conceived and designed with virtually no input from civil society. Then-President Gonzalo Sánchez de Lozado was actively involved, working closely with his key advisors. Even his Vice President at the time, Víctor Hugo Cárdenas, who was one of the most prominent political leaders of indigenous descent in Latin America, played almost no role.

Second, the decision to base LPP participation on OTBs meant that functionally based organizations were deliberately excluded. Ironically, this decision excluded the principal actor in Bolivian civil society advocating decentralization: civic committees. The rest of Bolivian civil society was relatively silent on the matter. Civic committees had become increasingly important as an alternative to Bolivia's corrupt political party system; they were largely urban and often had close ties to business groups, which were all sources of distrust among the LPP's architects.

Having excluded the principal groups demanding decentralization from the LPP framework, the ultimate success of the LPP was now dependent on sectors of civil society that had not participated in its elaboration and that were historically suspicious of the Bolivian state. With little or no social support for it, the government had to win over public opinion once the law was already in place in the face of a very effective opposition campaign against the "damned laws" (*leyes malditas*) that was able to mobilize substantial support from a variety of sources, including political parties, functional organizations and NGOs. Repression of protesters further clouded the legitimacy of the LPP when it was being implemented (Van Cott, 2000).

The key to successfully overcoming this problem inevitably became the availability of co-participation funds. As the intellectual author of the LPP and first National Secretary for Popular Participation, Carlos Hugo Molina, candidly explained, "the fundamental success for the consolidation of popular participation was the existence of resources. The people linked popular participation directly with resources" (personal interview, Santa Cruz, July 15, 1999). Within four months of the law's promulgation, particularly in rural areas, more resources had arrived than in the previous three years combined, and in many cases it was the first time they had received any resources from the state. Indeed, according to Molina, a central aspect of the government's campaign to raise support for the new institutions was to publicize how much money was arriving to local governments so that people would have an incentive to start exercising some control over its expenditure. Not surprisingly, one reason for the rapid legalization of so many OTBs was their desire to gain access to these resources—and in many instances it reflected the desire of political parties to get those OTBs most closely tied to them recognized so they could gain access as well (Booth et al., 1997, 23–24).

Aside from the obvious contradiction of creating participatory state institutions without any public input, the more fundamental contradiction relates to models of citizenship: the legitimation of institutional reforms embodying citizenship as agency was sought through recourse to a model of citizenship as cooptation. These mixed motives for the reforms only heightened the suspicions of poor, marginalized groups that already were fearful of state efforts to equate narrow political interests with the public good.

The decision to limit LPP participation to territorial organizations also raised serious questions regarding the representation of marginal groups and their manipulation by political elites. Demographics and migration from depressed rural areas meant that many OTBs were stagnant, moribund organizations that had lost their appeal to local inhabitants (Booth et al., 1997, 76). The sudden influx of central government resources gave them new life, but local political elites and political party representatives often soon dominated them. In other cases, organizations were formed without any real connection to society in order to channel funds. These problems were particularly acute in urban areas, where *juntas vecinales* are the principal form of OTB. The Programa de Las Naciones Unidas Para el Desarrollo (PNUD) study (1998, 17) found that fewer than 30% of residents participated in them, and that the principal participants were men over 30 from privileged socioeconomic classes. Political party influence was also quite noticeable (PNUD, 1998, 125–126).

More generally, there was little effort to mobilize citizen participation to get people to actually involve themselves in local politics (Booth et al., 1997, 86). This was particularly true for the young. A national survey conducted by PNUD (1998, 117–118) found that 73.7% of people 21–30 years of age had no contact with local organizations, and this was especially pronounced among women.

In contrast, the most dynamic organizations were often functional organizations, particularly committees formed to secure irrigation and potable water. These had something concrete to offer their members. Successful committees often did not disband once they obtained irrigation or potable water for their members, and have shown the capacity to move into other areas of activity related to community development.

The problem was particularly acute for women's representation, despite the LPP's formal commitment to providing equal opportunities for men and women. Female representation in municipal governments declined not only relatively, but also absolutely—despite the fact that the LPP more than doubled the number of municipal governments in Bolivia. The situation was sufficiently serious to lead reformers to institute a 30% quota for female candidates. While this led to significant relative gains for women, much of the quota's impact has been diluted by the fact that women have largely been relegated to positions of 'alternate', of which they account for 70%, who wait to replace actually sitting municipal counselors should they resign or ascend to the mayor's office (Kudelka, 2004). It reflects how men sought to control access to the new resources provided by co-participation, thereby pushing women (sometimes violently) to the sidelines (Kudelka, 2004). It is also a consequence of excluding women's organizations from participation in the LPP process because they were not considered to be OTBs. Men generally dominated OTBs, even before they had access to substantial state resources (Booth et al., 1997; Vargas, R., 1998).

These problems have been compounded by the way in which participatory budgeting and the vigilance committees function in practice. In terms of participatory planning, 'participation' by OTBs generally has been limited to setting priorities for expenditures and making demands, rather than actually participating in the planning process (Archondo, 1997; Vargas, R., 1998; Booth et al., 1997). This was partly because the planning process was not designed for more active inputs from civil society. It also reflects past patterns of a more paternalistic relationship between the state and civil society in which civil society looked to the state to resolve its problems.

The problem of limited participation was compounded by a lack of synchronization between the priorities established by the participatory budgeting process and actual municipal budgets. In 2000, only 23% of the projects funded by municipal governments originated through participatory budgeting processes,[13] yet actually making it into the city's budget is insufficient because budgeted programs frequently are not implemented. A study by Porcel and Thévoz of 151 municipal governments (1998, 103–114) found only slightly more than 50% of budgets were actually executed.

If OTBs are the foundation upon which the LPP rests, then the CVs are its central pillars. Creating 311 CVs proved to be a slow process. By December 1995, only 163 had been formed, so the government issued a decree stating CVs had to be formed by December 31 in order to be eligible for co-participation funds. "In 15 days all the political parties that governed municipalities created Vigilance Committees" (Ardaya Salinas, 1998, 25). Aside from raising questions about the representative quality of the CVs (Ardaya Salinas, 1998), this underscores a noticeable lack of social recognition of the role CVs potentially can play in empowering civil society. Institutionally, they were created by the state and lacked social legitimacy. The result is that the relationship between CVs and the communities they were supposed to represent is a formal one: "the base makes demands, but does not support" the CVs (Maydana, 2004, 204).

Not surprisingly, CVs were only rarely able to fulfill their oversight role (Maydana, 2004; Guzmán Boutier, 1998; Booth et al., 1997). In a study of 11 CVs, only two were functioning, with important qualifications in both cases. Their task is only made more difficult by the confusion over the actual role of the CVs, particularly regarding the exercise of social control over the expenditure of co-participation funds. Moreover, CVs depend on the municipal government for vital information, and the local government often simply refused to provide it. This can create a vicious circle of distrust and conflict between municipal governments and the organizations empowered by the LPP.

To the extent they are autonomous from their social base, CVs are vulnerable to manipulation by local governments and political parties. The LPP deliberately did not provide for financing the activities of the CVs, in a mistaken attempt to avoid turning them into a source of patronage.[14] Moreover, the task of fiscal oversight is a very technical one and few CV members had the necessary skills to fulfill these tasks. This further increases the vulnerability of CV members to political pressures from the municipality (Booth et al., 1997). As a result the members of CVs, particularly the CV presidents who often amass considerable influence over their respective CVs, were increasingly exposed to the patrimonial and rent-seeking dynamic of Bolivian politics in general (PNUD, 1998; Maydana, 2004).

Far from creating a model of citizenship as agency, the LPP fell victim to many of the worst aspects of the old model of citizenship as cooptation.

In a social atmosphere already characterized by high levels of distrust and skepticism toward the state, the creation of the LPP belied a strong civil society. Instead, as the political instability of Bolivia in the late 1990s and early 2000s dramatically demonstrated, social control and participation are increasingly following a logic of "civil society versus the state" (Maydana, 2004, 235).

The limits of the LPP's success offer important insights regarding the nature of communities and their relation to civil society. The recognition of OTBs reflected a deliberate attempt to connect communities with political processes in order to empower them and marginalize political parties and functional organizations that lacked any direct ties with communities. The process through which the LPP was designed and implemented alienated the communities with the strongest sense of identity that distrusted the top-down reforms, and the vacuum was filled by organizations from communities' weaker identities. These were the communities suffering most from poverty whose institutions had lost their ties to those same communities, paving the way for the reintroduction of many of the dynamics the LPP was intended to reverse. The success Morales had achieved in subsequent years appealed to these stronger communities based on his own indigenous identity. Ironically, however, the Movement Toward Socialism (MAS) that brought him to power had its roots in traditional labor organizing among coca producers and was strongest in areas of new settlement as indigenous people emigrated from the Andes to the rainforest in search of economic opportunities. In other words, to a certain extent Morales' success was a cause and consequence of the weakening traditional communities. Moreover, MAS' roots in organizing of coca producers as workers continues to divide the movement between supporters more closely associated with indigenous community identities and others more closely identifying with its trade union roots.

Participatory Budgeting in Porto Alegre

PB was first initiated in 1989 in Porto Alegre, a medium-sized city (population 1.2 million) in southern Brazil. While far less ambitious than the LPP in Bolivia, it similarly sought to create new institutions for realizing citizenship as agency at the local level where communities are strongest, but with considerably greater success. Indeed, its resounding success led to the adoption of similar programs in over 100 cities in Brazil, as well as many others throughout the world. By contrasting the relative success of PB with the LPP, important dynamics become apparent that help explain why citizenship as agency is often so problematic.

The impetus for PB came from the national level. In sharp contrast to the insulated, largely secretive process through which the LPP was designed, PB in Brazil was made possible by the 1988 Constitution that was crafted with considerable input from civil society. The new constitution made PB possible by granting greater authority to local governments to design new policy-making processes and recognizing the legitimacy of participatory institutions (Wampler & Avritzer, 2004). Rather than mandate a single institutional design for the entire country, Brazil's 1988 Constitution facilitated local experimentation, and Porto Alegre took up the challenge.

Several local factors heavily influenced the direction new reforms would take. Porto Alegre had enjoyed a relatively vibrant civil society, which grew in opposition to Brazil's military dictatorship (1964–1985). This experience ultimately was eclipsed by the 1986 electoral victory of the Democratic Labor Party (PDT), a left-wing populist party that demobilized civil society in order to reimpose a more traditional clientelistic government. The initial proposal for some form of participatory budgeting actually originated within civil society, in large part to allow civil society organizations to renew their own sagging legitimacy in the face of the pervasive clientelism of the PDT government (Avritzer, 2002; Baiocchi, 2002; Wampler & Avritzer, 2004).

The left-wing Workers' Party (PT) won the 1988 municipal elections, in large part because of public repudiation of the PDT. It was not yet a strong party in Porto Alegre. Despite divisions within the PT (Goldfrank, 2003), the party ultimately decided to make PB the cornerstone of its municipal policies (Baiocchi, 2002; Avritzer, 2002). Central to this decision were the close relations between the PT and the various civil society actors demanding greater popular participation in municipal government.

Despite these favorable circumstances, PB got off to a rocky start. Participation was initially relatively low and actually declined during its first two years (Goldfrank, 2003). The PT responded by working with civil society organizations, negotiating, and perfecting the institutions of PB. Funding levels were increased along with the scope of PB so that, by the late 1990s, 100% of all discretionary municipal expenditures were decided through PB (Wampler & Avritzer, 2004, 307). Deliberate efforts were also made to encourage local participants to think beyond their immediate communities and PB effectively began to address citywide concerns (Baiocchi, 2002).

PB operates on a yearly cycle. It begins in March, when assemblies are held in each of the city's 16 districts. Delegates are elected to represent their local communities in subsequent phases of the cycle. A 42-member PB Council is also elected to ultimately negotiate the final municipal budget with the local government. Budgets and projects from the previous year are reviewed. Delegates subsequently meet in intermediary meetings to determine regional priorities and discuss citywide concerns according to designated thematic groupings. The PB Council is also responsible for balancing competing demands, setting priorities, and distributing funds among regions and in accordance with larger citywide priorities. After negotiating the final municipal budget, the PB Council monitors actual expenditures (Avritzer, 2002; Baiocchi, 2002).

The end result of PB has been "a profound transformation of civil society itself" (Baiocchi, 2002, 23). The level of public participation continually increased, from just 976 in 1990 to 26,807 in 2000 (Wampler & Avritzer, 2004, 302). In contrast to the LPP, participation is open to all. Moreover, the number of social organizations increased markedly as a result of the PB process. Conservative estimates suggest that the number of neighborhood organizations increased from 180 in 1986 to 540 in 1998 (Baiocchi, 2002, 25). Ultimately, PB became an example of how "civil society organizations challenge old practices, such as clientelism and patronage, while simultaneously offering concrete alternatives" (Wampler & Avritzer, 2004, 291).

Most significantly, growing levels of participation and organization tended to concentrate in poorer areas, and people with lower incomes and levels of education tend to predominate in the PB process. This, plus the fact that municipal expenditures were deliberately redistributed toward poorer areas of the city, underscores the empowerment PB offers for disadvantaged groups. More precisely, citizens can see how their collective activities contribute to policy-making in positive ways, creating a potentially virtuous circle of growing civil society strength, dispersion of economic and political power and more inclusive democratic governance.

Community, Civil Society and the Quest for Inclusive Democratic Governance

It is important not to exaggerate the success of PB in Porto Alegre. It is clearly the most successful example out of more than 100 similar experiments, in a country with over 5000 city governments. However important it is for the citizens of Porto Alegre, PB still controls just 10–15% of municipal expenditures amounting to a meager per capita level of just over $200 (Wampler & Avritzer, 2004, 307). While it is unquestionably an important right of citizenship for people actually to decide where a school will be built, more fundamental decisions about school staffing and curriculum, for example, are made elsewhere. The ultimate challenge is to 'scale up' PB in the determination of national policies, and/or further decentralize decision-making authority to local governments so that larger issues can be addressed. Similarly, one should recognize that, despite its problematic inception, the PPL continues to function in Bolivia, having acquired increasing legitimacy through reforms and after the election of Evo Morales to the presidency.

More important are the insights the comparison offers for understanding the ambiguous relationship between civil society and communities. An important aspect of the success of participatory budgeting in Porto Alegre is intrinsically tied to its ability to incorporate communities as the basic territorial unit. It is at this micro level of small neighborhoods and streets that interests were initially identified and prioritized, and the success at this level proved a fruitful foundation for strengthening civil society. At the same time, the limits of PB reflected the limits of communities and their relationship to larger social and political dynamics. Like the impoverished indigenous communities in the Bolivian highlands that were alienated by the imposition of the PPL, the poorest segments of Porto Alegre's population largely remained outside the PB process, and in many communities the process has been increasingly dominated by local *caciques* who subverted the democratic values PB initially represented (Tranjan, 2016, 18). Just as the election of Morales contributed to the legitimation of PPL in Bolivia, the PT's close association with PB in Porto Alegre meant that when the PT lost control of the municipal government, the new administration deliberately reigned in its scope and participation subsequently declined, raising important questions about its longer-term sustainability (Oxhorn, 2016; Tranjan, 2016; Gugliano, n.d.; Rubin & Baierle, 2014).

The contrast between the two reforms also highlights the importance of state–society relations as a *process* in which the role played by civil society is decisive for determining the extent and nature of democratic inclusion. Communities are central to this as well, but their relation to civil society similarly determines their role. Whether communities contribute to the strengthening of civil society and, as a result, democratic governance will depend on a number of factors, of which organization and autonomy are central concerns.

Citizenship offers a useful lens for understanding these relations. Whether it be through citizenship as cooptation or citizenship as consumption, civil society is severely circumscribed. In these cases, communities face numerous challenges, including fragmentation and manipulation by elites in the pursuit of their own self-interest. Civil society, as understood from a collectivist perspective, provides the tools to avoid both, contributing to the strength of communities and their capacity to enrich democratic processes.

In the end, the problem is not social conflict, but the way in which it is mediated. Ignoring it or pretending that it has been eclipsed by modernity only risks perpetuating exclusion and ultimately the collapse of democratic institutions. While there are alternative ways for mediating conflict, the argument advanced here is that only civil society can do so in a way that supports inclusive democratic governance. As the sad history not of only of colonialism in the global South attests, but also the processes by which modern nation states in Western Europe and North America were created, this is the only way to preserve the true meaning of community. To understand this complex relationship, however, requires a truly interdisciplinary approach that transcends a tendency to examine both civil society and communities from the perspective of single disciplines, whether they are political science, sociology and normative theory in studies of civil society, or cultural studies and anthropology in research on community. As the various chapters in this volume attest, it will require a genuine dialogue between the humanities and social sciences.

Notes

1 Many of the ideas expressed in this section are developed in greater detail in Oxhorn (2011). An earlier version of the first part of this article was published as "Civil Society from the Inside Out: Community, Organization and the Challenge of Political Influence," *Pensamiento Propio* 19:40 (Argentina, July–December 2014), 63–91.

2 The following is based on fieldwork undertaken by the author in Santiago, Chile (1984–1987).

3 In fact, Olga was so ashamed of what happened to her that she refused to meet with me in subsequent trips to the shantytown.

4 It is important to emphasize that civil society organizations, particularly in developed democracies, frequently interact with their respective states at the local, subnational and national levels. Autonomy in this sense refers to the ability of civil society organizations to define and defend their collective dealings with the state, even when—as is frequently the case—they receive material assistance from states. Conversely, when civil society organizations do not interact with the state, they risk political marginalization, if not irrelevance.

5 While still inclusive, the increasing social mobilization around inequality that began with the Occupy Movement in the U.S. is a good example of the beginnings of a civil society reaction to growing problems of inequality in advanced market economies, particularly after the Great Recession of 2008. Earlier examples would include the Civil Rights and Anti-War movements in the U.S., as well as various other identity-based new social movements, particularly in Western Europe. For example, see Melucci (1985).

6 This was a particular problem for me in trying to do ethnographic research in Chile in the 1980s. As an outsider (particularly an American one), I was automatically suspect. Such suspicions were only reinforced by the regime's use of informants who, like me, wanted to learn as much as possible about civil society organizations in the shantytowns, and the harsh experience of repression after the 1973 coup. To overcome this, I literally had to earn their trust. See Oxhorn (1995b).

7 The collectivist perspective adopted here owes more to the work of Montesquieu. See Taylor (1990).

8 As Burdick shows in his study of religious organizations in Brazilian urban slums, such outcomes may be quite surprising. Progressive liberation theology in practice was actually quite exclusionary within poor communities. In part, this was because active participation requires a certain level of literacy to read and interpret the Bible, as well as an ability to articulate oneself effectively in group discussions. At the same time, Liberation Theology's links with social transformation emphasized the class nature of society, assuming that more economic equality would resolve problems caused by racism, gender inequality, and so on. Conversely, the requirements for participation in more conservative Evangelical groups were considerably lower—one merely had to believe. The strength of such beliefs, however, was associated with reductions in family violence, drug abuse and other real problems in people's day-to-day lives. Moreover, people were accepted regardless of their gender or skin color.

9 I will return to the problem of contested sovereignty below. It is also worth noting that Morales' national success was based on the successful organization of a new political movement, the Movement Toward Socialism (MAS). The movement transformed local community identity into a national force, reversing centuries of indigenous peoples' marginalization. As part of civil society, the MAS continued to help mediate conflict, both between the new indigenous movement and other civil society actors, as well as among the functional and territorially based organizations that sought representation through it.

10 The following is a revised version of Oxhorn (2009).

11 Of the 311 municipalities recognized by the PPL, 187 were new.

12 The LPP did play an important role in the rise of Evo Morales and, subsequent to his election 2005, it has been able to reverse these dynamics to an important degree. The link with the electoral success of Morales, however, raises questions about their sustainability after he leaves office.

13 A subsequent reform increased this to 45%. See Galindo Soza (2004, 112–113).

14 To address this, Social Control Funds were established in 1999 to finance CV activities. With some notable exceptions, this resulted in further questions about the CVs' social legitimacy without necessarily decreasing their vulnerability to political manipulation. See Maydana (2004).

References

Almond, Gabriel A., & Sidney Verba. 1963. *The civic culture: political attitudes and democracy in five nations*. Princeton: Princeton University Press.

Archondo, Rafael. 1997. "La aplicación de la Ley de Participación Popular." In *El pulso de la democracia* (Ed.). Secretaría Nacional de Participación Popular. La Paz: República de Bolivia, Ministerio de Desarrollo Humano, Secretaría Nacional de Participación Popular y Editorial Nueva Sociedad, 273–302.

Ardaya Salinas, Rubén. 1998. *El comité de vigilancia al auxilio de la democracia municipal*. La Paz: Instituto Latinoamericano de Investigaciones Sociales de la Fundación Friedrich Ebert Stiftung.

Avritzer, Leonardo. 2002. *Democracy and the public space in Latin America*. Princeton: Princeton University Press.

Baiocchi, Gianpaolo. 2002. "Synergizing Civil Society: State–Civil Society Regimes in Porto Alegre, Brazil." *Political Power and Social Theory* 15, 3–52.

Berman, Sherri. 1997. "Civil Society and the Collapse of the Weimar Republic." *World Politics* 49 (3), 401–429.

Booth, David, Suzanne Clisby, & Charlotta Widmark. 1997. *Popular participation: democratising the state in rural Bolivia*. Stockholm: Swedish International Development Cooperation Agency.

Burdick, John. 1992. "Rethinking the Study of Social Movements: The Case of Christian Base Communities in Urban Brazil." In A. Escobar & S.E. Alvarez (Eds.). *The making of social movements in Latin America: identity, strategy, and democracy* (171–184). Boulder, CO: Westview Press.

Bustamante, Fernando. 1998. "Democracy, Civilizational Change and the Latin American Military." In F. Aguero & J. Stark (Eds.). *Fault lines of democracy in post-transition Latin America*. Miami: North–South Center Press (University of Miami).

Cohen, Jean. 1985. "Strategy or Identity: New Theoretical Paradigms and Contemporary Social Movements." *Social Research* 52 (Winter), 663–716.

Foley, Michael, & Bob Edwards. 1996. "The Paradox of Civil Society." *Journal of Democracy* 7 (3), 38–52.

Fukuyama, Francis. 1989. "The End of History?" *The National Interest*.

Fukuyama, Francis. 2001. "Social Capital, Civil Society, and Development." *Third World Quarterly* 22 (1), 7–20.

Galindo Soza, Mario. 1998. "La participación popular y la descentralización administrativa." In J.C. Chávez Corrales (Ed.). *Las reformas estructurales en Bolivia*. La Paz: Fundación Milenio, 223–282.

Galindo Soza, Mario. 2004. "Diez años de planificación participativa en el proceso de la participación popular." In *Municipalización: diagnóstico de una década* (85–144). La Paz: USAID, Friedrich Ebert Stiftung, ILDIS.

Garretón, Manuel Antonio. 2003. *Incomplete democracy: political democratization in Chile and Latin America*. (R.K. Washbourne & G. Horvath, Trans.). Chapel Hill: University of North Carolina.

Gellner, E. 1991. "Civil Society in Historical Context." *International Social Science Journal* 129 (August), 495–510.

Goldfrank, Benjamin. 2003. "Making Participation Work in Porto Alegre." In G. Baiocchi (Ed.). *Radicals in power: the Workers' Party (PT) and experiments in urban democracy in Brazil* (27–52). London: Zed Books Ltd.

Gugliano, Alfredo Alejandro (n.d.) "A Caixa de Pandora da participação cidadã: O orçamento participativo e a governança solidária local em Porto Alegre." Porto Alegre: Universidade Federal do Rio Grande Sul.

Guzmán Boutier, Omar. 1998. "Denuncias del comité de vilancia o cuándo efectivo es el control social." In *PARTICIPACIÓN POPULAR. Una evaluación-aprendizaje de la Ley 1994–1997*. U. d. I. y. Análisis. La Paz: Ministerio de Desarrollo Sostenible y Planificación, Viceministerio de Participación Popular y Fortalecimiento Municipal, 132–153.

Habermas, Jürgen. 1992. "Further Reflections on the Public Sphere." In C. Calhoun (Ed.). *Habermas and the Public Sphere*. Cambridge, MA: Cambridge University Press.

Hann, Chris. 1996. "Introduction: Political Society and Civil Anthropology." In C. Hann & E. Dunn (Eds.). *Civil Society: Challenging Western Models*. London: Routledge.

IFAD. 2013. *Indigenous peoples: valuing, respecting and supporting diversity*. International Fund for Agricultural Development 2013 [cited October 2, 2013]. Available from www.ifad.org/english/indigenous/index_full.htm.

Kudelka, Ana María. 2004. "Análisis de las políticas de género desde un enfoque gerencial y su impacto a nivel municipal." In *Municipalización: diagnóstico de una década* (503–558). La Paz: USAID, Friedrich Ebert Stiftung, ILDIS.

Lagos, Marta. 1997. "Latin America's Smiling Mask." *Journal of Democracy* (8 July), 125–138.

Lehmann, David. 1990. *Democracy and development in Latin America: economics, politics and religion in the post-war period*. Philadelphia: Temple University Press.

Lehmann, David, & Humeira Iqtidar. 2012. *Fundamentalism and charismatic movements*. New York: Routledge.

Lipset, Seymour Martin. 1960. *Political man: the social bases of politics*. (1st ed.) Garden City, NY: Doubleday.

Mansbridge, Jane. 1980. *Beyond adversary democracy*. New York: Basic Books.

Maydana, Raúl. 2004. "El comité de vigilancia, la participación y el control social en el modelo municipalista de descentralización del Estado boliviano." In *Municipalización: diagnóstico de una década* (186–246). La Paz: USAID, Friedrich Ebert Stiftung, ILDIS.

Melucci, Alberto. 1985. "The Symbolic Challenge of Contemporary Movements." *Social Research* 52 (4), 789–816.

Melucci, Alberto. 1989. *Nomads of the present: social movements and individual needs in contemporary society*. J. Keane & P. Mier (Eds.). Philidelphia: Temple University Press.

O'Donnell, Guillermo. 1994. "Delegative Democracy." *Journal of Democracy* 5 (1), 56–69.

Oxhorn, Philip. 1995a. "From Controlled Inclusion to Coerced Marginalization: The Struggle for Civil Society in Latin America." In J. Hall (Ed.). *Civil Society: Theory, History and Comparison* (250–277). Cambridge: Polity Press.

Oxhorn, Philip. 1995b. *Organizing civil society: the popular sectors and the struggle for democracy in Chile.* University Park, PA: Pennsylvania State University Press.

Oxhorn, Philip. 2001. "La Construcción del Estado por la Sociedad Civil. La Ley Boliviana de Participación Popular y el Desafío de la Democracia Local." In *Documentos de Trabajo del INDES.* Washington, DC: Instituto Interamericano para el Desarrollo Social (INDES), Inter-American Development Bank.

Oxhorn, Philip. 2003. "Social Inequality, Civil Society and the Limits of Citizenship in Latin America." In S. Eckstein & T. Wickham-Crawley (Eds.). *What justice? Whose justice? Fighting for fairness in Latin America* (35–63). Berkeley: University of California.

Oxhorn, Philip. 2006. "Conceptualizing Civil Society from the Bottom Up: A Political Economy Perspective." In R. Feinberg, W.C.H. & L. Zamosc (Eds.). *Civil society and democracy in Latin America* (59–84). New York: Palgrave Macmillan.

Oxhorn, Philip. 2009. "La ciudadanía como consumo o como agencia: comparando las reformas democráticas en Bolivia y Brasil." In J. Bokser Liwerant, J.F. Pozo Block & G. Waldman Mitnick (Eds.). *Pensar la globalización, la democracia y la diversidad* (223–246). Mexico City: Universidad Nacional Autónoma de México, Coordinación de Estudios de Posgrado, Programa de Posgrado en Ciencias Políticas y Sociales.

Oxhorn, Philip. 2011. *Sustaining civil society: economic change, democracy and the social construction of citizenship in Latin America.* University Park: The Pennsylvania State University Press.

Oxhorn, Philip. 2016. "Latin America's Elusive Public Sphere." *Current History* 115 (778), 43–50.

Programa de Las Naciones Unidas Para el Desarrollo (PNUD). 1998. *Desarrollo Humano en Bolivia 1998.* La Paz: Programa de Las Naciones Unidas Para el Desarrollo.

Rubin, Jeffrey W., & Sergio Gregorio Baierle. 2014. "Democracy by Invitation: The Private Sector's Answer to Participatory Budgeting in Porto Alegre, Brazil." In J.W. Rubin & V. Bennett (Eds.). *Enduring Reform* (113–145). Pittsburgh: Pittsburgh University Press.

Rueschemeyer, Dietrich, Evelyne Stephens, & John D. Stephens. 1992. *Capitalist development and democracy.* Chicago: University of Chicago Press.

Rustow, Dankwart A. 1970. "Transitions to Democracy: Toward a Dynamic Model." *Comparative Politics* 2 (April), 337–363.

Secretaría Nacional de Participación Popular. 1997. *El pulso de la democracia.* La Paz: República de Bolivia, Minsterio de Desarrollo Human, Secretaría Nacional de Participación Popular y Editorial Nueva Sociedad.

Seligman, Adam. 1992. *The idea of civil society.* New York: Free Press.

Shils, E. 1991. "The Virtue of Civil Society." *Government and Opposition* 26 (Winter), 3–20.

Taylor, Charles. 1990. "Invoking Civil Society." In *Working Paper, 31.* Chicago: Center for Psychosocial Studies.

Tilly, Charles. 1996. "Citizenship, Identity and Social History." In C. Tilly (Ed.). *Citizenship, Identity and Social History, International Review of Social History Supplement 3.* Cambridge: Press Syndicate of the University of Cambridge.

Tranjan, J, Ricardo. 2016. *Participatory democracy in Brazil: socioeconomic and political origins*. Notre Dame: University of Notre Dame Press.

Van Cott, Donna Lee. 2000. *The friendly liquidation of the past: the politics of diversity in Latin America*. Pittsburgh: University of Pittsburgh Press.

Van Cott, Donna Lee. 2005. *From movements to parties in Latin America: the evolution of ethnic politics*. New York: Cambridge University Press.

Vargas R., Humberto. 1998. *Los MUNICIPIOS EN BOLIVIA. Son evidentes los avances con participación popular*. Cochabamba: Centro de Estudios de la Realidad Económica y Social.

Wampler, Brian, & Leonardo Avritzer. 2004. "Participatory Publics: Civil Society and New Institutions in Democratic Brazil." *Comparative Politics* 36 (3), 291–312.

Yashar, Deborah J. 2005. *Contesting citizenship in Latin America: the rise of indigenous movements and the postliberal challenge*. New York: Cambridge University Press.

Part II
Community

3 Modernized Honor Culture and Community

García Márquez's *Chronicle of a Death Foretold/Crónica de una muerte anunciada*

Gordana Yovanovich

While in modern theory, community has come to be "a word most agreeable to modern ears" and "one of the front-line feelings of our age" (Blackshaw, 2003, 19), a word that "stands out among other words" (Bauman, 2003), the notion of community is not always associated with an experience of a paradise or nostalgia for Paradise Lost. García Márquez's 1980 novel portrays an "imposed community" (Williams, 1973) with clearly defined roles that noticeably limit individual freedom and personal growth. The objective of the novel, however, is not so much to show obvious limitations of proscriptive communities, but to use the familiar as a stepping stone and starting place for transformation. As Argentinian writer and García Márquez's friend, Julio Cortázar points out in his *Hopscotch* (1966), the reader has become the most important character in the novel because the reader is the one who will participate in social change and in the reimagination of local and global communities. The Latin American Boom writers believed in the possibility of change and were convinced that literature had a role to play in it.

In the 1960s and 1970s, (left-wing) ideology played a strong role in the attempt to emancipate the proletariat and provoke change; however, Latin American intellectuals saw what happened in the Soviet Union and to some extent in Cuba and they advocated a more profound change, particularly at the level of everyday life. Instead of preaching with politicians for a new system which would replace the old one, or instead of circulating their views in journals, universities, and other civic forums as they did a century earlier, the Boom writers attempted to shape opinions by subverting and transforming existing norms. Their proposed (grassroots) change is/was to be instigated from inside because, as Julio Cortázar says, "we burn outwardly from within" (1966, 385). One of the first concerns was to make a connection with the reader, and then to get the reader to move "outwardly from within." To achieve this most Boom writers evoke the familiar, and when they are on the same page as the reader, the reader becomes "an accomplice," a travelling companion (*Hopscotch*, 397) in the recreation and transformation of the old.

To make the reader *un cómplice* in *Chronicle of the Death Foretold*, the Colombian Novel Prize laureate uses familiar established genres such as the chronicle and the detective story, and he creates recognizable characters based on stereotypes: men brag about their macho sexuality and drinking habits, while women are expected to obey and suffer raising their children, or they are to give men forbidden pleasures and understanding if they are working in a brothel. The familiar and the stereotypical connect the reader to the story, but the reader is made an accomplice in a more meaningful way when he or she is led to make sense of fragmented texts, when s/he has to believe in the supernatural as part of the natural (magical realism), or when s/he has to make sense of contradictions. The novel poses various problems and the reader is asked to understand multiple voices and negotiate new positions. Since the main unnamed narrator sympathizes with the controversial main character, a young woman named Angela Vicario, the reader is also led to see her in a positive light and to enter through her as well into a complex dialogical process which trains the reader for a more active form of association.

Crónica de una muerte anunciada (1980) portrays a small-town Latin American community shaped by its geographical location, fading Catholic values, and warped notions of honor. As mentioned earlier, the coalescing energy between men comes from their drinking together and sharing of prostitutes in the local brothel, while women are connected through gossip. The narrator's mother, for example, never goes out of the house but knows all that is going on in town and is one of the main sources of information in the novel. She brings together a system of gossiping voices which, together with the narrator's voice, make up the novel. The gossip that fuels the community and the novel in this instance is that Angela Vicario was returned on the night of her wedding when she told her husband she was not a virgin. According to the patriarchal system of honor, her brothers have to kill the man who took their sister's virginity and avenge their family, but it is never clear who the perpetrator is, why Angela points to a man who probably did not take her virginity, and why no one in town warns Santiago Nasar that he is going to be killed by the reluctant brothers, even though everyone knows that the honor killing is to take place.

The question that drives the reader to participate in the creation of the main story is why does the unnamed narrator come back to his community of birth 27 years after his friend Angela was taken back to her parents on her wedding night? The narrator explains that he came back to find out what really happened because the incident of the returned bride and subsequent honor killing had a profound effect on the whole community: "For years we couldn't talk about anything else. Our daily conduct, dominated then by so many linear habits, had suddenly begun to spin around a single common anxiety" (García Márquez, 1982, 96). He also addresses the moral question, why no one in the community prevented the murder given that the death was foretold? Driven by a collective anxiety, the narrator attempts to heal the common wound, and to suggest better ethical conduct for the future since a tradition, "so many linear habits," has been broken, and the community and the novel have to deal with a new vision of life and a new future.

The novel deals, above all, with the social structure in which honor culture plays a major unifying role. As *The Faces of Honor: Sex, Shame, and Violence in Colonial Latin America* shows, honor culture is at the core of Latin American group and individual identity. When the Spanish established colonies in the Americas they brought with them not only their language, religion, and institutions, but also their effective and intellectual traditions, and "among the more important elements of this cultural transfer was the notion of honor" (Johnson & Lipsett-Rivera, 2002, 1). The meaning of honor is place- and time-specific, however the central features of the culture of honor can be confidently asserted. In Latin America, as in the Iberian world, there were two complementary meanings of honor: status and virtue. These two distinct, but related, features of honor have been distinguished by two different words in Spanish: *honor*, which refers to the status of an individual, and *honra*, which is synonymous with virtue. In his most commonly used definition of honor, William Ian Miller explains that the relationship between the individual and the community in the honor culture is an emotional one. As Miller writes:

> Honor is above all the keen sensitivity to the experience of humiliation and shame, a sensitivity manifested by the desire to be envied by others and the propensity to envy the success of others.... The honourable person is one whose self-esteem and social standing is intimately dependent on the esteem or the envy he or she actually elicits in others.
> (1993, 84)

In such a setting, where the individual's identity is dependent on the approval of others, the community is built on a relationship of reciprocity: you will judge me, but I will judge you too, and we can impress or degrade and shame each other. If we compete to impress each other, or to help each other, as Robert Putnam suggests in the form of "mutual indebtedness" and "reciprocity" (Putnam, 2000) we are in a more desirable type of community, but if we are in a relationship of shaming or vendetta, that community is closer to a "nightmare: a vision of hell or prison," as Zygmunt Bauman says (2004, 61). García Márquez's novel portrays the second type of community, one that is afraid of shaming and is easily impressed by money and status. To change this situation it is not enough to replace the existing system with another one, but to change that system from the inside out. As James Bowman shows in his book, *Honor: A History* (2006), in the Western world the honor culture has been transformed through centuries, but it has never been supplanted altogether. He argues that even in the most freedom-oriented modern countries, despite the discrediting that honor cultures have undergone, "the basic honor of the savage—brevity in men, chastity for women—is still recognizable beneath the surfaces of the popular culture that has done so much to efface it." To test this claim, Bowman suggests calling "a man a wimp or a woman a slut" (Bowman, 2006, 5).

Chronicle of a Death Foretold parodies and examines the worldview in which men are to be strong and women are to be sexually pure. This view is not rejected by the novel but it is shown that, contrary to expectations, men are not strong and women are more concerned with forms that suggest purity than with ethical wholesomeness. Through Angela Vicario, a young woman in a small town, García Márquez suggests that honor should primarily be an emotion, that "*la honra es el amor*" (112), as Angela Vicario insists. Love, like honor, is not disconnected from the body, as the church has advocated since the Middle Ages. The relationship of the concept of honor to the body can be seen in the fact that we bow our heads to show honor to someone, or that someone is beheaded as a sign of dishonor. Similarly, slapping of one's face, or messing of one's beard are signs of taking away one's honor. In addition to observing the connection between honor, love, and the body, it is important to note that prior to the Middle Ages, in classical times, both male and female sexuality were associated not with control and prohibition but with vigor, vitality, and energy. As Carol Barton explains in *Roman Honor: The Fire in the Bones* (2001), "the *vir* (man), the *virgo* (woman), virility were virtues all expressed in youthful vigor, growth, fertility, freshness and energy" (Barton, 41). Linguistic connections are also telling in the fact that the word *emotion* comes from the Latin *emotus*, the past participle of *emoveo*, which means 'to move out or away.' As Barton explains, "Emotions were moving forces, motives, the source of energy and action" (Barton, 2). However, emotions are not encouraged in the honor culture of Latin America. Emotional experience was denied to Angela Vicario in *Crónica de una muerte anunciada*, because her mother, Pura Vicario, guided by the teachings of the Catholic Church, understood honor as abstention and obedience, rather than as life, love, and movement.

The culture of honor lost its connection to emotions and life-giving energy in Spain and especially in Latin America when, in the 16th century, the King promised emigrants to America the right to enjoy the privileges of the nobility. The majority of them came from Andalusia where less than 1% of the population was noble. But this was about to change because with the acquisition of wealth they could buy honor and social esteem. As Mark Burkholder indicates in his "Honor and Honors in Colonial Latin America," "[those who migrated] acquired in the Indies the two things they esteemed most but which they could not enjoy in Spain—wealth and nobility" (Johnson & Lipsett-Rivera, 1998, 24). Such a situation and the knowledge that the monarch could transform one's status led to a major shift in the honor culture. It created a new mentality which differentiated between the private and the public, making the relationship between the individual and the community less interdependent. As nobility now was closely linked to wealth, the nobility of soul, trust, and mutual support as unifying qualities of a community, remained mostly a classical ideal, which Angela Vicario attempts to revive in García Márquez's novel.

Chronicle of a Death Foretold is based on a newspaper article that reported a real honor killing. As Nora Viater (2011) explains, García Márquez read in the article that Miguel Reyes, who got married on January 21, 1951 in Sucre, northern Colombia, returned his bride Margarita Chica a few hours after the wedding ceremony because she was not a virgin. When she told her parents that the perpetrator was a young man in their village, the youth was assassinated in order to redress the family honor. The same basic scenario is then repeated in García Márquez's novel, but with significant changes. In the fictional story, Angela was forced by her family to marry a man she did not love because he had money that gave him his social status and *honores*, which Angela's family would gain through association with him.

When Angela's chosen husband arrives in the community of uneducated people, Bayardo San Román gains social esteem by impressing the local folk with his degree, by emphasizing that he is a track engineer, and by showing his wealth in the clothes he wears. The great majority is mesmerized by his wealthy appearance: "he arrived with saddlebags decorated with silver that matched the buckles of his belt and the rings on his boots" (25), as well as by his ability to assist the mass in Latin (27). "He arrived wearing a short jacket and very tight trousers, both of natural calfskin, and kid gloves of the same color" (26) and a young woman in town was so impressed by his entrance that she saw him as "a fairy" whom she could "butter and eat alive" (26). And eventually he becomes a legend for everybody as the community creates the myth that he is swimming in gold. The whole town murmured "that Bayardo San Roman not only was capable of doing everything, and doing it quite well, but also had access to endless resources" (27). Thus, when he chooses Angela Vicario to be his wife, her family is more than happy to move up the social ladder. The fact that Angela detests this man, "I detested conceited men, and I'd never seen one so stuck-up" (29), as she tells the narrator, is irrelevant because her sisters arrive with their husbands and the family pressure is such that, as an individual, she has no other alternative but to marry the rich man and give in to the pressures of the community.

> Angela Vicario never forgot the horror of the night on which her parents and her older sisters with their husbands, gathered together in the parlor, imposed on her the obligation to marry a man whom she had barely seen.... The parents' decisive argument was that a family dignified by modest means had no right to disdain that prize of destiny.
>
> (34–35)

Angela Vicario only dared hint at the inconvenience of a lack of love, but her mother demolished it with a single phrase: "Love can be learned too"

(34–35). The only other person who sees the honored man in a suspicious light is the narrator's mother; one of the most reliable characters in the novel. The old woman never leaves her house, but she hears everything through gossip, and her instincts tell her that the newcomer's fine clothes and his refined, effeminate gestures are signs that he should not be trusted. Hence, in her letter to her son, the narrator, she describes the man everyone is impressed with as a "*marica*" (33), or faggot. The term obviously does not refer to his (homo)sexuality but to the fact that he does not show strength of character.

Instead of attempting to be a part of the community, as expected from a man concerned mainly with appearances, Bayardo San Román places himself above ordinary people; his position in the community is not determined by mutual esteem, as it should be, but by social status which he buys and few can question. García Márquez exaggerates the position of his fictional character, but the novel makes the reader think about how much money is spent in our age of celebrities on appearances and glamor, and how much one wins a place in society by such means. The more media writes about certain events the more popular the celebrating person. Love is a part of the decor, but it certainly is not at the center of events. Thus, in the novel, Santiago Nasar, the wealthy man whom Angela Vicario names as the man who took her virginity, observes that for the preparation of Bayardo San Román and Angela's wedding, 40 turkeys and 11 hogs were killed. The bridegroom had also set up four calves to be roasted for the people on the public square, as well as 205 cases of contraband alcohol, which is almost 2000 bottles of cane liquor that was distributed among the crowd (18). Santiago Nasar then promises that he will have the same wedding, and that "Life will be too short for people to tell about it" (18), reaffirming that honor and recognition are gained in this community through material wealth and appearances. Spiritual values—in the secular sense of the word—are not even mentioned, but the absence of such values will lead the community and its individuals to a tragedy which will force them to re-examine themselves.

In addition to the above mentioned examples of hyperbole, the novel also addresses the question of lack of spirituality through the use of irony. All members of Angela's family are named after Christian saints but her two brothers, Pedro and Pablo, or Peter and Paul, are Christians only in form. The absence of true religious spirituality is shown also in the situation when the Bishop visits the town, but he never gets off his boat to meet the people. Angela's mother, who is significantly called Pura del Carmen Vicario, invokes the classical ideal of purity and chastity as well as the image of the Virgin Mary, and she blindly follows the rules imposed by the church and the patriarchal tradition, but there is little Christian spirit in her eagerness to marry her daughter against her will so that family can improve their social status. The mother is called not only Pura but also Purísima, the *Purest*. Such naming brings to mind the notion of competition which is at the center of the honor culture. Ironically, while she competes to be the best, she leaves her children little room for competition as she raises them to follow rigidly prescribed gender roles. She boasts that "The brothers were brought up to be men. The girls had been reared to get married. They knew how to do screen embroidery, sew by machine, weave bone lace, wash and iron, make artificial flowers and fancy candy" (31). The narrator's mother adds another significant factor, "Any man will be happy with them because they've been raised to suffer" (31).

The suffering takes place in the name of Christ, but García Márquez shows how ridiculous and abusive this way of seeing the world is. Through his famous technique of exaggeration he shows throughout the novel that the prescriptive patriarchal community is a place of shelter and belonging but that it has also destroyed the individual. The first victim is the mother herself who "devoted herself with such spirit of sacrifice to the care of her husband and the rearing of her children that at times one forgot she still existed" (31). But as she undermines her own self she demands the same of her children, leaving little room for individual freedom and choice. It is interesting to observe that the patriarchal honor culture is not only oppressive to women but to men as well, and the oppression is not carried out only by men but also by women. When Angela is returned by her husband on her wedding night because she is not a virgin, it is her mother who demands that her sons avenge the family honor. Clotilde Armenta sees the two brothers as "*poor boys*" and the honor killing as "the horrible duty that's fallen on them" (57). One of the brothers is so reluctant to carry out the vendetta and thus fulfill the social expectation that the other brother had to "put the knife in his hand and dragged him off almost by force in search of their sister's lost honor" (61). Regardless of their hesitation, however, the two men have to act or face shame; as Prudencia Cortes says, "honor does not wait" (62). The social pressure to avenge their sister's lost honor is widespread, but women seem to take the leading role in reinforcing the honor culture. Not only does the mother call for the honor killing but the other women in the family also make demands. Pablo Vicario's girlfriend explains years later that not only did she know the brothers were going to kill Santiago Nasar, but that she expected Pablo to kill a man to prove his manliness to her and to the community at large: "I didn't only agree, I never would have married him if he hadn't done what a man should do" (62).

If women have the power to preserve a culture, they also have the potential to change it, García Márquez suggests. He certainly believes in this, not only in this novel, but in his work in general. Perhaps his best example of women's courage and strength to act is the scene in *One Hundred Years of Solitude* when Ursula, the grand matriarch, threatens to kill her son, Colonel Aureliano Buendía in order to end the senseless wars. In *Crónica*, Angela Vicario is neither a strong matriarch nor a leader around whom a new community is to be formed, as Ursula is in his masterpiece, but her actions incite others, particularly the reader, to think about what is and what can be or could have been done differently. The young woman becomes the most important character in the story when she refuses to fake virginity on her wedding night. She could have continued to use manipulation as the second sex's best available method, but she chooses not to go along with the status quo, rejecting the instructions given to her by her experienced girlfriends. They tell her that when they are not virgins, girls usually get their husbands drunk in bed until they pass out, or they feign more embarrassment than really felt, so that with the light off, they stain the sheet in the darkness with mercurochrome (Márquez, 2012, 105). When Angela refuses to participate in social hypocrisy, and does not prepare the sheet for the following day when it is to be displayed in her bridal courtyard, but simply tells her husband the truth, she asserts that healthy unions cannot be built on deceit. As she explains to the narrator, "it was all something dirty that shouldn't be done to anybody, much less to the poor man who had the bad luck to marry me" (91). By holding such an attitude she shows honesty and integrity, which are essential for building good relationships and a healthy community. The statement may not be much by itself, but in the context of the whole novel this confession to her friend, the narrator, carries weight. Angela is not only the narrator's friend with whom she has moments of intimacy, but becomes the reader's friend as well. When she is returned as a young bride on the night of her wedding as if she were a head of cattle, and beaten by her mother who repeatedly slaps her and pulls her hair, the reader feels the injustice almost at the personal level.

It is never determined in the novel who took Angela's virginity; she identifies Santiago Nasar, but she does so only because she wants her mother to stop beating her and the torture to stop: "the only thing I wanted was for it all to be over quickly so I could flop down and go to sleep" (47), she tells the narrator. The enigma that is created regarding the real perpetrator against her virginity takes this work, which parodies a detective novel, away from the specific situation. The specific story turns into a general situation not only because of the mystery regarding the lost virginity, but because there are other situations in which the specific turns into the general. When Angela Vicario tells us that she named Santiago Nasar only because she was tired and wanted to go to sleep, she gives the impression that she is tired of living generally in gloom, "*en las tinieblas*" (57); her fatigue, as the novel implies, is not the exhaustion of one day, but of a lifetime, and of a particular way of life. The misfortune of being returned by her husband, she told the narrator, was only a cover up for "the other misfortune, the real one, that was burning in her inside" (91). The reader never finds out what exactly her deeper misfortune is, but there are a number of situations the reader can imagine. The novel deliberately omits this detail, leaving the reader to fill in the blank with some of his or her misfortunes, perhaps, and bring the novel closer to home.

The novel deals with a specific event which was reported in the local newspaper, but the specific and the local expand into the general as the newspaper story becomes a metaphor for a particular set of relations.

Santiago Nasar is named as the guilty person although he may not have necessarily committed the crime with Angela. The reader finds out that Santiago Nasar is guilty of sexual misconduct, like his father was, since both of them slept with women of the lower class, feeling that it was their entitlement. Hence, even if Santiago did not rape Angela, he could and would have abused or deceived her. Angela therefore does not commit injustice by naming him, disrupting thus "so many linear habits" (96). García Márquez's novel is not a call to arms, but it raises awareness regarding the question of social injustice and suggests, more importantly, that injustice can be addressed if people like Angela decide to do something about it. But the process of *conscientization* (Freire, 1993) has to take place first for underprivileged people to realize that they can gain agency because they can do things, or not do them, which will cause change from the lower level/grassroots. For example, in the case when a servant decides not to give Santiago the note that he is going to be killed, she does not act but her inaction has vital consequences. When the narrator interviews Santiago Nasar's servant, who could have acted to save his life, there is a strong implication that she chose not to act. The reader connects this with the information that Victoria Guzmán, the *mulata* family cook, had been seduced by Santiago Nasar's father, Ibrahim Nasar, "in the fullness of her adolescence. She'd made love to him in secret for several years in the stables of the ranch, and he brought her to be a house servant when the affection was over" (9). When the father dies, his son, who inherited "his father's Arab eyelids and curly hair" (7), perpetuates the abusive older male/boss–female/servant relationship with Victoria Guzmán's daughter. The young girl, Divina Flor, tells the narrator that Santiago Nasar used to grab her "*panocha*": "He grabbed my whole pussy" (13). Given that the girl is still a child, Santiago Nasar is a rapist. He could have or may have treated Angela Vicario in the same manner as he abused his servant's daughter and not felt responsible because they are from a lower social class, but the "linear habits" have to be broken. Angela names him and insists on naming him 23 years later because he *is* guilty of rape, though not necessarily her own.

Given the novel's fragmented nature, the reader connects resemblances and draws conclusions which make him or her very much a part of the novel. For example, there is a strong resemblance between the first scene in which the servant mother cuts up a rabbit and the way in which Santiago Nasar is butchered by Angela's brothers. Watching the mother with the knife as she warns him to stay away from her daughter, feeding the dogs with rabbit insides, and feeling her bitterness, Santiago shudders because he intuits that what she does to the rabbit she would have liked do to him. "Don't be a savage," he told her. "Make believe it was a human being" (10). At the end of the novel, it is a human being that is butchered like an animal and his insides are almost eaten by dogs. When Angela's brothers butcher Santiago, he is pursued by dogs, "soaked in blood and carrying the roots of his entrails in his hands" (120). Had the servant given him the piece of paper which warned him that he was going to be killed by the Vicario brothers, the death would not have occurred. In this way his death saves the servant's daughter from further abuse. The fact that it is never clearly stated that the mother intentionally withholds the warning note from Santiago makes the novel less about a specific murder and more about human relations in general. García Márquez's point is not that such and such a thing happened, but that the dishonorable behavior of the rich young man deserves punishment. In the mind of the servant, and in the reader's mind, the social status gained by money, without ethical behavior, should be and can be taken away.

The process of awareness-raising that the underprivileged can be empowered and that any individual can search for agency does not stop with the servants. Angela's example particularly leads to drawing such a conclusion. The novel shows not only that the marginalized should act; it also shows that they can find the strength and the ways to improve their position in their existing environment. The lesson is particularly directed to women because García Márquez has repeatedly stated that, in the family and in the community, women dominate in their control of everyday life. Hence they hold enormous potential for changing social conditions and gaining their own agency. For example, one should note that Angela is forced into an arranged marriage mostly by the women in her family: her mother and her sisters who arrived with their husbands on the engagement day. She is victimized by her mother during the wedding night, and she has been shaped to follow gender roles by her domineering mother. However, Angela learns from her mother (and other women in town) how to be determined. We know that her husband, who returned her on her wedding night, did not read any of the "almost two thousand letters that she had written him ... [because] they were all unopened" (95), but he was moved by her determination and the strength of her character. The extreme behavior was learned from Purísima, who never gave in to anything.

Writing about Angela Vicario, M.I. Millington (1989) called her and women like her "unsung heroines" because they have qualities like courage, determination, and honesty, but their positions are not recognized. In his study of male–female relationships in the novel, Millington shows that García Márquez's work displays the irony of the patriarchal system. While the system portrays men as the principal actors and while mothers teach their daughters to obey and suffer, as Angela's mother does, the real truth is that men are generally passive and women are the ones who act. In the novel, men are inactive except in sexual situations, as in their frequent visits to Mariá Alejandrina Cervantes' brothel, or in Santiago's and his father's pursuit and abuse of their young female servants. Men do not act to prevent the Vicario brothers from killing Santiago Nasar, and the brothers are reluctant to kill their sister's perpetrator but they are encouraged by their mother and their girlfriends. When they are out with their knives, the only person who attempts to stop the killing is again a woman, Clotilde Armenta. She calls on several characters to intervene, and when all fails she even attempts to physically obstruct the Vicarios herself: "Clotilde Armenta grabbed Pedro Vicario by the shirt and shouted to Santiago Nasar to run because they were going to kill him" (115).

An analysis of Angela's relationship with her mother shows that while this traditional gender-oriented community imposed certain roles and was a version of hell, as Bauman says, it left the core of the human being or individual undamaged. We read that the "stolidity her mother had imposed" hid and sheltered inside her "the pure decency" (91) which lead her not to deceive her husband on their wedding night. The same human decency leads her to reject her mother and gain her husband back on her own terms, years after he returned her on their wedding night. As Agnes Heller explains in his study of modern community, or "modern social arrangement" (Heller, 2005, 63) the main change that is taking place is that the individual is beginning to assume an active role and to negotiate his or her place: "men and women [can no longer] sleepwalk through their lives; [but have] to wake themselves up and make their destiny" (Blackshaw, 2009, 24). The idea of 'waking up' describes well what takes place in García Márquez's novel. In the novel, Angela Vicario awakens, first sexually and then mentally, and comes to despise her mother's adherence to the teachings of the church and tradition.

Angela tells the narrator that she fell in love with her husband on the night when she was returned by him and beaten by her mother: "When Mama began to hit me, I began to remember him. I wasn't crying because of the blows or anything that had happened. I was crying because of him" (91). Her reaction seems odd at first, but at this point Bayardo San Román is no longer a pretentious rich man but a victim, like herself. Her feelings for another fellow human being led her to write him one letter per week, for 17 years. However, as the story evokes 19th-century romances, the heroine is quite modern because her love is not romantic but sexual:

> She was awakened by the certainty that he was naked in her bed. Then she wrote him a feverish letter, twenty pages long, in which without shame she let out the bitter truths that she had carried rotting in her heart ever since that ill-fated night. She spoke to him of the eternal scars he had left on her body, the salt of his tongue, the fiery furrow of his African tool.
>
> (94)

Her own sexuality, the narrator tells us, made her strong, and interestingly, it made her a virgin: "She became lucid, overbearing, mistress of her own free will, and she became a virgin again just for him, and she recognized no other authority than her own nor any other service than that of her obsession" (93).

One of the advantages literature has over social sciences is the poetic licence to create situations which are contradictory or unusual, and encourage the imagination to see the world from a different perspective. As we

saw in our discussion of Roman honor, virginity is not synonymous with
the prohibition of sex but with creative energy and purity of life. Angela
becomes "a virgin again" because the notion of virginity in her way of
seeing the world is not related to the hymen, which can be repaired easily
as her friends know well, but to a state of mind and being. She has awak-
ened to be a strong woman, standing on her own two feet: "She became
lucid, overbearing, mistress of her own free will." Her attitude and the fact
that "she recognized no other authority than her own" make her a modern
woman, a feminist, but also relates her to the women of classical Rome
who, as Barton explains, competed in the contest of purity just as strenu-
ously as the men competed in the contest of virtues such as *labor, indus-
tria, disciplina, diligentia*. "For the Roman women, to be *pura* and *casta*
required an ardent will," Barton writes (37).

Angela becomes "mistress of her fate for the first time" (93) when she
allows herself to experience feelings. They lead her to recognize that "hate
and love are reciprocal passions" (93). With the awakening of love for
herself first and then for her husband, she begins to despise her mother:
"For the first time since her birth, Angela Vicario saw her as she was: a
poor woman devoted to the cult of her defects" (92). "Just seeing her
would turn my stomach" (93), she told the narrator. But the novel as a
whole does not focus so much on the dislike of the patriarchal tradition,
honor culture, and oppressive women as it invites the reader to think about
different possibilities. As Carlin Barton wrote, "We cannot, any more than
the ancient Romans, live without honor" (Barton, 2008, 92). The novel
portrays traditional Latin American honor culture in order to reform it
from inside. Why do we need honor, asks the hungry wife in García Márquez's *No One Writes to the Colonel* (1961), it does not give us anything
to eat? We cannot eat honor, but it nurtures us, replies the wise Colonel (*el
honor no se come, pero nutre*).

As Bowman points out in his detailed study of the history of honor, the
notion of honor has been defined differently in each culture because each
time period has brought conditions and ideologies of its own which change
the classical concept. However, the notion of honor has never disappeared.
The biggest challenge in the history of honor has come since 1975, particularly since the Vietnam War, the rise of feminism, and the myth of individualism. However, as we have seen in García Márquez's novel, feminism
and individualism can form a dialogue with the honor culture. The culture
of honor influenced by the teachings of the church controlled women's sexuality and often led to violence. But with the invention of the pill there is
no longer the need to control women to prevent unwanted pregnancy.
Hence, sexual relationships before marriage or outside of marriage do not
need to be so zealously guarded.

As Angela suggests in the Colombian novel, virginity is not so much
related to hymen as it is to a particular type of being and acting; a type of
being that is necessary if human associations are to be meaningful. Qualities recognized and awarded by honor culture are not irrelevant or

antiquated, but our understanding of honor culture has to be broadened. In his study of honor, Bowman reasons, now that women have fought for "woman's right to a full measure of humanity and it is here to stay honor must accommodate itself to that concept or become irrelevant" (Bowman, 319). The struggle for rights, associated with the idea of civil society, has certainly brought great improvement, but human community benefits if and when the idea of rights is accompanied by the practice and ideology of the honor culture in which individuals keep each other in balance in their everyday lives: you will impress me and I will impress you because we depend on each other in our construction of identity and happiness, or we will shame each other in order to prevent unfair behavior and unhappiness. Honor and shame are two sides of the same coin.

If communities are to be built on trust and on strong actors, as all social theorists argue, literature like García Márquez's novel plays a role in teaching the value of trust and in motivating the reader to understand how and why some values from traditional society are important in elevating both the individual and the community. The short novel discussed here shows that women are pillars of community but that they have to recognize their own potential and the fact that they can influence change and improvement. Men are ridiculed for their aimlessness, drinking, and the machismo revealed in their relationship with prostitutes. Sexuality is an important topic which today does not need so much to be freed as it needs to be examined in a larger human and social context. Like other freedoms, sexual freedom also should come with responsibility, the novel suggests. No one prevents Santiago Nasar's death because the community instinctively felt that a man who believes that his social status gives him the right to abuse deserves to die. The novel does not advocate honor killing and violence, but it uses a case of honor killing as a metaphor to examine the question of human association. It strongly suggests that trust is an important aspect of community-building, and that women in particular need to 'awaken' and recognize their own potential and heritage which gives them the strength to make changes and a healthier relationship between the community and the individual.

References

Barton, Carlin. 2001. *Roman honor: the fire in the bones*. Berkeley: University of California Press.

Bauman, Zygmunt. (2004). *Identity: conversations with Benedetto Vecchi*. Cambridge: Polity Press.

Blackshaw, Tony. 2010. *Key concepts in community studies*. London: SAGE Publications.

Bowman, James. 2006. *Honor: a history*. New York: Encounter Books.

Britton, Celia. 2008. *The sense of community in French Caribbean fiction*. Liverpool University Press.

Burkholder, Mark. 1998. "Honor and Honors in colonial Spanish America." In L. Johnson & S. Lipsett-Rivera (Eds.). *The faces of honor: sex, shame, and violence in colonial Latin America* (18–45). University of New Mexico Press.

Cortázar, Julio. 1966. *Hopscotch: a novel.* New York: Random House.

Delanty, Gerard. 2010. *Community.* New York: Routledge.

Freire, Paolo. 1993. *Pedagogy of the oppressed.* New York: Continuum.

García Márquez, Gabriel. 1981/2009. *Crónica de una muerte anunciada.* Mexico: Random House, cuarta edición DEBOLSILLO.

García Márquez, Gabriel. *Chronicle of a death foretold.* Gregory Rabassa (Trans.). 2003. (All text in English is from this edition.) New York: Vintage International.

Heller, Agnes. 2005. "The Three Logics of Modernity and the Double Bind of the Modern Imagination." Thesis *Eleven.* 81 (2005), 63–79.

Johnson, Lyman, & L. Lipsett-Rivera, Sonia (Eds.). 1998. *The faces of honor: sex, shame, and violence in colonial Latin America.* Albuquerque: University of New Mexico Press.

Miller, William Ian. 1993. *Humiliation and other essays on honor, social discomfort, and violence.* Ithaca, NY: Cornell University Press.

Millington, M.I. 1989. "Unsung Heroine: Power and Marginality in *Crónica de una muerte anunciada.*" *Bulletin of Hispanic Studies*, 73–85.

Putnam, Robert D. 2000. *Bowling alone: the collapse and revival of American community.* New York: Simon & Schuster.

Viater, Nora. 2011. "Garcia Márquez le Gano un juicio a uno de sus personajes." Literatura, *Diario Clarin*, primero de diciembre.

4 Reframing the Archive and Expanding Collective Memory in order to Bridge the Divide between Community and Civil Society in Yxta Maya Murray's *The Conquest*

Pablo Ramirez

In the 1960s and 1970s, the Chicano Movement began to actively engage a collective memory that included the myths of an indigenous Mexican past. At the time, the U.S. was experiencing the largest waves of Mexican immigration in its history. The American media cast these immigrants as an invading horde. Chicano nationalists countered these negative representations by utilizing collective memory, specifically the myth of Aztlán, in order to reframe Mexican immigration. According to the myth, around the 10th century AD the god Huitzilopochtli told the Aztecs to leave Aztlán, their homeland, and travel south until they saw an eagle perched on a cactus, devouring a snake. In 1328, the prophecy is fulfilled, and they establish their empire in Tenochtitlan, the site of present-day Mexico City. However, it was prophesied that during the era of the Fifth Sun the Aztecs would once again return to Aztlán, which is believed to be located in the U.S. Southwest. It was no coincidence, Chicano nationalists claimed, that this mass migration was happening just as the era of the Fifth Sun had begun. This was a clear fulfillment of an ancient prophecy; Mexican immigrants were not an invading horde of foreigners, but a people reclaiming their ancestral homeland.

As we can see from the above example, collective memory is not simply a matter of content; it is a structure that responds to political and social upheaval and crisis by using memories and history to interpret and create the present. It provides a framework that helps to articulate how and why a group remembers. As Iwona Irwin-Zarecka explains, collective memory allows a community to "frame" a certain event in order to shape how it is read and remembered (Irwin-Zarecka, 1994, 5). Collective memory, in other words, is a dynamic process that responds to political and social circumstances in the present by using the past to reframe current events and crises (Irwin-Zarecka, 1994, 7). The myth of Aztlán, for example, has no inherent political significance. Chicano nationalists engaged collective memory in order to reframe an event (mass immigration from Mexico), transforming Mexicans from outsiders to heirs and, in the process, galvanizing a community to political action. As one can see from this example of the myth of Aztlán, collective memory is not static; it must be continually shaped and reshaped in order to address contemporary political and cultural situations.

Unfortunately, Chicano nationalists turned Aztlán into an identitarian myth, a strategy nations have used to create a homogenous people within a set of closed borders. Suddenly there were insiders and outsiders. Chicano nationalists' vision of an authentic Chicano community was a patriarchal one, which silenced the voices of Chicana feminists and queer activists in order to create a unified cultural front. Looking at the history of the Chicano Movement, we can see how even a community that brought about so much positive political and cultural change can lapse into totalitarianism. But how do we form a community without lapsing into totalitarianism? This is a major concern for continental philosopher, Jean-Luc Nancy. As Todd May explains, Nancy uses the term 'totalitarianism' to refer to "narrow constraints placed upon individual and social identity and behaviour rather than just to a type of state" (23). This is a danger for both the Left and the Right. For the Right, totalitarianism may involve imposing a set of traditional values upon the unwilling (May, 22); for the Left, it may involve having a "respect for others ... overridden in the name of obligation" (May, 22). For Nancy, the moment a community defines a common nature that characterizes its members is the moment when the community begins to veer dangerously close to a state of totalitarianism. This moment of articulation must be avoided in favor of a focus on what cannot be reduced to a single meaning or definition.

As a corrective to the normative, totalitarian nature of the Chicano Movement, many Chicanx[1] embraced Gloria Anzaldúa's concept of the borderlands. Like the Chicano nationalists, Anzaldúa engaged Chicanx collective memory in order to imagine community. Although Gloria Anzaldúa, author of the seminal *Borderlands/La Frontera*, does not use the term 'collective memory,' reading her work it is clear that for her what helps to (re)constitute both the individual and the community is an immersion in collective memory. Instead of using collective memory to focus on the collective or fashion a history of a people, which is what Chicano nationalists attempted to do, Anzaldúa engages pre-Columbian myths and goddesses in order to develop a program of self-care for Chicanx. Anzaldúa charges the Chicanx community with a serious mission: to put "history through a sieve, winnow out the lies" and reinterpret "history and, using new symbols ... shap[ing] new myths" (Anzaldúa, 82). She encourages people to create an identity by negotiating between two or more cultural frames of reference, sifting through history and not relying on a monocultural historical narrative.

Anzaldúa argues that Chicanx need to create a knowledge system that deals with two or more seemingly antithetical cultural frames of reference in order to open up possibilities of alliance and mixture that have been foreclosed by nationalism. Anzaldúa aims to heal the open wounds of a borderlands experience, which may involve *choques* or clashes and shocks that sometimes occur from living between two nations and multiple frames of reference. One of the main methods of healing such border wounds is to enable Chicanx to narrate their individual lives through an engagement with collective memory. Although collective memory is the common foundation for both community and individual, an engagement with collective memory does not produce a homogenous community or a single type of Chicanx. In other words, the borderlands approach to collective memory does not create an identitarian myth for a community, but an ethical program that heals the self and allows us to connect with others to end oppression. Instead of building a nation, this group exists between borders, in the borderlands, finding new ways of coming together outside the tactics and strategies of nationalism. Her focus on the ethical program of building alliances with other oppressed peoples changed the vision of community from a closed group into an open community that is constantly in the making.

Members of the Chicanx community must create what Michael Hames-Garcia, in his reading of Anzaldúa's *Borderlands*, calls an "original relation to history," which would allow one to create a new way of relating to the past in order to respond to one's political, communal and personal relations and circumstances (Hames-Garcia, 2000, 113). Chicanx may share a collective memory but, for Anzaldúa, an engagement with this collective memory is about choice and a respect of difference. By encouraging Chicanx to create an original relation to history, Anzaldúa hopes to foster difference within the Chicanx community instead of having the individual subsumed by a homogenous culture. While history often functions as a national narrative that tells its citizens what and how they should remember events, collective memory does not. As the pitfalls of Chicano nationalism make clear, collective memory is not supposed to form a nation but a community—two very distinct entities. Moreover, while history tends to establish a linear, progressive narrative, collective memory must return to the past in order to move forward. By embracing the cyclical time of myth and the linear trajectory of history, the Chicanx community returns to the past in order to move forward into the future. It is this return–forward movement that establishes a close relationship between the past and the present.

But what if such a mission to create an original relation to history becomes too heavy a burden for a single community member to bear? What if a community needs to expand and/or supplement collective memory to remember? Yxta Maya Murray explores these questions in *The Conquest* in which Sara, a Chicana book restorer who works for the Getty Museum, comes across a book written by a mad Spanish monk in the 16th century. It is the story of Helen, an Aztec princess and juggler who disguises herself as a man and boards a ship for Spain. Reading the 16th-century book, which is also titled *The Conquest*, Sara remembers the Aztec and

Mexican myths and legends her mother told her as a child and is certain that the book is not a work of fiction but an autobiography, written by an indigenous woman disguising herself as a monk. By establishing the provenance of Helen's story, Sara sees an opportunity to use the archive to honor her deceased militant mother and recuperate the Chicanx past.

However, to expand collective memory to include official archives constitutes a significant departure to how Chicanx remember the past. While collective memory consists of a great many different kinds of materials and narratives, Chicanx collective memory places a great deal of importance on an oral tradition in which parents and grandparents transmit stories and events to their children through storytelling. Therefore, participation in civil society through an engagement with public institutions, such as archives, is a path that the Chicanx community has only begun to explore. For the longest time the Chicanx community was unable to access the archives upon which official historical discourse is based. As a result, to remember the past meant relying on a community-based transmission of collective memory. Chicanx are still suspicious of archives and museums, and with good reason. Archives, after all, were created and maintained by the victors and the powerful, who worked very hard to erase the history of the conquered, the marginalized, and the powerless. Museums and archives tend to be seen as instruments of the state rather than as civic institutions. Collective memory and the archive therefore represent two opposite approaches to the past that even borderlands Chicanx find difficult reconciling. *The Conquest*, however, illustrates not only the necessity of the archives, but the possibility of transforming the archives into a space of civic engagement.

In *Archive Fever*, Jacques Derrida states, "[T]here is no political power without control of the archive, if not memory. Effective democratization can always be measured by this essential criterion: the participation in and access to the archive, its constitution, and its interpretation" (4). Sara is convinced that she can democratize the archive by making it a civic institution where Chicanx collective memory can thrive. Sara needs the archive because the responsibility of not only her mother's memory, but also the myths and tales transmitted to Sara are too heavy a burden and prevent her from going forward. Without the mediation of the archive, she becomes haunted, and her body becomes an archive that flesh-and-blood humans were never meant to be: "But I was afraid to forget her, and collected everything that I could and stored her inside of me—every eyelash, the tones her voice could take, the clicking of the beads around her wrists and throat" (Murray, 2003, 43). Bridging the divide between community and civil society, collective memory and archive, will allow her to pursue both collective rights (recovering the Chicanx past) and her individual goals (marry her white American fiancé).

The Conquest, in other words, imagines how an interaction with a public institution can help bolster and enrich collective memory by transforming an engagement with collective memory into both a community practice and a form of civic engagement. By focusing on a book that is both archival object and text, *The Conquest* shows how practicing narrative ethics (i.e., an ethics of reading) can accomplish both kinds of engagement. If collective memory recreates the past in order to reframe or recontextualize the present, narrative ethics recreates the text through reinterpretation. By immersing herself in the collective memory of the Chicanx community, Sara is able to transform an archival European cultural object into a Chicanx text. In other words, narrative ethics becomes a radical act when a Chicana rereads the novel that is supposed to have been written by a mad European monk and transforms the book into a text written by one of her cultural ancestors. In doing so, *The Conquest* helps the reader imagine a different relation to the past, one that creates a contact zone between the archive and collective memory, orality and textuality, and community and civil society.

Collective Memory and the Chicanx Community

In his book *The Inoperative Community*, Jean-Luc Nancy examines the important constitutive role community plays in the formation of the individual, which he prefers to call "singularity." Instead of seeing the individual/singularity as a pre-existing and self-enclosed entity—something that exists prior to its immersion in community—Nancy argues that individuals are formed by what is outside of them, and that the line between inside and outside is so blurry that it renders these terms inadequate. This approach to the individual establishes a major point of intersection between Anzaldúa and Nancy. For Anzaldúa, her program of individual self-care and self-making requires an engagement with the collective (especially collective memory). This requires the individual to remain open to multiple frames of reference, multiple narratives, and multiple alliances. Similarly, for Nancy, if an individual were completely enclosed, then that individual would not be able to connect with others. However, it is important that we not simply do away with the boundaries of the individual. If the individual had no boundaries, then the individual would be completely immersed in some common substance or experience. To better explain the complicated nature of inside and outside, Nancy focuses on the practice of sharing, which renders these boundaries neither fixed nor demolished.

For Todd May, Nancy's main contribution to the discussion of communities is his emphasis on how the community helps constitute the individual as a being-in-community. But Nancy, for May, concentrates almost exclusively on the normative aspect of community—what a community must do to avoid lapsing into totalitarianism—and not very much on the constitutive aspect of community, which would address how communities are created and sustained. May asks, without any shared experiences, values, or goals, how does a community come into existence and thrive? He suggests that "community is defined by the practices that constitute it"

(52). He argues that "introducing the concept of practices allows us to see both what constitutes a community and what it is about communities that is constitutive of individuals" (53). There does not have to be a normative aspect to such practice. In other words, "the point in isolating the concept of practice is not to tell people how to act" (53). An individual can belong to different communities and engage in very different practices.

The Conquest, I argue, explores how an engagement with collective memory becomes a practice (among many) that constitutes the Chicanx community and therefore Chicanx individuals at the same time. *The Conquest* represents Chicanx ethnicity as the acceptance of an obligation to remember; it is this engagement with collective memory that constitutes our membership in the Chicanx community. Similar to the practice that May defines, an engagement with collective memory is historically contingent, socially significant, and political in nature. As the text illustrates, not all members engage in this practice (engagement with collective memory) and when they do, they do not engage in this practice in exactly the same way. *The Conquest* presents three approaches the Chicanx community has taken to deal with the past: the assimilationist approach adopted by the Mexican American generation (1930–1960), the nationalist approach of the Chicano Movement (1960s and 1970s), and the borderlands approach championed by most contemporary Chicanx writers and intellectuals. Although these approaches to the past arose as a result of specific historical circumstances, *The Conquest* illustrates how the Chicanx community today embraces all three modes of remembering and forgetting, thereby showing that there is no uniform approach to the past.

This does not mean, however, that the text presents all three forms of remembering as equally effective or ethical. The two earlier forms of remembering (assimilationist and nationalist) can lead to some ethical failures and a distorted relationship to the past and the future. Sara's father, for example, represents the assimilationist approach to the past adopted by the Mexican American generation. Political organizations like The League of United Latin American Citizens (LULAC) adopted a model of assimilation that stressed Mexican Americans' status as native-born American citizens in order to secure their civil rights (García, 1989). Sara's father voices the Mexican American generation's assimilationist approach when he tells Sara to forget the past and embrace the privileges that come from being a U.S. citizen: "Everything here … It's your birthright. You're born here, wham. Everything for you. Your problems are tiny problems.… All you've got to do is close your eyes on the bad" (170). Sara's father may embrace the benefits of citizenship, but that does not mean he embraces civil society, as well. As Philip Oxhorn points out, civil societies promote more inclusive democracies that allow people to pursue *both* individual and collective rights (28). Sara's father, however, focuses solely on individual rights, urging Sara to forget about collective rights and collective memory.

Assimilationists, like Sara's father, have no use for collective memory. On the contrary, the assimilationist encourages immigrants and members of ethnic communities to forget their ethnic pasts and embrace a homogenous American future. Once one forgets, one can embrace the American neo-liberal definition of the autonomous individual who has the freedom to pursue his or her self-interests. His assimilationist amnesia, however, is represented as the repression of traumatic memories. He used to be a man with a "perfect memory" and would remember every injustice and brutal act of physical violence that he suffered at the hands of white Americans. He went so far as to inscribe these memories of racist violence on his body in the form of a tattoo. He couldn't forgive them, so he decided to forget in order to let go of his corrosive anger. No longer consumed by remembering and hating, he becomes an American success story, establishing a successful construction company. However he does so at the cost of his past and community.

Oxhorn reminds us that there is a difference between community and civil society. While a community is based on trust and cooperation, civil society allows us to pursue collective rights in the absence of trust and close-knit ties (31). Despite the difference between the two, communities can effectively participate in civil society. For Sara's mother, Beatrice, however, there can be no point of intersection between the Chicanx community and public institutions, which means there can be no meaningful civil society for the Chicanx community. For her, there is no space between community and the state. Beatrice is clearly motivated to pursue collective rights such as recovering the Chicanx past, but she tries to achieve these goals by focusing solely on community and maintaining a strong distrust of public institutions.

In this manner, Beatrice represents the Chicano nationalist approach to collective memory. It is Beatrice who introduces Sara to Chicanx collective memory through her storytelling, passing on to her daughter a fierce desire to recuperate the Chicanx past. Beatrice's engagement with collective memory, especially indigenous myths and history, allows her to make sense of her political situation and to forge a connection with Sara. Beatrice, however, is incredibly suspicious of archives and museums. When Beatrice takes Sara to see an exhibit of pre-Columbian artifacts, she tells Sara that the museum-goers might as well be gawking at them; Chicanx are the ones on display. Enraged, Beatrice reaches into the glass display case that a guard forgot to lock and takes a Mesoamerican incubala. For her, taking the remnant is not theft but a reclamation of the past. For Beatrice, the archive, as represented by the museum, can only be an instrument of the state and never be a site of memory for the Chicanx community.

Both of Sara's parents reject civil society. Sara's father rejects it in favor of the state and individual rights; Sara's mother rejects it in favor of collective rights and community. However, the character who has the most ambivalent relation to both collective memory and civil society is Sara's colleague, Teresa, a woman who had once been the best conservationist until her successful battle with cancer makes her realize her mortality. She then loses all interest in preserving objects for future generations: "Everything should be used up, swallowed up! Not saved. Not hoarded like the bones of saints. And I do see this place [archive] as a fantastic tomb" (48). She cuts herself off from both the past and the future and, in doing so, becomes an autonomous individual who is determined to live in the present. She is presented in an ambiguous manner. On the one hand, she is depicted as someone who is determined to enjoy life, but her enjoyment is always shadowed by her mortality.

She has an admirable rebellious spirit, but her rebellion also entails an attempt to subvert the museum as a space for civil society, where the public can connect to the past. Teresa transforms the museum from a public institution into a private space when she holds an after-hours party. The academics she invites use the preserved museum objects to create a strong, tactile connection to the past. As Sara runs around making sure the objects are not harmed, Teresa stands at a distance, enjoying the sight of these objects being used up. Since she can only see herself as an individual, instead of as a member of a community, she sees no reason to preserve the past for future generations. Without a community, she lives as someone who has no future because she can only see herself as someone who is about to die. Consequently, she has no interest in preserving the museum as a civic institution.

How a Counterstance Makes Memory an Act of Paralysis

Oxhorn points out that civil society "is a mechanism for non-violent resolution" (29); civil society, in other words, allows members to deal with conflict in a productive manner. By rejecting civil society, Sara's father avoids conflict altogether by repressing his traumatic past while Sara's mother is driven to wage war against white Americans and their institutions. Sara hopes to use the archive as a way to resolve her conflict between her promise to her mother to recuperate the Chicanx past and her promise to marry her white American fiancé. The major obstacle to a peaceful resolution, however, are the promises the daughters make to their dead parents to avenge their people. In other words, the parents make their daughters promise to wage war. These promises threaten to rob Sara and Helen of their agency and their right to create an individual relation to history. Worst of all, what both parents ask their daughters to do is to connect memory with vengeance, thereby forcing them to adopt a counterstance in regard to their enemies.

The Conquest represents this counterstance as both an unethical approach to collective memory and a barrier to civil society. The text echoes Gloria Anzaldúa's advice to Chicanx to reject Chicano nationalism's counterstance because it simply encourages one to react (rather than think) and define oneself in simple contradistinction to the 'enemy' or the other. A counterstance, in other words, encourages us to react and define ourselves in contrast to another group. It is a self-defeating political stance that simply "locks [us] into a duel of oppressor and oppressed" when we should strive to stand "on both shores at once" (Anzaldúa, 78).

The Conquest illustrates that a community is neither a reproduction of the past nor a reproduction of the parents' or ancestors' identities. A community must change over time. One generation connects to the future not by hoping the next generation will be like them, but to help them grow and develop into a different group of people that can adapt and respond to change. Indeed, Sara and Helen are very different from their parents and cannot put limits on their hearts; they fall in love with the enemy. Sara falls in love with a white American soldier and Helen falls in love with a white European woman, as well as European literature, food, and culture. This is why both Helen and Sara must break their promises to their parents. In *The Conquest*, one must abandon the counterstance to pursue a path that allows the Chicanx community to participate in civil society in order to engage memory in a healthy manner.

Forgiveness as an Ethics of Memory

To bridge the divide between collective memory and archive (and hence civil society) one must abandon a counterstance in favor of forgiveness. While people often associate forgiveness with forgetting, *The Conquest* shows how forgiveness allows us to remember who and what is important. Helen's promise to her father, for example, creates a morality of memory rather than an ethics of memory. Unlike ethics, Margalit explains, "we need morality precisely because we do not care" (2003, 288). Helen does not care for Charles V, but her promise to her father is a constant reminder of the murderous emperor. This constant reminder threatens to establish a stronger relationship between Helen and the emperor than the one between Helen and her father. Reading Murray's *The Conquest*, one cannot help but ask, what is the cost of remembering people we hate, people we do not care for, and who do not care for us?

If Anzaldúa argues that a counterstance locks us into an eternal duel with our enemy, Yxta Maya Murray shows how a counterstance asks us to remember our enemy and not the people we care about. Helen realizes this the moment she is finally given the opportunity to carry out her father's wishes and has the emperor at her mercy. Just as she steels herself to kill the old, feeble man on his deathbed, he calls her "mother." It turns out that the dying man responsible for decimating her people only wants to be held by his mother. Helen is filled with pity:

> Each time I bent down to his ear and whispered, "Suffer not old man," and "Sleep peacefully, King, without pain," I imagined that I did not care for the Emperor who killed us, but instead comforted my beloved father's starved body, giving him a succor I could not when he died.
>
> (261)

As Margalit argues, "Forgiveness is an ethical duty, it is a duty in that special case of ethics, namely a duty to ourselves" (2003, 1710). In other words, it is a duty we owe to ourselves in order to free ourselves from hate and anger. By forgiving the emperor and replacing him with her father, Helen succeeds in separating her father's memory from the emperor. By letting go of the emperor and her promise, she can better remember her father. Forgiveness becomes a refusal to let your enemy or evil define you; it encourages a remembering that liberates you from your oppressor. Forgiveness allows Helen to abandon her counterstance and to remember in a way that is both beneficial and nourishing.

Narrative Ethics and Reframing the Archive

The text illustrates how a borderlands approach to narrative ethics can help bridge the divide between archive and collective memory, as well as community and civil society. In narrative ethics or the ethics of reading, stagnant print is brought back to life—rendered different and new—each time one rereads a text. An interpretation is supposed to re-create the text and make it live. In *The Conquest*, an ethics of reading makes it possible for Chicanx collective memory to appropriate an archive and civil society through reinterpretation. When Sara encounters *The Conquest*, a book supposedly written by a mad 16th-century European monk, she is certain that it is written by an indigenous woman instead. Although she has no proof, her connection to Chicanx collective memory allows her to recognize the book as part of Chicanx history. To prove the provenance of the book, however, she must employ the materials from the archive itself in order to introduce *The Conquest* into Chicanx collective memory. To do so she must shift from oral myth to text, whose intertextuality is not separate from European texts but informed by them. That is to say, that while it is collective memory that allows Sara to penetrate the disguise of the text (a disguise that enabled it to be preserved) and to see its Aztec origins, the process of establishing its proper provenance has very little to do with cultural purity or authenticity. In fact, the only way to reclaim the text is by depending on other European texts. Finding herself in the archive, in other words, is the result of a process of intertextuality. She begins to look for Helen in the archive's old European texts, eventually accumulating enough traces of Helen to prove her theory and establish *The Conquest* as both a European and Chicanx text. Sara reclaims the book through interpretation, but she does so not to establish an exclusive claim or an origin as nations do. Helen's book becomes part of Chicanx collective memory, not by separating it from Europe, but by connecting it to other European texts. In doing so, Sara transforms the archives from a site of European history and theft to a site of reclamation and memory.

It is the text's intertexuality that begins to break down this myth of authenticity and genealogies. In this way, *The Conquest* connects the ethics of reading with an ethics of remembering. Not only does Sara work to conserve the book-as-object, she transforms the object from a book into a text—open to new interpretations and new labels. Rereading becomes reframing. Sara's rereading/reframing does not attach Helen's *The Conquest* to its original context—Europe—but to an intercultural nexus of connections. By reframing the archive through a rereading (or reinterpretation) of *The Conquest*, Sara enables Chicanx collective memory to provide an entirely new context (Chicanx and Latin American) that the creators of the archive never imagined for its European collection. The intercultural nexus that Sara creates through her attempt to reframe/reinterpret Helen's text goes against the nexus established by rich old J. Paul Getty, who as a collector creates a collection that, in Stewart's words, "marks the space of nexus for all narratives, the place where history is transformed into space, into property" (1984, 251). The collection, in other words, is the property of J. Paul Getty and is supposed to function as a testament to his greatness as a collector. However, what Sara does is transform this archive from a rich white man's property to both a borderlands space and a space for civil society in which Chicanx can create an original relation to history that would allow them to recuperate their memories in order to recuperate themselves amid objects of great European literature and culture. *The Conquest* shows the power of collective memory to defeat the very power dynamics that make the archive possible. Sara's rereading brings the rare books in the collection into dialogue with one another in order to establish a new context from which to read Chicanx history or Chicanx collective memory.

Conclusion

In the end, *The Conquest* imagines the expansion of Chicanx collective memory to include official archives. However, this expansion affects the civil sphere, as well. By merging collective memory with the archive and civil society, the reality that the archive renders intelligible is radically changed, as well. What Sara has done is to transform what was considered a work of fiction, which involved magic and myth, into an autobiography, meaning that myth, magic and ghosts are presented as real:

> I think there's just enough between these pages to dynamite a small section of reality.... If *he* could be *her*, then what else have we got wrong? they'll wonder. I'm liable to believe anything now. Maybe there *are* Sirens beneath the ocean. Maybe that cold wind spooking you *is* the breath of the dead and buried clamoring for justice.
>
> (283)

Chicanx collective memory enchants the sphere of civil society. Chicanx collective memory proves Margalit's assertion that shared memory is caught up between myth and history, that is to say "between viewing the world as an enchanted place (myth) and viewing the world as a disenchanted place (critical history)" (544–545). Chicanx literature, in its attempt to explore the uses and opportunities of collective memory, affords the Chicanx community a site that negotiates between myth and history. Chicanx literature, in other words, becomes a site that explores both myth and history in way that the realism of everyday life and institutions resist.

By claiming that the Chicanx community lives with myth through an engagement with collective memory, I am not simply saying that the community takes myth as a literal truth, but as what Margalit calls a "noble lie," in which the community shows a willingness "to shape their lives in light of the myth" (553–557), thereby transforming myth into "a sacred story ... connected with revivifying elements from the past" (561–562). Myth is an essential element of collective memory in the Chicanx community because it involves changing the way one usually sees causality and history. As Margalit explains,

> In the disenchanted world of critical history, there is no backward causality. We cannot affect the past; we cannot undo the past, resurrect the past, or revivify the past. Only descriptions of the past can be altered, improved, or animated.
>
> (565–567)

Collective memory, on the other hand, can make the past anew. In other words, collective memory encourages members to recreate the past in order to reframe or reinterpret the present. The present will always make new demands on the past, so the past is constantly reinterpreted, remade, and rediscovered. With the proper provenance of *The Conquest* established, the Chicanx community can now use the archive, a civic institution, to preserve their own mythical perspective—together with collective memory.

Note

1 'Chicanx' is a gender-neutral term; unlike 'Chican@,' which includes both the feminine and masculine –a and –o respectively, the term 'Chicanx' rejects this gender binary. 'Chicanx' can be both singular and plural.

References

Anzaldúa, Gloria. 1987. *Borderlands: the new mestiza/la frontera*. San Francisco: Aunt Lute.

Crane, Susan A. 1997. "Writing the Individual Back into Collective Memory." *The American Historical Review* 102(5), 1372–1385.

Derrida, Jacques. 1996. *Archive fever: a Freudian impression*. Chicago: University of Chicago Press.

Garcia, Mario T. 1989. *Mexican Americans: leadership, ideology, & identity, 1930–1960*. New Haven: Yale University Press.

Halbwachs, Maurice. 1992. *On collective memory*. (L.A. Coser, Trans.). Chicago: University of Chicago Press.

Hames-Garcia, Michael Roy. 2000. "How to Tell a Mestizo from an Enchirito®: Colonialism and National Culture in the Borderlands." *Diacritics* 30(4), 102–122.

Irwin-Zarecka, Iwona. 1994. *Frames of remembrance: the dynamics of collective memory.* New Brunswick, NJ: Transaction Publishers.

Margalit, Avishai. 2003. *The ethics of memory* (2nd ed.). Cambridge, MA: Harvard University Press.

May, Todd. 1997. *Reconsidering difference.* University Park, PA: University of Pennsylvania Press.

Nancy, Jean-Luc. 1991. *The inoperative community.* (P. Connor, Trans.). Minneapolis: University of Minnesota Press.

Ramirez, Pablo. 2010. "Toward a Borderlands Ethics: The Undocumented Migrant and Haunted Communities in Contemporary Chicana/o Fiction." *Aztlán: A Journal of Chicano Studies* 35(1), 49–67.

Stewart, Susan. 1984. *On longing: narratives of the miniature, the gigantic, the souvenir, the collection.* Baltimore: Johns Hopkins University Press.

5 Memory and Temporary Communities in Laura Restrepo's *The Dark Bride/La novia oscura*

Maca Suazo and Lisa Bellstedt

This chapter explores how different types of community are formed in *The Dark Bride*, a novel by Colombian author, Laura Restrepo. While the communities portrayed in the novel are fictitious, they are based on real communities that have existed in Colombia's history. After a brief summary of the novel's plot, this chapter highlights the connections between its main characters, Sayonara, El Payanés, and Sacramento, and examines the formation of a union between the Tropical Oil Company workers and the prostitutes in the La Catunga neighborhood of Tora. Both communities play important roles in the so-called 'rice strike,' a major event that drives the novel's plot. The larger community of workers and prostitutes comes together in solidarity against the oppression of a larger power, but is eventually defeated by the Colombian government, the Tropical Oil Company, and Colombia's military forces. While the community's temporal formation does not lead to major victory, it offers the underprivileged some comfort and satisfaction by simply having existed.

It is worth noting that the Tropical Oil Company did exist in reality in the Barrancabermeja region of Colombia (where the novel takes place) between 1919 and 1951. There is documentation that six strikes were held against the company, much like the one that transpires in the novel. Restrepo's depiction of the strike offers a critical interpretation of the oppression suffered by similar communities in Colombia's history and imagines a scenario in which these communities have the potential to rebel against oppressive forces. In this study, Michael Taylor's and Mariane Krause Jacob's definitions of community inform the discussion.

The story of Sayonara (a prostitute who becomes a legend due to her rebellious and exotic nature) is intertwined with those of Sacramento and his best friend, El Payanés—a worker who, like many others, comes to the town in search of work and a better life, arriving on foot from the Popayán region (hence his nickname 'El Payanés'). Each of the three protagonists becomes involved in the rice strike in his or her own way. The story of Sayonara develops in the background in order to shine a spotlight on the entire community's action sparked by the strike, effectively reclaiming the memory of strikes in the past. The strike erupts as a consequence of the poor working conditions imposed by the Tropical Oil Company (the

Troco), specifically the abysmal meals provided to the workers consisting of balls of rice floating in a tasteless brown sugar broth. The prostitutes join the workers "for nearly twenty days and nights" (Restrepo, 1999, 87) to confront the oppression, driven by both the oil company and the military, with a determination equal to that of the oil plant workers. In spite of their efforts, the oil company defeats the strikers through various intimidation tactics, causing the community to disband. The story revolves around its protagonists, culminating with an ambiguous image that the reader is left to interpret on his or her own.

According to Claire Lindsay (2003), the novel takes place in the oil region of the Magdalena Medio of Colombia, in a village that is now called Barrancabermeja. Citing Robert Davis (1993), she writes that "Tropical Oil was a subsidiary of Standard Oil of New Jersey. They held the concession of Barrancabermeja from 1919 until 1951" (Lindsay, 2003, 51). During the time in which the novel takes place, the country suffered a period of extreme violence. Lindsay writes that the transitional period between Liberals and Conservative Republicans was "a particularly turbulent period of Colombian history, marked by repeated electoral fraud, a belligerent labour movement and ubiquitous violence throughout the country" (Lindsay, 2003, 51). The rice strike in the novel is a fictitious representation of a series of strikes that, according to Enrique Valencia (1984), occurred in Barrancabermeja during the 1930s and 1940s. Lindsay (again citing Valencia, 1984, 40) writes that "[t]here were six strikes total held by the *Unión Sindical Obrera* against the Tropical Oil Company" (Lindsay, 2003, 51). While the dates are historically accurate and the oil company as well as the strikes did exist in reality, the novel recounts a version of events based on memories shared by characters who are interviewed by a fictitious narrator. As Deborah Martin (2008) explains, Restrepo's novel

> is concerned with the new cultural identities created by changing configurations of wealth in Colombia in the 1940s, especially with those new communities formed around flows of capital from North America in the creation of an oil industry in the north-east of the country.

As the oil industry developed, communities of prostitutes started to appear to provide services to the employees of the foreign-owned petroleum plant. While the male workers were happy with their presence, the prostitutes faced a campaign of discrimination led by the Catholic Church against them specifically and the women of La Catunga in general, while the Colombian government enforced health regulations in order to control the prostitutes and later intimidate them with the use of military force as punishment for their support of the strikers.

Community, Belonging, and Solidarity

Michael Taylor (1982) argues that community is an *open concept*, based on three universal characteristics: that a community is a group of people that shares specific beliefs, values, ideologies and myths; that a community shares codes and symbols used to communicate and coexist with each other; and that members of a community will establish different kinds of social relationships (Taylor, 1982, 18). In the novel, the oil plant workers and the prostitutes both express the need to belong and share with each other the experience of oppression and the language and symbols of the oppressed. Communication is essential to their sense of community, as is mutual understanding. Speaking from a Latin American perspective, Mariane Krause Jacob (1999) also argues that the concept of community possesses three main characteristics: belonging, interdependence, and communication (Krause Jacob, 1999, 49). She particularly emphasizes that community members share ideals or problems (55), as well as a similar interpretation of daily life (56). Krause Jacob also emphasizes that communities are constructed and reconstructed through communication, which is an important defining characteristic of the communities in Restrepo's novel.

An example that illustrates the concept of community as belonging can be found in the community of the petroleum plant employees, who travel together on paydays to La Catunga using trucks that are converted into buses. As one of the characters, Sacramento, insists, the petroleum plant employees are united by a sense of pride which stems from the affection the prostitutes show towards them by calling them "*los peludos*" [the shaggy men]:

> They called us the shaggy men because an oil worker was proud of arriving in La Catunga looking tough, hairy and bearded. But clean and smelling fine, wearing leather boots and a white shirt, with a gold watch, and a ring to show off his salary. And always, as if it were a medal, his company ID visible on his lapel. The ID that identified you as an obrero petrolero, an oil worker. That, hermano, was our badge of honour.
>
> (Restrepo, 1999, 2)

In addition to their sense of pride, the community of petroleum plant workers also shares a defining image of a working man who can afford to wear an expensive ring and who can show off his Company ID. The community of this group of men who visit La Catunga is defined and united by its members' common profession. Their sense of identity comes from being a part of this group, and being a 'shaggy man' is synonymous with being honorable.

In the novel, the *feeling* of belonging extends beyond the local boundaries of the community as Frank Brasco, a North American engineer, unites with the workers and later with the Colombians during the rice strike because he is attracted to the group's sense of belonging and togetherness. He also shares with them a longing for a world that rejects exploitation. While visiting the home of Todos los Santos, where the strikers and the prostitutes who supported them stay on the night that the strike begins, Frank Brasco observes that: "despite the tension and the overpopulation, there was harmony in the sleeping house, and [...] the warmth of close bodies staved off any danger" (Restrepo, 1999, 88). Despite his education and origin from a very different culture and society, Brasco appreciates the animalistic feeling of togetherness of this "human flock" or "the affinity of the human flock when it finds itself gathered" (Restrepo, 1999, 89). He longs to be a part of this community in a meaningful way: "he realized with happiness how much it pleased him to feel like a member of the clan" (Restrepo, 1999, 89).

As an example of Krause Jacob's characteristic of interdependence, the novel explores the interrelation in the community of women from La Catunga, whose complex web of interactions is based on the need for survival and their ability to support themselves through their work as prostitutes. This interrelation is established by a determined hierarchy that exists in La Catunga, according to the "tariff" that each of the women is able to pay. The women hang different-colored light bulbs above their doorways to inform clients of how much money each of their services will cost, effectively creating a hierarchical system. Each woman's price is set according to "how exotic and distant a woman's nationality [is]" (Restrepo, 1999, 3).

> Green for the blond French women; red for the Italians, so temperamental; blue for all women from neighboring countries; yellow for the colombianas; and common, ordinary white—vulgar Philips bulbs—for the pipatonas, who only aspired to a crust of bread to feed their children.
>
> (Restrepo, 1999, 5)

The women of La Catunga are bonded by a sense of shared suffering. This suffering is partly due to the nature of their profession and the fact that it is viewed in their society as a permanent condition. Once they dedicate themselves to the profession, they can never cease to be prostitutes: "for us, once we become a puta there's no way back. It's like becoming a nun. A woman with this life dies being a woman of this life" (Restrepo, 1999, 56). While the women carry this burden, it also seems that they are capable of separating their identity from their profession. It is interesting to consider the interrelation that exists between each woman's profession and her idea of self. Much like the gynecologist, Doctor Antonio Maria, observes, the prostitutes express the following dichotomy: "generally they behave like split beings: From the waist up is the soul and from the waist down, business" (Restrepo, 1999, 168). This separation could be seen as a way of expressing a complex interrelation between themselves and their community, as each woman is faced every day with the same dichotomy, while they collectively share a 'soul' that is not sold in the transaction of their business. This dichotomy seems to be part of the shared suffering that they all endure. Thus, the community of prostitutes is formed not only because of various characteristics they share but by a fixed outside opinion over which they have no control.

The women of La Catunga are not only united through their profession and the consequences and discrimination that come with it; the social 'category' that is ascribed to them by the church as an institution is also important. While the prostitutes are rejected by the Catholic Church, they still place an importance on communicating their shared spiritual beliefs. For example, they agree to meet *in front of* the Catholic church, as they are banned from entering the building: "The parish priest had forbidden them to enter unless they had publicly renounced their profession" (Restrepo, 1999, 67). Because they are banned from entering the church, the prostitutes celebrate their own "Stations of the Cross," observing the Catholic tradition of commemorating Jesus' suffering during *Semana Santa*. The prostitutes lead a procession from their houses towards the Patria Theatre where they attend a private matinée screening of the film *Jesus of Nazareth*. "The Maundy Thursday sky dawned, vaulted over with dark clouds, and the streetwalkers of La Catunga, following tradition, dressed in mourning, covered their faces with Spanish mantillas, and went barefoot, in a vow of humility" (Restrepo, 1999, 66). Once in the theater, shortly after the film starts, the women begin to sob in a kind of collective catharsis: "the women of La Catunga burst into tears. They gave free rein to a cascade of warm and comforting tears" (Restrepo, 1999, 67). The women accept the fact that they will never enter the church, even dead, but still take it upon themselves to act out the rituals of purification inside a theater. As they watch a film about Jesus Christ and Mary Magdalene, the women are able to identify with the story so much that they imagine that they are performing a collective act of pardoning their sins, which in this case is expressed through their tears:

> They didn't stop crying until they heard the celluloid Mary Magdalene swear and swear again that she had seen Christ resplendent, his wounds healed and gloriously resuscitated, and then they left the Patria Theatre feeling lightened, free of guilt and empty of tears, prepared to bear another year without complaint or protest.
>
> (Restrepo, 1999, 67)

This excerpt clearly illustrates a sense of belonging that arises not only through the beliefs and traditions of their shared culture, but also through their shared suffering and the stigma of their profession that will follow them to their graves and beyond, bonding them as a community of outsiders.

According to Karen Fog Olwig (2002), there are two kinds of communities: *face-to-face* communities, whose members are personally acquainted and form local groups, and *global* communities that are born out of an "idea." People belonging to a community of ideas are not necessarily required to have been acquainted in person. The author proposes that another kind of *temporary* community can also exist for a determined period of time until it is broken up, but that for groups whose members retain a memory it is possible to reintegrate in the future. To illustrate this point, Iwona Irwin-Zarecka (1994) argues that "one need only think of class reunions [...] a brief exchange of favorite old stories brings back the bonds, however altered by the passage of time" (Irwin-Zarecka, 1994, 55).

The emotional connection that forms within a community, whether it is classified as face-to-face, global, or temporary, can come to be so important for its members that they create collective imaginations for which they are willing to fight, or as Vered Amit (2002) puts it, "are willing to die for such limited imagining" (Amit, 2002, 17). This collective imagination helps to construct a "visceral" aspect that evokes profound emotions of belonging and identification: "the visceral nature of community [...] is not coldly calculated contracts, but embodied, sensual and emotionally charged affiliations" (Amit, 2002, 16). Tony Blackshaw (2010) suggests that community is an "idea" that, when shared, creates values and ideals such as solidarity, honor, respect, and guilt that are maintained and passed on through generations. These ideals, according to Blackshaw, "[fire] the imagination like no other idea: to pursue an ideal, to embody a dream, to struggle against loss" (Blackshaw, 2010, 173). In the pursuit of dignity or honor, all three types of community are evident in Restrepo's novel. Regardless of whether the communities are face-to-face, global, or temporary, each one exhibits a strong sense of cohesion, purpose, and solidarity.

According to Jorge Larraín (2002), "[t]he experience of solidarity and communal participation in the resolution of problems may partially restore trust by showing [that] the external world is not always hostile and threatening and that common action can get positive results for all" (Larraín, 2000, 200). This belief in the importance of collective action, based on the concept of solidarity, leads the community members in the novel to risk their personal safety in the pursuit of a common good. Robert Nisbet (1953) argues that "human beings do not come together *to be* together: they come to *do something* together" (Nisbet, 1953, 43). Thus, in the novel there is a connection between the action and the feeling of being together; the community is encouraged by its own togetherness and decides to carry out actions with a belief in the possibility a common benefit.

The prostitutes join in on the workers' action not just with banners and protests, but also by refusing to work on the basis of a shared feeling of solidarity and an enthusiasm for the possibility of a better life:

> Infected with rebellious passion led by La Machuca, the prostitutas of La Catunga went on strike with legs crossed in solidarity with the

petroleros and stayed out of the café. They traded dangly earrings and diadems for red rags that they tied around their heads and took to the streets, along with the general populace, to participate in the manifestations that arose on every street corner and to join protests and massive acts of resistance in support of the lists of demands. And, out of an extra sense of civic concern, they demanded an aqueduct and sewers in the neighbourhoods of Tora.

(Restrepo, 1999, 254)

Through their participation in their cross-legged strike, the prostitutes not only support the solidarity of the workers, but also motivate the village to come together for the sake of obtaining positive changes for the general community, as is seen in the example of the sewage system installation.

The Tropical Oil Company makes every effort to destroy the community's solidarity. The company uses military force to deter members of the community from letting strikers stay in their homes "to prevent solidarity with Lino el Titi and the rest of the members of the strike committee" (Restrepo, 1999, 254). Military force is also used to severely punish those who show any support for the strikers' cause:

The arrested, nearing a hundred in number, were kept under the rays of the sun and the chill of the moon on the baseball field, which had been converted into a temporary prison. And during a brutal siege, General Valle's men beat Chaparrita to death and left Caracoles paralyzed on one side of her body, for the simple crime of having hidden several strikers under their beds.

(Restrepo, 1999, 255)

This example sheds light on the level of commitment that the community is willing to undertake in the name of "solidarity with the cause." They participate in the strike because they share the experience of injustice, believing that together they have a chance to address and obtain a common good. Their solidarity acts as a unifying force that gives them purpose and cohesion.

The Community's Actions

The temporary communities that exist in the novel are bound together and fight against a common oppressor in two different ways. The first instance is through spontaneous action, which is evident in the scene with the men in white lab coats. The second is based on an agreement between the communities of prostitutes and oil plant workers during the rice strike. In the first example, the prostitutes are required to renew their health cards every week. In order to get the green light they are made to endure humiliating examinations:

Every Tuesday by law, week after week, the prostitutes of La Catunga had to appear at dawn in the center of town, on Calle del Comercio, and stand in line in front of the antivenereal dispensary to have their health cards renewed.

(Restrepo, 1999, 59)

The women object to this humiliating ritual as they discover through communication that they are all forced to endure the same poor treatment. This awakens a shared feeling of injustice among them:

Leaning against a wall, all identical in the eyes of the corrupt officials, with no preferred lightbulb status or nationality or fee differential, no color of skin better than any other. On Tuesdays the dignity of any of them was worth fifty centavos, not one more or one less.

(Restrepo, 1999, 60)

Their unity and sameness is created by the treatment they receive from the outside world, and by a consequential internal feeling that they have been robbed of their dignity. Their dignity is further harmed by the doctors who disrespectfully order them to take off their underwear: " 'Off with the underwear!' [ordered the] men with white lab coats" (Restrepo, 1999, 60). The community responds to the doctors' abuse through an act of rebellion instigated by a young Sayonara. She becomes infuriated upon witnessing the verbal abuse suffered by her godmother, Todos los Santos, and shouts at the doctor: "She is not climbing up or opening her legs, you shitty bastard!" (Restrepo, 1999, 61). Another prostitute pitches in, shouting insults at the doctor and amidst the laughter of the other prostitutes, a spontaneous uprising is instigated:

first a little, then more, beginning as the chatter of schoolgirls, then becoming the harassment of mutinous putas, hurling insults, trash, and rocks at the dispensary doctors who, without knowing how, managed to lock the door and barricade themselves against the revolt that was mounting outside.

(Restrepo, 1999, 62)

The women scream and throw objects while the men in white lab coats fire back with insults: " 'Son-of-a-bitch whores!' Answered masculine voices from behind the barricades. 'Syphilis spreaders!' " (Restrepo, 1999, 62) to which the women respond with more rocks and an avalanche of burning clothing, starting a fire: "This is for all of our friends who were raped and abused in this dump! trumpeted the vodka-soaked voice of Analia, and a bottle crashed against the window of the dispensary, shattering the glass" (Restrepo, 1999, 62).

The struggle of the underprivileged, even when it is an expression of the whole community, is not easily won. As expected, their rebellion is met with a military intervention, forcing the women to escape and hide themselves as quickly as possible. Nonetheless, their uprising is not in vain. The men in white lab coats find themselves

> asphyxiated by the smoke, their eyes reddened and teary, and their arms raised high, like freed puppets, the besieged doctors exited in surrender at the very moment that men in olive green appeared, jogging down the street, holding their weapons.
>
> (Restrepo, 1999, 63)

Ignoring the military presence and encouraged by their numbers, the women of La Catunga are united by their uprising. While they are unable to defend themselves otherwise, they fight with their words, not only for their own cause but against exploitation of all women in the town: "Death to all the sons-of-bitches who exploit the women of Tora!" (Restrepo, 1999, 64). In this example of a spontaneous act of rebellion, the solidarity between the women leads to a positive outcome in the community's fight for justice, even if their victory is only temporary. In this example of a communal triumph in the pursuit of social change, the action of the prostitutes leads to a creation of a new dispensary with a new gynecologist who is dedicated to service, who cares about treating their ills, and who puts an end to the health-card system.

The second example of a temporary community challenging a dominant power is through the collective action of both groups during the rice strike. The prostitutes and the oil workers of Plant Number 26 join together to form a larger community of strike-sympathizers that combines forces and supports each other for the strike's duration. The rebellion against the oppressive Tropical Oil Company is not an organized act, but a spontaneous reaction to days of exploitation and abuse. The rebellion starts with "a ball of rice" (Restrepo, 1999, 182) as the employees at Plant Number 26 object to the fact that the lunch provided by the company consists only of "watery molasses and rice balls" (Restrepo, 1999, 212). As one of the characters expresses, the standard meal is a disgusting monstrosity that "[is] not even fit for prisoners, hermano, there's no right" (Restrepo, 1999, 212). A conflict is sparked when the workers begin to throw the inedible balls of rice at each other in a playful interaction. El Payanés throws a rice ball at a framed photo of Mister Maier, the general manager, unsuspecting "that he was living the first moments of what from then on would be the forever famous rice strike, the fifth and most violent of the so-called primitive, or heroic, strikes by the Tora union" (Restrepo, 1999, 214). Unfortunately, the community that emerges as a result of the uprising does not last long as the Tropical Oil Company recognizes a threat to their position of power. To maintain its control, the company attempts to divide and conquer, first separating the prostitutes from the workers by breaking up the La Catunga neighborhood: "the Tropical Oil Company had made the profitable, corporate decision to redeem all the prostitutas in the area" (Restrepo, 1999, 279).

The company also offers houses to workers who aspire to have a traditional family with a wife and children. Plant Number 26 is also easily brought back into operation after the strike as the company hires other people in the immediate and surrounding area who are in need of work. As one of the strikers, Don Honorio, explains:

> We workers hadn't counted on the eighty survivors of the killing spree at Orito, who had arrived in Tora two weeks before the strike, looking for a petrolero's salary [...] or the forty-some families made homeless by the flooding of the Rio Samaná; or the group of recent arrivals from Urumita, Guajira, who offered themselves for work; or the one hundred sixty Pipatón Indians recently expelled from their ancestral lands by the Troco itself in its project to expand operations.
>
> (Restrepo, 1999, 258)

This example shows how difficult it is for the community to have its demands heard due to circumstantial competition with other, less fortunate communities. These communities are willing to accept the company's conditions as they are in order to survive, which weakens the legitimacy of the strikers' demands. The irony of the situation adds salt to the wound of the striking oil plant workers, whose demands are not met. They are easily replaced by new employees that have already endured exploitation at the hands of the Troco. As the example illustrates, the Pipatón Indians are expelled from their ancestral lands by the oil company which is willing to employ them in another location to replace the striking workers. As a result, the community that is born out of a just cause is broken up by dominant powers. The character, Horacio Laguna, muses: "It's true that the rice strike achieved almost none of its demands and that it ended in failure [...] but it was a valiant, dignified failure, and that's fairly close to a victory" (Restrepo, 1999, 259). The workers have not won the war, but they have won a battle. In its fight for the common good, the community has started an awakening of the masses in solidarity, and the mobilization of the community to take action has brought its members a feeling of satisfaction, dignity, and courage, leading them to conclude that their effort was "fairly close to a victory."

While the company can use various strategies to weaken local communities and impose its power, and while the military can use its power to control the prostitutes and striking workers, there are intangible aspects of life which they cannot control, that the community can also use to empower itself. The following conversation between prostitutes is revealing:

> Did Correcaminos's father ever forgive her? Or Delia Ramos's mother?
>
> 'Not them or anyone,' shouted Fideo. 'You can go from there to here, but from here to there all the doors are locked.'
>
> 'All,' adds Olga, 'except for those of your memories.'
>
> (Restrepo, 1999, 81/SL 2002, 57)

Memory plays an important role in the novel, allowing the characters to return to a common past even when they feel that doors have been closed for them in the present. This return through the use of memory can be seen as a symbolic link between traditional communities and the imaginary ones that exist in the novel. As Celia Harris, Helen Paterson, and Richard Kemp (2008) write, the retelling of stories by a group of people allows its members to agree on a common language and construct a similar world-view. In *The Dark Bride*, memory is constructed through a collective retelling of stories about how the women come to work as prostitutes:

> It happened to Correcaminos,[1] as it did with so many others, who in twenty-four hours go from being virgins to being putas. She was a decent, illiterate girl from a poor family who one day lost her virginity, became pregnant, and was transformed into the dishonor of her family [...]
>
> 'Can you imagine that?' said Olga indignantly, listening to us as she chopped parsley to add to a compress for Fideo,[2] who lay in a hammock due to her chronic illness. 'Everything was taken from her and her child with only six words: You are no longer my daughter.'
>
> (Restrepo, 1999, 56)

The women then tell their stories from their own perspectives. As they do this, the act of remembering erases the barrier between whoever is listening and the character telling the story as "the three interrupt each other, remembering the misadventures of Melones"[3] (Restrepo, 1999, 57). Once the memory is 'shared' as a collection of thoughts, it contributes to the cohesion of the community and then becomes a collective memory. The collective memory fuels the community's shared enthusiasm to fight against oppression: "With the imminence of disaster, the old union spirit for fighting is reborn. It had been dormant for a couple of years after a slew of debilitating strikes that ended in deaths and massive layoffs" (Restrepo, 1999, 217). Thus, when the community of prostitutes, workers, and the people of Tora face fear, their spirit for fighting emanates from their memory:

> Lino el Titi resumed control and decreed that the strike must continue until victory or death. And this news, which spread like wildfire, caused the initial fear, confusion, and chaos to yield to greater fervor, worker unity, and a feverish determination to fight.
>
> (Restrepo, 1999, 249)

A "roar" awakens a strong sense of cohesion within the community and impels it to act: "[T]he old leaders [...] came out of their slumber to roar again like shaggy beasts, and their roars were recognized by the multitude" (Restrepo, 1999, 217). This roar is recognized by the multitude as it awakens its collective memory of past rebellions in the name of survival.

According to Harris et al. (2008), "[a] major function of collective memory is to serve the needs of the group in the present. These needs include the formation of and maintenance of a sense of group identity, group cohesion, and group continuity" (Harris et al., 2008, 214). The roar alludes to something that the members of the community know instinctively, something that is buried in their memory. For example, when the leader, Lino el Titi, entrusts Sacramento with the job of finding La Machuca in order to bring back the publication of "the strike bulletin" (Restrepo, 1999, 251) and gives El Payanés the responsibility of ensuring its clandestine distribution, he assures them that the people will know what to do: "You'll give the bulletins to the neighbourhood leaders and they will give them to the block coordinators, so that they can be circulated to everyone" (Restrepo, 1999, 252).

When El Payanés asks him how he is expected to identify the neighborhood leaders and block coordinators, Lino el Titi responds:

> They know who they are, they know from the last strike, and they will come forward ready to do their part as soon as they see the first bulletin passing from hand to hand. The bulletin is the heart of the strike [...] As long as the bulletin goes out, the strike will remain alive.
>
> (Restrepo, 1999, 252)

In this case, the community's collective memory is complemented by the written political message distributed in the bulletin. The modern means of political propaganda is then added to their memory, as the following excerpt illustrates: " 'This sheet of paper,' she tells me, 'represents perhaps the most important thing we have done in our lives' " (Restrepo, 1999, 254). The character, La Machuca, keeps a copy of the newsletter in her keepsake trunk: "[she] has kept this copy of the Boletín de Huelga number six safely stored for years" (Restrepo, 1999, 254), as this edition contains evidence of her shared memory: "All of Tora tense, awaiting their bulletin to prove that the strike was still alive, that in spite of all the repression the leaders hadn't given up, that in spite of the difficulties, victory was within reach" (Restrepo, 1999, 256). The community's sense of unity and its spirit for fighting are bound together in its memory of previous rice strikes, which they hope to repeat and record for future reference.

According to Robert Bellah:

> people growing up in communities of memory not only hear the stories that tell how the community came to be, what its hopes and fears are, and how its ideals are exemplified in outstanding men and women; they also participate in practices—rituals, aesthetic, ethical—that define the community as a way of life.
>
> (Bellah et al., 1985, 153)

This 'way of life' is reflected in the community of memories that includes and is constructed by folklore—particularly through myths and legends—

which are transmitted through collective memory. Alberto Padrón specifies that the word 'folklore' is of English origin and is "used to construct common knowledge," adding that "the definition should be utilized from the perspective of a social group that uses certain cultural goods serving a particular function according to the needs of the community" (Padrón, 1985, 4). An example of the community preserving its 'way of life' through cultural folklore can be seen when Frank Brasco listens to the workers as they retell their versions of Colombian legends: "they sat around a pot of coffee, under a riot of stars and cicadas, to tell stories of ghosts and spirits who wander around doing things that an Anglo-Saxon like him found improbable" (Restrepo, 1999, 215). As someone who comes from a world where a culture of folklore has arguably been extinguished, Brasco approaches their stories from a rational perspective, intervening frequently with the question "Why?" leading the workers to give him the nickname "*Dime-por-qué/*Tell-me-why" (Restrepo, 1999, 284/SL 2002, 215). When, in the following dialogue, Brasco asks the workers about the meaning of the legends of Mohán and Luz-de-la-Cienaga, it is quite clear that the Colombian vision of the world goes beyond simple logic:

> 'But tell me why … Mohan carries girls off to the bottom of the river if he could make love with them more comfortably and without getting wet on the shore?'
> 'Mister has already started with his tell-me-whys,' they would laugh. 'Well, because he lives down there and that's where his sumptuous palaces are.'
>
> (Restrepo, 1999, 215)

> 'But tell me why Luz-de-la-Cienaga eats little children when there are so many pigs and chickens and fish…'
> 'Because if he doesn't eat children he's not scary, mister Brasco, and his stories wouldn't interest anyone, not even you.'
>
> (Restrepo, 1999, 215)

While the logic behind their myths and legends is foreign to Frank Brasco, for the members of the community the world of the supernatural that intervenes in their lives is quite common and helps to shape the common language shared by the community members. This cultural folklore is meaningless to the American, but for the locals and their community, myths and legends connect them to the wisdom of the past and help them cope with the present.

Bellah (et al.) argues that "if the community is completely honest, it will remember stories not only of suffering received but of suffering inflicted" (Bellah et al., 1985, 153). The (prostitute) community of memories remembers its pain and suffering, but it also chooses to remember its spirit for fighting, which helps them to fight against the men in white lab coats. They defend themselves through collective action, but they also make mistakes.

This is seen in the case of the prostitutes tormenting the new gynecologist who arrives not to humiliate but to help the women infected with syphilis. Doctor Antonio Maria Florez

> had come to Tora to replace the previous charlatans in white lab coats, driven out of town by a ferocious collective vengeance, which one day took the form of a cruel joke and the following day became a threat or a serious hint.
>
> (Restrepo, 1999, 164)

The prostitutes do not immediately trust the new gynecologist: "The girls [...] welcomed him the very first night by fouling the door to his house with the fetid corpse of a hanged cat" (Restrepo, 1999, 164). They collectively continue to attack the doctor and his family, including the doctor's wife: "from a high window the dirty contents of a chamber pot were emptied on her head" (Restrepo, 1999, 165). Even after the doctor plans to provide care to the women free of charge, eliminates the health-card system, and rebuilds the doctor's office with his own hands, the prostitutes preserve the idea of vengeance in their memories: "the anger of the women of La Catunga, goaded by the fresh memory of disgrace they had suffered, refused to give up the sweetness of their revenge" (Restrepo, 1999, 165). The memory of pain and suffering prevents the women from recognizing the new doctor's good nature. As Bellah says, "if the community is honest," it must admit that it is capable of collective vengeance even when there is no reason for such a reaction. Suffering endured in the past can keep communities from the acceptance of positive forces and opportunities for improvement in the present.

Conclusion

Laura Restrepo's *The Dark Bride* presents a vision of various types of community, each adding a unique element to the novel's plot or message. Central to the novel's plot is a temporary, face-to-face community that is born during the rice strike. This community is made up of the smaller pre-existing community of the prostitutes in Tora and the community of oil plant workers. The two groups form a larger community on the basis of understanding and solidarity during the rice strike as a consequence of the abuse of a North American oil company, the Troco, which exploits the workers and terrorizes the prostitutes. By coming together as a larger community, the prostitutes and striking workers experience a feeling of solidarity which gives them the strength to survive and also to rebel against the oppressor. The groups experience a strong sense of community because they share humanistic values, as well as the belief that rising up in a strike and mobilizing the masses to act together will ultimately lead to positive change. To describe the union in this temporary community, Restrepo uses the image of "*la manada humana*" or a human flock, which alludes to the instinctive or animalistic nature of the group's formation in the face of oppression. The irrational union is further strengthened by myths and legends from the past which both warn against danger and help to enforce the spirit of struggle and survival. Their call to action of the 'roar' is a part of their collective memory which helps the multitude to remember the strikes of the past and prepare to rise up against the powers that oppress them. The success of the strike-oriented community's uprising is short-lived. The centers of power recognize that the groups united in a larger community have the potential to be successful in their uprising and use economic means to divide and conquer them. In the end, the workers of the oil company or '*los peludos*' and the prostitutes cannot claim a large victory, but they enjoy a "sort of victory" in their union as a result of their mutual respect, their solidarity, and their feeling of belonging.

While the larger community of strikers and its sympathizers does not achieve its goals, the smaller successes of the community of prostitutes are important. The women receive better treatment from a kinder gynecologist after years of abuse and mistreatment from their previous doctor. This would not have been possible if the women had not come together in an uprising against the men in white lab coats. Another victory won by the prostitutes is the installation of a sewage system in Tora, which can also be seen as a smaller victory achieved by the rice strike. Lastly, the communities of memory that exist in the novel are important as they are essential to the women's ability to come together during the strike with such ease and determination. By keeping the memory of past strikes alive through communication, the women are able to support the strikers in a meaningful and efficient way.

Notes

1 *Correcaminos*: a nickname meaning 'roadrunner.'
2 *Fideo*: a nickname that means 'spaghetti' or 'noodle,' used for someone who is extremely thin.
3 *Las Melones*: a nickname that means 'the melons.'

References

Amit, Vered. 2002. *Realizing community. Concepts, social relationships and sentiments*. London and New York: Routledge.
Bellah, Robert N., Richard Madsen, William M. Sullivan, Ann Swidler, & Steven M. Tipton. 1985. *Habits of the heart, individualism and commitment in American life*. University of California Press.
Blackshaw, Tony. 2010. *Key concepts in community studies*. SAGE Publications: London.
Davis, Robert. 1993. *Historical dictionary of Colombia*. Metuchen and London: Scarecrow Press.
Flores Mercado, Georgina. 2011. "Comunidad, Individuo y Libertad," TRAMAS 34, UAM-X México, 15–46.

Fog Olwig, Karen. 2002. "The Ethnographic Field Revisited: Toward a Study of Common and Not so Common Fields of Belonging." In A. Veret (Ed.). *Realizing community: concepts, social relations and sentiments* (124–145). London: Routledge.

Gladwell, Malcolm. 2008. *Outliers*. New York: Hachette Book Group.

Harris, Celia B., Helen M. Paterson, & Richard I. Kemp. 2008. "Collaborative Recall and Collective Memory: 'What Happens When We Remember Together?'" *Memory*, Vol. 16 (3), Psychology Press, Taylor and Francis Group.

Irwin-Zarecka, Iwona. 1994. *Frames of remembrance: the dynamics of collective memory*. New Jersey: Transaction Publishers.

Krause Jacob, Mariane. 1999. "Hacia una Redefinición del Concepto de Comunidad-Cuatro ejes para un análisis crítico y una propuesta." *Revista de Psicología de la Universidad de Chile*, Vol. X, No. 2, 49–60.

Larraín, Jorge. 2000. *Identity and modernity in Latin America*. Cambridge University Press.

Lindsay, Claire. 2003. "'Clear and Present Danger': Trauma, Memory and Laura Restrepo's *La novia oscura*." Hispanic Research Journal, Vol. 4, No. 1, 41–58.

Martin, Deborah. 2008. "Mothers and Nomadic Subjects: Configurations of Identity and Desire in Laura Restrepo's 'LA NOVIA OSCURA.'" *The Modern Language Review*. Vol. 103, No. 1. Modern Humanities Research Association, 113–128.

Nisbet, Robert. 1953. *The quest for community*. New York: Oxford University Press.

Ocampo, Javier. 1988. *Mitos Colombianos*. Bogotá: El Áncora Editores.

Padrón, Alberto. 1985. "El Folclore y la Cultura Tradicional Popular," *Aguayro*, No 162. Digitalización realizada por la Biblioteca Universitaria, 2010, MdC, Memoria Digital de Canarias.

Restrepo, Laura. 1999. *La novia oscura*. New York: Harper Collins.

Restrepo, Laura. 2002. *The dark bride*. (S.A. Lytle, Trans.). Toronto: Harper Collins.

Taylor, Michael. 1982. *Community, anarchy and liberty*. Cambridge: Cambridge University Press.

Valencia, Enrique. 1984. "El Movimiento Obrero en Colombia." In P.G. Casanova (Ed.). *Historia del movimiento obrero en América Latina* (9–51). Mexico City: Siglo Veintiuno.

6 Community and Learning

The Process of *Conscientization* Among Nicaraguan Peasants through Song

Mery Perez

The lasting effects of the way in which a group of Nicaraguan peasants lived in community in the 1960s and 1970s is still felt in Nicaragua today. This experience has been embodied in music and continues to inform and move civil society in this Latin American country and its neighboring region. The community of Solentiname was born in the southeast area of Lake Nicaragua, and was originally shaped by its geography and colonial history. Its remarkable transformation from individuals living on scattered islands into a community of learning began with the arrival of Nicaraguan priest and poet, Ernesto Cardenal. Cardenal, who was later nominated for the 2005 Nobel Prize in Literature, is certainly a controversial figure for his alignment with Liberation Theology and his role as Nicaragua's minister of culture from 1979 to 1987. He was publicly chastised by Pope John Paul II during his 1983 visit to Nicaragua for this alignment. Nevertheless, the process of learning facilitated by Cardenal led to a rebuilding of community in this remote area. In this discussion of Nicaraguan rural communities, Etienne Wenger's concept of communities of practice and social learning (2000) as well as Paolo Freire's concept of *conscientization* (1993) are used as the theoretical framework of analysis. This chapter will show that what began as a sharing of faith, Bible readings, and music, eventually led the peasants to become aware of their social reality. This helped them view their future from a different perspective. The *conscientization*, or consciousness-raising, brought concrete implications: community members became involved in improving their immediate situation, and they later engaged in revolutionary action. This chapter analyzes the sociopolitical context out of which the Solentiname community emerged, and it discusses how the community developed with the help of the musical work entitled *Misa Campesina* by Carlos Mejía Godoy, which incorporated local musical instruments and familiar song forms in the community's reinterpretation of the Bible. The chapter will conclude with an analysis of two songs which where key in the creation of community, reimagined by a learning experience.

Prior to 1966, the archipelago of Solentiname on Lake Nicaragua was just a remote and lush tropical place, far from the reach of progress (Cardenal, 2003). "We only had a place to live, as if we were birds on the island"[1] states Mrs. María Guevara, a 63-year-old woman who has lived on San Fernando Island for most of her life (personal interview, December 23, 2013). Life changed gradually yet dramatically when the newly ordained Catholic priest and poet, Ernesto Cardenal, arrived on Mancarrón Island. He came looking for an idyllic, natural environment where he could lead the isolated, contemplative life he had always dreamed of. It was not long before his plans began to change as the inhabitants of these small islands flocked around him looking for leadership and belonging. Rather than becoming a silent contemplative community, this group evolved to become a community deeply engaged with the social reality of Nicaragua.

Community is considered by many social scientists to be an essential yet illusive concept. A number of theories and definitions have emerged in the past few decades and some scholars have argued that the term 'community' has become vague and almost meaningless (Plant, 1978). However, extensive reflection and research also show that the notion of community has evolved over time along with various changes in society (Bauman, 2004; Wood & Judikis, 2001; Clemens, 2008). Furthermore, engaging individuals in conversation, one cannot help but notice that however illusive the term is, the experience of community is of utmost importance in the lives of people (Cardenal, 2003; Dueñas de Polavieja, 2012). It allows individuals to forge strong connections with each other which assign meaning to their lives (Wood & Judikis, 2001) and contribute to their overall health and well-being.

In their *Conversations on Community Theory*, Wood and Judikis (2001) state the following:

> Community can be defined as a group of people who have a sense of common purpose(s) and/or interest(s) for which they assume mutual responsibility, who acknowledge their interconnectedness, who respect the individual differences among members, and who commit themselves to the well-being of each other and well-being of the group.
>
> (12)

With this definition in mind, I explore the role of community in the process of *conscientization* of the Nicaraguan peasants living in Solentiname in the 1960s and 1970s. Community, for them, proved to be an essential element in a process whereby they became active agents of social change and revolution.

Community and Learning

For Etienne Wegner (2000), community is intimately connected to the process of learning, because learning is not something that we do in isolation; it is, rather, a deeply social activity. We know what we know, he argues, because we engage within very complex social, cultural, and historical systems that accumulate knowledge over time and share it with us through life-changing experiences and through information transfer (225). Wegner refers to these complex systems as communities of practice which build a reservoir of knowledge obtained through decades of research and experience. This reservoir is available to its members and, to some extent, those that come close to the community's frontiers. For example, he suggests that we know that the earth is round, not because we have seen it, but because the scientific community has convinced us that it is. Developing a sense of belonging or relationship with these communities is crucial as: "these relationships are what enable you to 'know' about the earth's position in the universe. In this sense, knowing is an act of participation in complex 'social learning systems'" (226). Belonging can, in turn, take place in three modes: engagement, imagination, and alignment.

Wegner argues that such a social component of learning is not something new since it is recorded that human beings have

> formed communities that share cultural practices, reflecting their collective learning: from a tribe around a cave fire, to a medieval guild, to a group of nurses in a ward, to a street gang, to a community of engineers interested in brake design.
>
> (229)

Social learning, however, is not limited to the agency of what we nowadays may define as a professional group or discipline; it can take place among any group that shares in collective learning practices. Learning takes place for individuals as they interact with other members of the community, but the community also learns as it comes into contact with other communities and external bodies of knowledge that approach its borders. New ideas and situations may challenge its core values and require an adaptation on behalf of the community, but such dynamic community engagement is "at the very core of what makes us human beings capable of meaningful knowing" (229).

For learning to take place, it is important that the individual engaged in a community feels a sense of belonging and identity. Engagement is, for Wegner, the first step in attaining this sense of belonging because when we engage in conversation, in doing things together, in producing artifacts, we "shape our experience of who we are" (232) and "learn what we can do and how the world responds to our actions" (Wegner, 227). The artifacts may include things such as songs and musical instruments, which will be discussed later in this chapter, and they are used within rituals and conversations, two important means of engagement that were crucial in the Solentiname learning process and the reimagination of community. Finally, belonging requires alignment of behavior and activities, having them correspond with the sense of who we are and our community. Wegner defines alignment as follows:

Making sure that our local activities are sufficiently aligned with other processes so that they can be effective beyond our own engagement ... the concept of alignment as used here does not connote a one-way process of submitting to external authority, but a mutual process of coordinating perspectives, interpretations and actions so they realize higher goals.

(228)

Through alignment, the individual gets a sense that his or her actions are part of a greater picture, an ideal that goes beyond themselves. Action, then, becomes an expression of community membership. The ideals that were shared by the Solentiname community brought about inevitable changes. For the men and women living on these islands, alignment had specific repercussions as new ways of doing things and sharing became part of their daily lives and faith. For some of the young men, this meant deeper engagement in the revolution.

Brazilian education theorist, Paolo Freire (1993) also considers that the role of community is essential to learning, since learning for him was a participatory process of awareness-building or *"conscientization."* *Conscientization* is the process of developing a total vision of one's surroundings. It is also a critical appraisal of the social setting, and a process that is key to bringing about change to society. Freire contrasts this engaging process of *conscientization* with that of "banking education," the authoritarian model that sees learning as a transfer of knowledge between the expert and the learner. "Banking education" sees reality as "motionless, static, compartmentalized, and predictable" (Freire, 71) and assumes that the individual is an empty recipient incapable of much reflection. Humanity is here seen as isolated from the world that surrounds it. In Freire's words, "The objects that surround me are simply accessible to my consciousness, not located within it. I am aware of them, but they are not inside me" (76). In the banking education model of learning, the expert has possession of all truth regarding a particular subject. Words are "hollow" and "alienated" (71) and they lack the power to transform.

Conscientization, on the other hand, considers that the individual is engaged with his or her reality as well as with other human beings. The individual has the capacity to reflect, to become troubled by what he or she sees, especially if what they are exposed to stands in contradiction to what they already know. Freire argues that once individuals are "posed with problems relating to themselves in the world and with the world, will feel increasingly challenged and obliged to respond to that challenge" (Freire, 81). Once faced by real challenges and situations, people cease to be docile listeners and become "critical co-investigators" (Freire, 81) who become immersed in reflection and action. The community here discussed certainly faced numerous and serious challenges, as the next section will reveal. As Freire argues, the possibility to engage in critical conversation elicited a concrete response to these challenges on behalf of the community.

The Case of Solentiname Community

The archipelago of Solentiname is made up of 36 islands, the largest of which is Mancarrón where Ernesto Cardenal established his community. This group of islands is located in the southeast area of Lake Nicaragua, between 10 and 30 kilometers from the port city of San Carlos. The natural beauty surrounding these islands is characterized by lush rain forest, and birds such as herons, parrots, and golden orioles, among others (Cardenal, 2002; Dueñas García de Polavieja, 2012). Its name is derived from the Nahuatl word '*Celin-tenametl*,' which means place for many guests (Cardenal, 128), which it certainly became after Cardenal's arrival. Prior to Ernesto Cardenal's arrival, however, the Solentiname community was defined by a harder reality than the reality of other regions in Nicaragua. It was "outside of the road of progress and outside of the roads of transportation, and outside of history, and it would have been outside of geography if this had been possible" (Cardenal, 94). In addition to the legacy of the colonial system of encomienda and the history of vicious enmity between the two main political parties in Nicaragua, the isolated location left the community without an easy access to the market where they could sell firewood, eggs, and the few things they produced on the islands. The uneven landscape as well as the dry soil made agriculture a very cumbersome enterprise which did not leave them very much monetary gain (Dueñas García de Polavieja, 2012). They also lacked electricity and construction materials to build their homes and lived in huts "made out of palm branches" (4). The stark difference between the rich and the poor was most evident in Solentiname.

By the time Ernesto Cardenal, born in Granada in 1925, arrived to Solentiname, he was an ordained Catholic priest whose longing for contemplative life had sent him on an international quest. He spent a few years in a Trappist monastery in the United States where he was a novice under the tutelage of Thomas Merton. He later studied theology in Mexico, finalized his priestly formation in Colombia, and was ordained in Nicaragua in 1965 (Cardenal, 2002). Cardenal's initial intention when he arrived in Solentiname was to establish an isolated contemplative community. However, when he discovered slowly that peasants living around the area he had purchased were looking to him for leadership and guidance, he assumed the role of a community leader (Cardenal, 2002). He tells us about the first community calls:

> I think that the first visit we had was that of Marcelino who arrived with his machete to see who we were. His farm was close by; he was not interested in religion but with us he changed completely and became one of the best commentators of the Gospel during the Mass.
>
> (105)

The community continued to form around engaging weekly Gospel discussions and soon the peasants became aware of the unjust living conditions that surrounded them (Kirk, 69). These consciousness-raising discussions were recorded and later transcribed by Cardenal and published under the title *The Gospel in Solentiname*, a book described by John Kirk (1992) as an "anthology of religious-political reflections" (69). They also found expression in art, as many of its members learned the primitivist style of painting and sculpture from Cardenal. These eventually became a way of sustenance for them since the land was not conducive for large-scale agriculture (Cardenal, 2003). Others used their musical talents to add to their religious gatherings and in 1968 contributed to the creation of the *Misa Popular* which made use of the popular Nicaraguan rhythms which were familiar to the peasants. Through rhythm and lyrics, this Mass showed, even if in a subtle way, that Christ was, like them, a "poor worker" (Kirk, 70).

Cardenal's unorthodox masses were strikingly different from the previous church experiences of the inhabitants of Solentiname. He modelled his work on the archipelago after the ecclesial base community of San Pablo in the outskirts of Managua, which was guided by the Spanish priest, Father José De la Jara. His approach to pastoral work inspired Cardenal because it remained in close contact with the reality of the poor. Cardenal learned from Father De la Jara not to preach a sermon but to allow for a dialogue on the gospel, thus creating an environment of trust, participation, and critical analysis (Cardenal, 198). As Mrs. María Guevara explains: "Before Ernesto lived here, we had another way of seeing the Church, another way of seeing how priests preached" (personal interview, December 23, 2013). According to her, prior to the arrival of Cardenal in Solentiname, church experience was marked by silence, distance, and disengagement: "Going to Mass was something very quiet and, as Christians, we could not participate in anything of the Mass. Only if we had to receive communion, we received it and that was it." Unlike traditional priests, Cardenal's preaching did not always limit itself to teachings from the Bible. He considered that regular, mundane things had to be addressed before people could be receptive to the Gospel. In his memoirs, for example, he relates how, during the first Mass he celebrated in Solentiname, he preached about the best place to build a latrine so as to prevent people from getting sick. He comments that he did this because, before teaching catechism to the children, he needed to ensure he actually had healthy children to teach (Cardenal, 108). Thus, the new Masses of the community were a new experience, in the full sense of the word, where people not only participated actively but experienced their faith and their everyday life as something deeply intertwined.

Since the Masses in the community of Our Lady of Solentiname always began with singing accompanied by guitars and drums, it was easy for young people to become engaged. After the Mass, the people gathered for lunch where everyone took part preparing the food. The food was also shared in the midst of singing and guitars which made these lunches "truly a communion" (Cardenal, 199). This fostering of a true sense of communion has been explained by Mrs. María Guevara Silva in the following way:

It was as if we had arrived at a party and someone said: 'Come in, come and serve yourselves, let's see what we are going to do.' It was as if we had joined a great assembly where everyone had to participate.

(personal interview, December 23, 2013)

Mrs. Elba Jiménez also remembers these gatherings with affection: "We all used to gather in the church and after, once he finished his Masses, we used to have lunch" (personal interview, January 13, 2014). The sharing of food and music as a part of engagement with their faith generated a sense of belonging among peasants which they cherished and expressed with the enthusiasm reflected in their voices during the interviews carried out for this project.

Conscientization

Mrs. Esperanza Guevara Silva believes that the weekly Mass celebrated with Cardenal proved to be an important factor in their process of *conscientization*; the process of becoming politically aware. She affirms that the first conviction that emerged out of their participation in the Mass was that they lived in an unjust society, one that was far from displaying any traits of true Christianity. For them, the Mass allowed for a questioning of themselves regarding what they could do to change that reality. She states:

You came to know, through each Gospel that there was injustice, and that the first one who had given his life because of an injustice on this earth was Christ. That was discovered and it was very unsettling for some young people.

(personal interview, January 13, 2014)

Thus, for many of the young men and women of the community, the Gospel was troubling because it posed them with a call to action, aligned with this new understanding of who they were.

Reading the newspapers and listening to revolutionary music was as central to the community of Solentiname as their Gospel-sharing. Cardenal (2002) recorded that they read together not only the newspapers, but also poetry and politically charged texts, such as Che Guevara's biography. As Esperanza Guevara Silva testifies in a personal interview, the community came together by listening to musicians who represented the Nueva Canción movement in Latin America, a movement which started in the 1950s and sought to bring about political change by recovering national identity through the use of folk sounds and rhythms (Tumas-Serna, 144). This community's identity solidified as they listened to songs by artists such as Alí Primera, Joan Manuel Serrat, Quilapayún, and Carlos Mejía Godoy. They also listened to Silvio Rodriguez and Pablo Milanés through the clandestine broadcastings of Radio Habana from Cuba and they sang their songs in their social gatherings (Dueñas García de Polavieja, 14).

The new awareness that emerged out of this sharing of literature and music proved to be unsettling for everyone in the community. Fernando Cardenal, Ernesto's brother, also a Catholic priest, suggests that his brother did not agitate the masses, so to speak, but rather fostered awareness regarding the situation of Nicaragua (Dueñas García de Polavieja, 12). As community members mention, once they were questioned by their own reality, a response began to gestate. Their later involvement in the revolution can be directly related to the process of community engagement and learning. The Solentiname community believed that the realization that they were living in an unjust society led them to ask: "What do you do so that it is not? This is what brought us to participate 10 years later in the demise of the dictatorship" (personal interview, January 13, 2014). They also argue that it was the weekly gathering for the Mass where they grew in awareness. Esperanza Guevara expresses this as follows: "And the Mass played a big role. It was the Mass. The Poet never sat down with us to ask 'What do you see?' But 'What could you do?'" For Cardenal, the process of *conscientization* and radicalization happened as a result of living in close contact with the peasants' reality. This experience allowed him to identify his belief in Christ with the poor. He recalls in his autobiography: "And the contact with the poverty of Solentiname's peasants as well as the national reality which was getting worse, also contributed to me and the community becoming politicized and radicalized" (Cardenal, 206). His political convictions and his faith began to mingle, and he expressed this to those around him. For him, the people of Nicaragua, particularly the poor, were the embodiment of the sufferings of Christ.

The surviving members of the Solentiname community still remember how their celebration of faith became a process of *conscientization* and subsequent political commitment. The celebration of the Mass which was linked to their daily lives was a group exercise which, as the members testify, made them "commit ourselves as young people to the community, to be concerned with the people of the community, with the sick, to support the poorest, to help with the building of their houses, to be attentive to the community lunches" (personal interview, December 23, 2013). They were thus taken away from rituals and led to direct action. When they added this element of action to their faith, they became aware of the things they were missing, not only as members of Solentiname community but as members of Nicaraguan society. In a personal interview, María Guevara Silva states:

> After, little by little, we gradually realized what we did not have. It was as if we lived in a state where nobody knew anything about us and as if we did not have rights to anything, we had no school, we had no health, we had no transportation, well, we had practically nothing.

They came to understand that their rights as members of Nicaraguan society were not being taken into consideration and that this omission was the cause of many of their hardships.

The process of awareness and politicization that Dueñas García de Pola-vieja sees as a natural process arising from reflecting on a liberating view of the Gospel had concrete repercussions in Solentiname. Once troubled by the awareness that the unjust society in which they lived did not have to continue to exist as it did, the members of this community could not help but take the action they felt was necessary. For example, many of the young men from Solentiname joined a Sandinista group in the attack on the San Carlos military headquarters on October 13, 1977. This new reading of the Gospel, one deeply connected to the community, a community that suffered and lacked many basic things, proved to be unsettling and brought many to become involved, despite the risks.

Musical Expressions

The very engaging experience of community produced a number of artifacts in Solentiname. These included paintings, songs, and musical instruments, among other things, as the excitement of sharing exposed people to new ways of artistic expression. While many of them learned the primitivist style of painting and sculpture from Ernesto Cardenal, not only as a reflection of their reality but also as a means to support themselves (Cardenal, 2003), others used their musical talents to add to their religious gatherings. Music became, for them, a way to express who they were as working peasants as well as a way to explore how this peasant identity was profoundly linked to faith. With their homemade instruments they contributed, for example, to the writing of the *Misa Campesina*, a Mass reflecting liberation theology in its music, instrumentation, and lyrics. The community moved away from using the organ, the instrument usually upheld by the traditional church as the instrument of choice during liturgy, and turned, instead, to instruments that would have been part of the daily lives of their young people:

> The young people liked to play the guitar and they played. Drums were made with cow and calf skins to use at Mass. The youth painted a drum beautifully in black with birds and fish around it. It looked like a piece of art and it played well. Someone else came up with maracas which were also painted, as well as a guitar which had flowers and birds.
>
> (María Guevara Silva, 2013)

These instruments, familiar to young people because they were made and decorated by their own hands and had images and styles that were highly valued in Solentiname, strengthened the sense of community, as they provided a familiar means of expression.

By the mid-1960s, the unique characteristics of the small Solentiname community began to attract an increasing number of visitors, usually young people both from Nicaragua as well as from abroad. Among those young people who arrived hoping to be immersed in the reality of this community was Nicaraguan musician, Carlos Mejía Godoy. Ernesto Cardenal explains that Carlos Mejía Godoy's music was already both well liked and well understood by Nicaraguan people by the time he arrived on the islands. He became a sort of scribe who captured the wisdom and reflections of the community and incorporated them into the *Misa Campesina*. This Mass became an exemplary musical creation because it is simultaneously an expression of the community's spirit as well as an agent of fortification of community learning and imagination (Cardenal, 2002, 255). Through it, the peasants begun to situate themselves in a newly imagined and newly articulated place in society and in faith because by its very creation this Mass challenged the social and religious structures lived in Nicaragua prior to the revolution. Following the basic liturgical structure, this music turns the world upside down by bringing God into close proximity with the poor and lets the poor address him in their own language through word, rhythms, and instrumentation. Here, God also aligns himself with the struggle of this community instead of aligning himself with the ruling class.

Community members still remember that "Carlos was constantly taking notes," listening for the deeply felt expressions of how the Gospel was lived in Solentiname (Esperanza Guevara Silva). The weekly Masses with the peasants' commentary on the Gospel as well as their festive Sunday lunches were the source of wisdom for the creation of the text of the Mass. For Mejía Godoy, the people of Solentiname were "true prodigies of imagination, synthesis, wisdom, intuition and, at the same time, of religiosity and fervor" (personal interview, January 2, 2014). He insists that he had to pay close attention to everything that was around him so as not to miss the knowledge that flowed from the people. He had to remain attentive because "Sometimes a woman who is serving coffee says a phrase and that is the phrase we have been looking for because we are not looking for high literature but popular sensitivity" (personal interview, January 2, 2014). This Mass was first recorded in 1975 and eventually became the Mass of choice in communities that lived in poorer sectors of Nicaragua, as well as in Central America, such as Father de la Jara's Managua community. Even though it continues to be played in popular circles and has been recorded by well-known artists such as Miguel Bosé, Nana Mouskori, Ana Belén (Mejía Godoy, 1979) and many others in Latin America and the world (K. Cardenal, 2006), the *Misa Campesina* is known for being a truly popular musical expression. Mejía Godoy himself expresses this in a most heartfelt way. He states: "I don't feel like a full author but a coauthor of a work that was written by the Nicaraguan people with their sacrifice, their faith, their fervor, their ideals and their dreams" (personal interview, January 2, 2014).

The songs of the *Misa Campesina* stand as a most vivid embodiment of the community's engagement and *conscientization* and the inevitable connection they felt between faith and action. This is especially evident in the 'Communion' and the 'Dismissal' songs, where the joy of praise and faith-sharing is linked to everyday action. After reflecting that God is with the community, that God works alongside the poor and gives inherent dignity to the occupations of the working class, the Mass calls for concrete actions in daily life. Through the use of a natural environment familiar to the people and deeply connected to the Solentiname experience, the Communion Song describes the culminating point of the gathering. Here, the voice of the people describes the table of the Eucharist as a plantation of corn, an essential element in the Nicaraguan diet and economy and the most likely workplace for peasants: "Let's go to the cornfield, the cornfield of our Lord. Jesus Christ invites us to his harvest of love. The cornfields shine with the sunlight. Let's go to the cornfield of communion."[2] Nature joins in the celebration felt by the community as the verses describe the fish found in Lake Nicaragua, naming them by their local names: "The little fish of the lake want to accompany us and they jump overjoyed as if they were filled with fraternity: laguneros and róbalos, guapote and gasear, mojarras, guabinas and even the sardines seem to sing" (Communion hymn of the *Misa Campesina*). But this joy, this experience of communion and worship brings with it a serious commitment as it is expressed in the final verse: "Communion is not an inconsequential or empty myth, it is commitment and living, a becoming aware of Christianity, it is to say I am a Christian and you can count on me my brother" (Communion hymn). Going to Mass and receiving communion is far from being the disconnected experience that Mrs. María Guevara Silva describes as being part of their life before Cardenal's arrival in Mancarrón. Participating in this communion is a joyful feast and a profession of their commitment to their community and their country.

This significant and joyous experience of the Mass comes to an end after communion, but the participant is reminded here, through the closing song, that everyday life is inextricably connected with what they celebrated. The peasant, the agricultural worker, expresses a resolution as he or she articulates the sadness caused by separating from the community. The closing song states that gathering in fraternal communion is a beautiful thing, mentions individual people of the community by name, and describes them as joyous in the midst of this celebration: "There is nothing as beautiful as seeing Chenta Calero with her four children and Gaspar, her happy companion. From here I can see the fisherman Presentación Ortíz singing happily with his entire family." This happiness, sings the peasant, will overflow into life and will be the reason for him or her to carry out their work with more dedication: "Now that I return to my house filled with joy, I am going to clean my garden with more devotion." Finally, the last verse is an invitation to join their efforts in defending and strengthening the community: "Let's join hands to make a strong wall to always defend the community." It is a final commitment to safeguard the community against anything that may threaten it from the outside.

Conclusion

During the period prior to the triumph of the Nicaraguan revolution of 1979, *Misa Campesina* and the learning experience created through the reading and interpretation of the Gospel, kept alive a community in the full sense of Wood and Judikis' definition. The community was engaged in concrete actions, but also had a common interest at heart: the improvement in their quality of life and that of Nicaraguan peasants. They acknowledged that they were interconnected, and they committed themselves to the well-being of each other and expressed this most eloquently through song. Their conversations based on the Gospel, their exposure to various ideologies through reading and music, as well as their constant awareness of the social reality of Nicaragua's peasants, facilitated a process of learning that brought with it an unsettling awareness that they could not ignore. This community was certainly a community of practice as they learned methods of artistic expression through painting and music and became knowledgeable in practical solutions to the troubles of living in the archipelago of Solentiname. The songs that were born out of the intimacy of community sharing served not only to strengthen their sense of identity and engagement but facilitated their alignment with the values they discovered in their faith-sharing. The song of the *Misa Campesina* also served as a way for the Solentiname peasants to inform and engage other communities that came into contact with them. The people of Solentiname experienced a new view of the Gospel and practiced religion in a way that validated their sufferings and their way of life. They also learned that it was not right that a political dynasty ignored their plight and stripped them of land and resources. They saw, if only for a short time, that they could redefine their place in Nicaraguan society and the church. They also learned that they did not have to live in isolation from each other, but that they could live in a community which was formed around their learning experience and practicing religion. Their community was a place for a process of *conscientization* that changed their lives dramatically and moved them to become involved in the process of revolution.

Notes

1 Interviews cited in this chapter were translated by the author from the original Spanish script.
2 Texts from the *Misa Campesina* cited here are all translations by the author.

References

Bauman, Z. 2004. *Identity: conversations with Benedetto Vecchi*. Cambridge, UK; Malden, MA: Polity Press.
Berryman, P. 1984. *The religious roots of rebellion: Christians in central american revolutions*. Maryknoll, NY: Orbis Books.
Cardenal, E. 2002. *Las ínsulas extrañas: Memorias 2*. Madrid: Editorial Trotta.

Cardenal, K. 2008. *Misee for Kari Og Ola/Misa Campesina*. [CD]. Norway: Kirkeling Kulturverksted.

Clements, D. 2008. *The future of community: reports of a death greatly exaggerated*. London: Pluto Press.

Deere, C.D., & Royce, F.S. 2009. *Rural social movements in Latin America: organizing for sustainable livelihoods*. Gainesville, FL: University Press of Florida.

Diamond, S.F. 2013. *Rights and revolution: the rise and fall of Nicaragua's Sandinista movement*. Lake Mary, FL: Vandeplas Publishing, LLC.

Freire, P. 1993. *Pedagogy of the oppressed* (New rev. 20th-anniversary ed.). New York: Continuum.

Gobat, M. 2005. *Confronting the American dream: Nicaragua under U.S. imperial rule*. Durham: Duke University Press.

Guevara Silva, María. Personal Interview. December 23, 2013.

Heyck, D.L.D. 1989. *Life stories of the Nicaraguan revolution*. New York: Routledge.

Kirk, J.M. 1992. *Politics and the Catholic Church in Nicaragua*. Gainesville, FL: University Press of Florida.

Mejía Godoy, C. 1979. *Misa Campesina*. [CD]. Managua: CBS.

Plant, R. (1978). Community: concept, conception, and ideology. *Politics & Society, 8*(1), 79–107. doi:10.1177/003232927800800103.

Tumasserna, J. (1992). The Nueva-Canción Movement and its Mass-mediated Performance Context. *Latin American Music Review/Revista De Musica Latinoamericana 13*(2), 139–157.

Wenger, E. (2000). Communities of practice and social learning systems. *Organization, 7*(2), 225–246.

Whitford, B. & Paskievich, J. (Directors). (2009). *The gift of diabetes* [Video/DVD]. Montreal: National Film Board of Canada.

Williams, P.J. (1985). The Catholic Hierarchy in the Nicaraguan Revolution. *Journal of Latin American Studies, 17*(2), 341–369. doi:10.1017/S0022216X00007926.

Wood, G.S. (2001). "Conversation 1: Defining Community." In J.C. Judikis (Ed.). *Conversations on community theory*. West Lafayette, IN: Purdue University Press.

7 Community and the State

Piecing Together Differences in Alejandro Brugués' *Juan of the Dead*

Miharu M. Miyasaka and Patrick X. Horrigan

In Cuba's post-1959 'realist' cinema, horror films are not common and monsters have nearly vanished from the national audiovisual imagination. In the film *Juan of the Dead* (2011), written and directed by Alejandro Brugués, this rarity is a mix of nationality and genre: a Cuban film about zombies. Following Jeffrey J. Cohen's lead and exploration of "what happens when monstrousness is taken seriously, as a mode of cultural discourse" (1996, viii), and his reasoning of "why we have created them" (1996, 20), the specific ways that Brugués' film questions what is represented as a monstrosity are addressed. This chapter explores the notions of 'cultural zombies,' arguing that the anxiety over being a zombie-like follower leads to a fragmented identity. In *Juan of the Dead*, characters fight off a zombie outbreak, which leads to their rediscovery of social responsibility and the meaning of community.

The newly formed community displays the potential for groups to overcome oppressive national structures and threatening situations through collective action. In relation to this achievement, and the borrowed genre of horror cinema, a group of Cuban filmmakers joined forces on May 4, 2013 to challenge a long-standing state cultural policy that tried to limit their artistic license and dictate their production. While the 'unofficial' Cuban filmmakers' guild negotiates the scope of its authority within the state, the film characters' behavior in response to the zombie outbreak takes on monstrous dimensions. Despite any differences, however, there is an attempt to legitimately *piece together* differences, rights, and order, in a way that balances the anxiety of being swallowed by the *whole* and monsters that poke *holes* in the centers of meaning.

In *Juan of the Dead*, Brugués explores the confrontation between 'cultural zombies' and 'zombie ghouls'[1] as society fragments and crumbles under a situational crisis. Survival is dependent upon individuals' ability to draw together and build on common interests like business, family, and friendship. Affecting this "zombie revolution"—as the film is described on its promotional website—requires a display of initiative that gives individuals the power to overcome the zombie ghouls despite the absence of an effectual official order. Alejandro Brugués and his community of filmmakers experience a similar obstacle in a seemingly zombified state institution that limits authentic artistic production. The filmmakers' project depicts the ghoul as an odd presence, rather than *good* or *bad*, and while they are not directly connected to a social movement, they challenge public practice and develop serious negotiation strategies. For the filmmakers, one of the most important aspects of their community is its ability to utilize various networks of communication. Their use of Internet and other discussion forums gained widespread support as the community overcame such obstacles as distance and other communicative difficulties. This approach allowed the filmmakers to forge an authentic community that effectively challenged the Cuban institutional goliaths. Moreover, to overcome these ghoulish figures both the filmmakers and the characters in *Juan of the Dead* embrace a mindset of inclusiveness and negotiation, understanding permanent and provisional elements, 'biological' and 'adopted' offspring.

Waves in the Water

In the opening scenes of *Juan of the Dead*, the first zombie ghoul appears as a foreigner, emerging from the paradisiacal waters that bathe Havana's seawall, wearing an orange uniform from the U.S.-controlled Guantánamo Bay Naval Base prison. From this point on, 'zombie ghouls,' otherworldly flesh-eaters, unbearably threaten the existence of the Cuban 'cultural zombies,' who still behave as humans. Despite Brugués' representation of Cubans in a state of cultural stillness, or zombification—first apparent in the protagonist Juan's opening lines, glorifying life in a place where everything is a matter of sitting in wait for the fruit to fall from the tree—the suggested cultural lack of drive seems preferable to foreign and irreversible change. As the film unfolds, Juan's determination to preserve his carefree Cuban lifestyle is staggered only by his love for his daughter, Camila. Juan's love for Camila and his desire to protect her guides him through a prodigious transformational period, as he realizes his potential as a leader and, ultimately, sacrifices his own safety for that of the members of his community.

Juan's ability to perceive the subtle differences between zombie ghouls and cultural zombies gives him an advantage over other civilians who remain unaware of the imminent threat. After being bitten by a ghoul, life continues as a form of existence characterized by an exaggerated "loss of something essential that previous to zombification defined it as human ... the person is no longer a person in either an existential or metaphysical sense" (Boon, 2011, 7). Being a mobile, brainless corpse that "will not know itself as subject, only as pure body" exaggerates an absence of will; thus, monsters embody the worst outcome of a previous crisis (Cohen, 1996, 4). Ghouls in Cuba seem so frightening in comparison to Cuban zombiness due to a total absence of differentiation: humans inhabiting a nationally and culturally indistinguishable world—as if homogeneity among Cubans was preferable/different from all zombies being the same. In regards to the film itself, *Juan of the Dead* is a Cuban–Spanish co-production based on a global horror genre with no local tradition and well positioned towards an international market.

Brugués' film depicts the potential for a constructive and fruitful relationship between national and international entities as long as it is a fair, cooperative endeavor. At the same time, it represents as humanly essential a connection between an individual and a national project. In this state–society connection, where society is made up of groups and individuals, social participation must be the product of free will. Juan's transformation throughout the film, from a self-indulgent, irresponsible, apathetic individual to a zombie executioner for the sake of the nation, depicts a hope that Cubans (in Cuba) will join his fight against the foreign enemy. However, Juan's attempt to protect his nation does not assume or force participation; rather it provides an opportunity, a framework to bring together groups and individuals who share similar goals. This interaction fosters a sense of community that is more profound than with cultural zombies, a structure that is non-existent as a zombie ghoul. Zombification *à la ghoul* represents "cannibalism as incorporation into the wrong cultural body" of sameness, which ultimately eradicates any trace of the individual (Cohen, 1996, 14).

In other Cuban–Spanish co-productions, cinematic scholar, Mariana Johnson interprets similar *anxieties of authenticity* in relation to an international reality of "globalization and mobile capital, deterritorialisation and resettlement, and migrations imagined and real, [that have caused] a shift ... from the myopics of national culture to the relationality of transnational flows" (Johnson, 2008, 278). Whilst this trend towards a more global appeal is evident in the increasing variety of production models, postproduction locations, aesthetics, and genres in contemporary Cuban cinema—of which *Juan of the Dead* is a paradigmatic example—the threat of a global ghoul still affects "how ... Cuba [is] negotiating its entry into the global film marketplace, and what is at stake" (Johnson, 281). Predictable tensions from an encounter of national and international practices intensify in Cuba, where the state-owned Cuban Institute of Cinematographic Arts and Industry (ICAIC)[2] officially centralizes all processes of filmmaking, e.g., production, postproduction, distribution, exhibition, archives, laboratories, studios, and nationality of films, among others. Some 'anxieties of authenticity' relate to the institutionally unified body refusing to accept its 'monstrous' nature made of different national and international parts. In the film, the arrival of the zombie ghouls precipitates a nationwide negative reaction that is particularly driven by the constant association of the ghouls with U.S. instigators or dissidents—an idea frequently promoted by the state-owned media networks. As a cinematic production, *Juan of the Dead* exemplifies this national anxiety over outsiders threatening Cubans' will, as it is produced independently from ICAIC. However, as is also the case with the film, external threats are not necessarily what they appear to be and the answer is not always alienation and total control. In some instances national and international cooperatives allow both parties to achieve more as a unit than was ever possible as singular entities.

The national zombies in *Juan of the Dead*, however, had already lost something previous to being horrified by the ghoul's appetite. The film's *habaneros* embody a terrifying feature of (pre-Romero) living dead as described in the film *The Ghost Breakers* (George Marshall, U.S., 1940), which, surprisingly, takes place in Cuba: "[They] ha[ve] no will of [their] own. You see them sometimes *walking around blindly*, with dead eyes, *following* orders, not knowing what they do, *not caring*" [italics added]. In the initial sequences of *Juan of the Dead*, the Havana dwellers seem to fit accurately within this description. Juan seems to hold a particularly uncaring attitude towards official institutions, e.g., the state television and the Committee for the Defense of the Revolution (CDR), although he apathetically *follows* a routine of watching the TV news and going to CDR meetings. The arrival of the ghoul leaves people provisionally stateless, with no official discourses, mechanisms and/or institutions to guide them. The general population is unable to notice a distinct shift from cultural zombie to ghoul, and their blind acceptance of state-led propaganda draws them nearer and nearer to a point of zombification.

Juan, on the other hand, seems aptly capable of developing alternative ways to survive from within the social collapse—something that he proudly claims to have also done in pre-ghoul times. While he used to experience a zombie-like indifference towards other zombie-like practices within Cuba, through his uncaring attitude Juan gains some power to cheat the game by not following all its rules. However, in order to really snap out of the zombie mode and attain a more powerful position, he needed to be able to negotiate the legitimacy of his vision of/for the game. Juan had to be able to form an authentic community, within which he could find the power and support to overcome oppressive national structures. The new community gave him a say in those aspects of a social design that previously made him react like a tricky player, and the arrival of the ghouls allowed him that opportunity by provisionally turning things upside down.

In another interpretation of zombie symbolism, J.J. Cohen describes the "monster [as] an extreme version of marginalization, an abjecting epistemological device basic to the mechanics of deviance construction and identity formation" (ix). When foreign and soon-to-be 'nationalized' ghouls are placed alongside a notion of sameness (us, living Cubans), they expose suture mechanisms that are used to patch (living-dead) holes in the national uniform. In the case of Cuba, appeals to genuine homogeneity often try to contest the horror of an artificial sameness in other parts of the world (or globalization gone wrong); the former representing a total and consensual interconnection between governing institutions and governed individuals (and among themselves). In *Juan of the Dead*, the state promotes the idea that the ghouls are U.S. dissidents in an attempt to unify the nation against an identifiable enemy. The media becomes an outlet to instill a fear of foreign offensives that threaten the Cuban way of life. While some Cubans have had a tendency to romanticize the Cuban situation, as exemplified by Juan's character, the film also suggests the importance of realizing that not everything foreign is a threat and that there can be life beyond Fidel's Cuba. While unity within a nation is important, society must also emphasize free will and freedom of choice: Cubans cannot be manipulated into staying in Cuba; it has to be an authentic, thoughtful decision. In order for the Cuban community to be as strong as possible, Cubans need to want to be a part of it, not because of fear or power but because of want, trust, and a belief in solidarity.

Indivisibility within such communities functions as a reassuring national truth in times of transnational uncertainties. In the case of the zombie invasion, to challenge the community's structure for some is to effectively *let the ghouls in*, and while this fear is slightly irrational it is not completely unfounded. The film shows that a complex dynamic of social practices is taking place between community and civil society, and not giving them a place at the debating table, fostering awareness and understanding, furthers the gap between what people do and what is officially represented and interpreted as being done. *Juan of the Dead* shows a reality zombified by pre-ghoul followers and fragmented by post-ghoul groups of Cubans surviving on common interests like business, family, and/or friendship. This individualism exaggerates a prior disconnection with official principles and communities that ordered national life, e.g., the network of Committees for the Defense of the Revolution and the media. The media's portrayal of the outbreak of, and subsequent call for, a mass protest does little to counteract the 'dissident' attacks. The attempts made by the state and its military counterparts are ineffective in organizing the survivors and do little more than introduce another threat to their community and livelihood. The symbolic and administrative mechanisms used for social cohesion fail to lead or even propose an effective social response to the outbreak. In the absence of an effectual official order, to remain a 'living' Cuban and to have power over the dead becomes a matter of both individual initiative and a community-oriented mentality; for strong communities are made up of strong individuals.

Brugués' film presents a problematic approach towards community and processes of fragmentation, which plays very well with the figure of the ghoul. Humans/Cubans become living pieces of flesh: creatures dragging limbs, half-torsos and severed parts. They are partial bodies that live off pieces of flesh; a person is not eaten completely, but the brain and some parts of the body are left to *survive* and move. Comparable to this not-fully-operative disjointed system, Juan's individualism, though essential for short-term survival, stands opposite to what gradually becomes clear to him: a national project represents the most genuine and sustainable way to live. This logic explains his decision to ship off, or better, to raft off the subjects of his private interests—his daughter and friends/associates—away from Cuba, while he stays to save the whole nation. It is this meaning that ultimately gives sense to his new empowered existence as a member (on his own terms) of a bigger community.

In the film, the problem of the 'cultural zombie,' or follower, and the 'zombie ghoul,' or fragmented, is resolved by invoking the principle of the '(w)holly' nation. But what does Juan have in mind? Will he lead the survivors, or rely on reinstating official networks? Will he negotiate with groups effectively practicing their own survival strategies? What if others have a vision of a mixed zombie society? The film rightly addresses current Cuban anxieties over more social participation, active involvement in public affairs, and individuals' rights to their own beliefs, even if these differ from an official imagination. Juan uses the shifting circumstances to create his own "extermination" business, capitalizing on the hardships of others. Even within his immediate community, Juan initially shows little compassion for his neighbors and rarely negotiates his costs of doing business. The film circumvents the complexity of the problem by pointing to a national project devoid of the multifaceted negotiation necessary to define between governing bodies and citizens' visions of a post-ghoul society, which will still be inhabited by the "monstrous" presence of "difference[s] made flesh" (Cohen, 1996, 7).

This is not to deny that "histories of imperialist oppression and economic powerless[ness] in the Third World practically demand the construction of national authenticity and cultural heritage as strategies of self-determination" (Johnson, 2008, 283). However, an exaggerated emphasis on this xenophobia and fear of iconoclastic behavior tends "to fetishize cultural authenticity along nationalistic lines," and limits the dynamic of international and national propositions and influences (Johnson, 283). In the film, an authoritarian character is seen from the start forcing his will on his fellow Cuban neighbors. This man, described by Juan as "a sodomite ... a chemical substance," sports a military-style outfit and, while he boasts his power over others—a characteristic also endorsed by his son—he ultimately ends up a zombie ghoul and is overcome by Juan in the final scenes. This is a monumental shifting point in the film as Juan sacrifices himself to save another, a change that exhibits the strength of the individual over ghouls and a militarized, authoritative power. Ideally, non-authentic human *and* Cuban behaviors would be banned from a future social project as monstrous "violation[s] of a cultural code" (Cohen, 1996, 11).

It is interesting to discuss this approach to nationality in relation to the film enterprise itself, which expands the horizon of Cuban cinema by connecting it to a global genre and to a generation of independent filmmakers that are outsiders in *their* local tradition of institutional cinema. Even if *Juan of the Dead* moves fluidly in these (trans)national waters, the protagonist of its story exhibits an excessive one-sided will to define a factual center of meaning; Juan is a fragment of society assuming what all others will share and have to follow. These anxieties can be resituated in the context of a contemporary Cuban audiovisual sphere and its ongoing debate over interpretations of national cinema as institutional or professional practice. The confrontation between 'cultural zombies' and 'zombie ghouls' resembles the current power struggle between "icaicentrism"[3] and the acceptance of ICAIC's guidelines, and film independency, which is praised *and* feared for its appetite for creation/production self-governance. Recently, a group of Cuban filmmakers started a process of negotiations with the state in order to resolve this cultural tension. What is promising about their project is that it is not a one-man show, but a collective in dialogue with a complex reality of professional self-determination and cultural policy, i.e., a variety of experiences, competencies, and guiding principles.

An Alternative to 'Zombification'

On 4 May 2013, after prior communication via email, a community of approximately 70 filmmakers and industry professionals gathered to discuss long-due changes in the Cuban audiovisual landscape. In 1959, the ICAIC was created under Law no. 169 to channel all national and international activities related to Cuban filmmaking. To this day it is still officially recognized as Cuba's major cinema company (the others also being state-owned), and in the eyes of the Law it is the *right*ful way to make films in Cuba. In practice, most films produced in Cuba after 1989 under the banner of national cinema have been co-productions with foreign companies. In the last decade especially, many films have been produced independently through national and/or international private funding. The state's cultural policy grants ICAIC an almost exclusive role as the institution that formally governs film practice (administrative, commercial, technical, and creative), leaving other forms of production and films in a limbo of legality, productivity, and public recognition. For decades, this 'icaicentrism' has functioned like a "monster [that] prevents mobility ... delimiting the social spaces through which private bodies may move" (Cohen, 1996, 12). In this context, ICAIC can be seen as a monster, or zombie ghoul, because it creates institutional *sameness*, an aspect that was critically discussed at the so-called 'filmmakers' encounter.'

 In the following pages, two aspects that have been instrumental in positioning the group as a legitimate and powerful negotiator, *piecing together* a cultural vision and practice, are discussed. Using modern media resources to reimagine its own community (for professional peers), the filmmakers' project functions on the premise of representativeness, competence, achievement, reciprocity, and transparency. Through the use of digital platforms such as email, blogging, and websites, it stabilizes a connection with its membership (and other interested parties in/outside Cuba), while also creating virtual spaces for public participation. The filmmakers' initiative addresses a long-due deconstruction of Cuban cinema as a complex and dynamic network of state-funded, (semi)independent and (inter) national propositions and influences, allowing for cultural meaning— Cuban cinema—to catch up with the cultural practice—Cuban filmmaking—that it is supposed to represent. The initiative's communicational power stems from its focus on actual problems that affect many filmmakers, exploring official and non-official channels of communication, having the means and will to share, accept, and debate ideas in a quick and open way, and setting concrete and often short-term objectives.

To put it simply, the meeting on 4 May and its subsequent proceedings have been a fast-tracking intent by a specific group, i.e., people with common professional interests trying to negotiate directly with the state to implement a particular agenda that not only impacts the group but society in general. It is a bottom-up strategy in a context characterized by a top-down way of governing that tends to move at a very slow pace. For instance, the filmmakers had officially presented their project in a document called "Proposals for the Renewal of Cuban Cinema" (*Propuestas para la renovación del cine cubano*), during the VII Congress of Cuba's Union of Writers and Artists (UNEAC) in 2008. Their objective was to dialogue their way into an "active involvement in the design of cultural policies" (*Palabras al Consejo Nacional*, 2013); however, five years went by without any response from top institutions such as the Ministry of Culture. In light of normal channels of communication with the state via intermediary institutions proving ineffectual, a more direct alternative was deemed necessary. The issues documented in 2008 were not exceptional but systemic. In fact, the main problem was that Cuban cinema had not been adequately represented by a National Film Law recognizing a plurality of practices. Unlike Law no. 169, which was created as a legal framework to establish an institutional monopoly over all activities related to filmmaking, a film law should consist of a network of institutions and relations functioning jointly as well as independently. In this scenario envisioned by the filmmakers, ICAIC exists as an inclusive film institute rather than a state production company, as one part of a complex system made up of many different experiences and *wills*. What *haunts* the filmmakers is an autopilot mode set to only *follow* official coordinates of what is possible and impossible.

In this scenario, the state displays little desire to intervene and solve any persisting problems. In order to effect significant change, groups and individuals must take the lead and fight for their vision. In *Juan of the Dead*, Juan experiences a similar disinterest in addressing the reality of his situation, as he decides to lead his own initiative to overcome the ghouls. The strength of his newly formed community, similar to the filmmakers' endeavor, is founded upon an emphasis on both individual and collective importance. On their own, few of the individuals would have survived, however, as a whole they are able to work together to conquer their enemy and achieve their goals. While in pre-ghoul times some of the members of Juan's team were seen as marginal members of society—manipulators and thieves, lazy and unintelligent—in this new scenario their strengths are emphasized and their weaknesses are overcome. The authenticity of this new community is founded heavily on this aspect of encouraging participation from all members despite perceived, not necessarily real, disadvantages.

The legitimacy of the filmmakers' group and its proposals rests in their commitment to representation, acknowledging the work of active filmmakers with and without official affiliation to institutions such as ICAIC. This sense of growth and inclusivity is illustrated by their first improvised and informal encounter on 4 May, which gathered approximately 70 people, and their subsequent meeting on 18 May, which hosted approximately 100 industry professionals. Among them were National Film Awardees; various generations of filmmakers with different academic and professional formations, who, as was publicly recognized in one of their official documents, "[were all included] regardless of their aesthetics, contents or group interests" (Cineastas cubanos por el cine Cubano, 2013). This inclusivity depicts the potential for individuals to overcome their differences to fight for a change that benefits their collective goals and interests, deconstructing any homogenizing structures that culturally distort diverse artistic productions.

Similar to *Juan of the Dead*, the specter of cultural zombification or a culture of followers is troubling in audiovisual waters. In their first meeting, film director, Enrique Colina spoke about filmmakers' right to participate in matters of decision-making that have systemically ignored the professional base legitimizing its representativeness (Segunda cita ... de cineastas Cubanos, 2013). By voting to establish an official Filmmakers' Workgroup, playfully nicknamed G-20 due to the number of its members, filmmakers instrumentalized an alternative form of representation. As publicly stated by Cuban scriptwriter, Arturo Arango, the group works independently from ICAIC's own workgroup and is the only one in charge of representing the filmmakers and their demands. The latter is a very important aspect because the initiative speaks for very specific, persisting problems, which are predicated and accepted on the basis of their practicality and relativity to current filmmaking, without forgetting that their decisions pave the way for a future vision of national cinema.

The relationships between Juan, his community, the state, and the zombie ghouls draw strong connections to the relationship between G-20 and ICAIC. Where ICAIC's affiliation with the state prevents the filmmakers from producing authentic, independent works, so too does the Cuban State, as represented by the mainstream media and military organizations, try to prevent Juan and his companions, as symbolic of the larger Cuban population, from surviving independently. The media tries to mislead them by calling attention to an imagined dissident attack while the military attempts an unnecessary takeover to control the outbreak. This relationship is symbolic of the Cuban situation as groups and individuals are limited in their ability to gain independence from the state. While neither Juan nor G-20 seek complete independence from the state, their efforts to create private businesses and partnerships challenges the state's strength and authority. The inevitable confrontation that arises from this duality is predicated upon the state's behavior towards these groups.

Whose competence is this? Colina connects the guild's right to participate in official decisions to their role as producers and main protagonists of cinematographic activities (Segunda cita ... de cineastas Cubanos,

2013); therefore to him it is a matter of professional competence. The legal limbo that marginalizes independent production in Cuba illustrates one of the problems that arise when players do not have a say in the rules of their game. As is presented in *Juan of the Dead*, consistent state intervention and prevention results in the inevitable demise of its institutional structures, as the media personnel are contaminated, the military is overcome, and the symbolic buildings are turned to rubble. With regards to G-20, the friction between ICAIC and the independent production companies could force a more severe split than anything previously imagined. Over the last decade, an increasing number of filmmakers have begun working through private production companies that have not been granted legal status, a standing that affects funding mechanisms such as bank loans, employment recognition, and social benefits, among other conditions. This should come as a surprise since some of these films were shown in local theaters, featured Cuban actors, technical and creative personnel, and exhibited in national and international film festivals. They have been instrumental in reviving the prestige of Cuban filmmaking, as is the case for *Juan of the Dead*, independently produced through 5th Avenue Productions (*Producciones de la 5ta. Avenida*). Brugués' film was voted 'Most Popular Film' at the Havana International Film Festival (2012), it won the Goya Award for Best Ibero-American Picture (2013), and it was the second Cuban film in recent decades to be screened at the Toronto International Film Festival (2011). At this point it is important to address the fact that ICAIC lost its traditional state funding in 1989, entering a precarious self-sustaining mode that considerably limited its presence in Cuba's audiovisual landscape (Getino, 2007, 190).[4]

Despite the contributions made by independent production companies, the first setback in the G-20's meetings with state representatives from the Ministry of Culture was precisely the legalization of such companies (*Otro intercambio*). But, why make more difficult the work of those players to whom the game owes part of its existence? Professional (cinematographic) and governmental (legal–administrative) competency means a publicly recognized authority decides what is possible in terms of culture and policy. Any power struggle between these groups over cultural policy would seem deconstructive since it reveals a guiding principle that "originates in process, rather than in fact (and that 'fact' is subject to constant reconstruction and change)" (Cohen, 1996, 14–15). The increasing presence and relevance of independent practices shows the possibility to legitimately challenge the whole—but not holy—narrative of a national state cinema. In challenging the state narrative, however, it is important to negotiate a mutually beneficial outcome that does not undermine either party.

For the filmmakers, in order to implement a new general policy, i.e., a new National Film Law, negotiation is an important, if not necessary, strategy. The work of the G-20 embodies a negotiated autonomy because it questions the legitimacy of a specific cultural state of affairs without confronting the political and economic status quo to which it directly and indirectly relates. For this reason the group contends the notion of a state cinema while unquestionably supporting the governmental body that designed and implemented a culture of exclusively centralized audiovisual practice. On the premise of dialogue, the filmmakers still grant ICAIC a central position in the audiovisual sphere though recognizing the incompatibility of its centralized nature; the same lead institution will *revive* in a new form characterized by a different leading method.

In their efforts to reconstruct the institutional character of filmmaking in Cuba, the filmmakers combine formal and alternative ways of production and communication. For instance, their webpage *Cine Debate* is hosted by UNEAC's website, and their meetings take place at ICAIC's Strawberry and Chocolate Cultural Center. This all works towards the notion of reciprocity—an important aspect in community-building—in the sense of proposing changes and accepting influences, and expecting the same from others. Filmmaking is to a certain professional extent a one-group show, but to empower its cultural scope in the Cuban context some degree of institutionalization is necessary. Otherwise, as it currently happens, the increasing production of independent films will not translate into more screen time in national theaters, remaining an informal presence in the people's imagination (who nonetheless have proved resourceful in accessing these works and connecting them to a narrative of national cinema). The filmmakers recognize that "[their] proposals ... will have to go through a complex process of negotiation and *defense* with those institutions in charge of approving them and sometimes transferring them to higher levels" (Actualizando las citas, 2013 [italics added]), and that they will have to learn the rules of the legal game. But one important premise of this negotiated approach is to not always follow things to the letter. The state's proposed deferral of the debate regarding the status of independent production companies was not accepted by the filmmakers and will be further reviewed.

The notions of transparency and public engagement have also contributed to the group's position as a legitimate and powerful negotiator. On numerous occasions the G-20 has connected openness to authentic representation, giving members the right to know and appraise the work of those who speak on their behalf and collectively retain or remove them. Hence, the group has set an example of public accountability. The most challenging part of making further achievements is obtaining concrete results within a short time-span. Some of their claims entail: legal status for independent production companies; official Registry and Regulations for the Audiovisual and Cinematographic Professional (his/her social and labor rights and duties); a Film Institute with a Council or Parliament of Filmmakers; a Cinema Development Fund; and a revised National Film Law. In the meantime, by way of their initiative they have succeeded in publicly interpreting Cuban cinema as a complex network of symbolic, social, professional, and economic factors that combine state and/or independent, institutional and/or private, national and/or international practices. The filmmakers' project attempts to piece together a functional creature, keeping at bay the dysfunctional 'cultural zombie' that tends to follow with 'monstrous' indifference. The meaning that gives cohesive power to their project is that of their envisioned National Film Law; an order that needs to be multifaceted, participatory and dynamic.

Let the Right Ghoul In

At the time of the outbreak, Juan turned to national media sources to gain information. To communicate with other members of his community, Juan must rely primarily on traditional means of communication such as land-line phone or word of mouth. From the perspective of Juan and his companions, Cuba is completely disconnected from modern digital technology. There is no Internet or Intranet to search about the epidemic; personal or public computers are not in sight, and neither is the act of texting, typing, blogging, or emailing. Had there been such means of communication, perhaps the survivors could have immediately and visibly grouped together in a virtual space in light of the ghouls' threat to the physical sphere. The only mention of a digital world comes from Juan's vague and almost disdained mention of a blogger who lives in his building. The blogger, Sara, is one of the first to leave Cuba in the wake of the epidemic. Perhaps, because of her access to digital networks, she is more aware of the reality of the situation, as opposed to those Cubans who are disconnected from such digital realms of information.

Such disconnection is likely to characterize poor environments like Juan's, who also does not have a profession that in Cuba would grant him official access to Internet or digital technology, e.g., some sectors in the fields of Education, Arts, Medical Sciences, Foreign and State Business, Technology, and Government. Far from Juan's level of disconnectedness, many—though not all—Cuban filmmakers routinely use Internet; they have email, Facebook accounts, and access to personal and public computers, a familiarity reinforced by the profession since nowadays most films are made in digital format. Some use personal blogs or other social media networks to share ideas about their work and express opinions on current national and/or international issues. Coexisting with a virtual reality, however, is a modern trait that most Cubans still find off limits, and it would be fair to say that even those connected must face many limitations and the quality of their access depends on the financial or institutional means of each person. Despite all this, what is noticeable about the filmmakers' initiative is that, unlike Juan, they rely heavily on digital technology and are engaged in a global dialogue. To further discuss this, their presence in digital spaces as well as the global scope of their webpage is examined.

As previously mentioned, the filmmakers used email to inform each other about the May 4th meeting; they restructured their community through digital networks that relied on technological outlets. The G-20's official form of contact with fellow filmmakers, or other interested parties, is a Gmail address that appears on the *Cine Debate* webpage. Also, their proposed National Registry of the Audiovisual and Cinematographic Creator requires future legally registered filmmakers to provide an email as personal information, and address and phone number are also included in the same category. This speaks to a digital way of doing things that is becoming normalized, electronic correspondence now representing a common practice in Cuba. Apparently not for Juan and *his dead*, however, who do not seem to be *living* in a national cyberspace only inhabited by approximately 1.4 million official Internet users from a population of 11 million (Venegas, 2010, 13). In theory, filmmakers (as artists and culture professionals) are part of a community characterized by *right*ful connectedness. Some have access to Intranet and/or Internet services from home, specific state institutions such as ICAIC, or abroad. Many Cuban filmmakers function in digital/global terms via trips directly and indirectly related to the profession, as well as co-productions that entail foreign personnel, post-production locations, and commercialization; they attend international film festivals, or study at the International Film and Television School (EICTV) alongside non-Cuban professors and classmates. This constant dialogue of national and international practices has translated into and, at the same time, resulted in an increased use of digital technology, up-to-date with global practices. As a film, *Juan of the Dead* is a great example of this with its state-of-the-art website and a series of promotional teasers on YouTube.

In light of all this, Juan's disconnected existence seems very foreign. His primary means of information-gathering is a pair of binoculars and a rooftop which, while providing him with adequate insight into the ghoulish transpirations, still leaves him unable to effectively communicate with others. As mentioned earlier, Juan's neighbor Sara, the blogger, quickly becomes aware of the need to leave Cuba to avoid becoming affected. From Juan's perspective, a cloud of suspicion hangs over her character due to her *untraditional* digital knowledge. Furthermore, she almost causes a break between Juan and Lázaro in her efforts to lead Lázaro astray; fragmenting an otherwise 'natural' camaraderie. In this sense, Juan's digital disconnectedness prevents him from allowing members of his community, as well as himself, from leaving their oppressive pasts behind. Had Juan followed Sara and Lázaro, instead of convincing Lázaro to return and consequently sacrificing Sara to the underwater ghouls, perhaps he may have been able to avoid the ensuing hardships that still led him to similar conclusions. To this extent, while certain forms of media impede the creation of authentic communities, other types of communication that are built upon similar communication networks have great potential to bring people together and foster genuine communicative forums.

All of this puts into play good, bad, and 'weird' views of fragmentation, in the sense of global and digital influences. An ordered Internet/Intranet connectedness designed by the state is made accessible to the right sectors of society. Cristina Venegas points out that the Cuban State has made great investments in digital technology for social and commercial purposes and, as such, it founded the University of Information Sciences (UCI) to function as "[p]art educational institution, part software factory" (2010, 3). "Since … 1996, the increase in the number of official Cuban websites has provided evidence that the government uses the Internet to position itself as a player in the worlds of capital and digital capitalism" (Venegas, 159). By way of illustration, ICAIC's website *Cubacine* includes a virtual store called *mallcubano.com*, "dedicated to the commercialization of all genuinely-cuban [sic] cultural products and services and it is composed of diverse departments *focusing on the new marketing trends through Internet*" (Mall Cubano, 2014 [italics added]). The global scope of this online business that sells "movies," "cultural services," and "smoking products," among a long list of other consumer goods, is visible in its exclusively foreign currency options: Euro and U.S. dollar. Also, the way it markets its national delivery service oddly appeals to a global appetite: "From anywhere in the world to anywhere in Cuba." Based on this official financial enterprise it would be interesting to see how the state deals with 'online shopping' *à la* crowdfunding. In 2013, the Cuban independent production company, 5th Avenue Productions, started an international crowdfunding project on Indiegogo in order to finance Cuban filmmaker, Miguel Coyula's film *Blue Heart*. More of these initiatives are only to be expected, in tune with a dynamic that Johnson would associate with "globalization and mobile capital" (2008, 278), up to date with a "good" official predisposition towards the outside virtual world. The question is if new production trends through Internet, such as crowdfunding, will fit the 'right' criterion.

Negative perceptions of a global/digital ghoul relate to the loss of a permanent and stable center of meaning. For Juan, the nation is the essential symbolic and physical space that Cubans share, giving them an objective right to not be like others; a geographic determinant literally meaning self-determination to culturally self-differentiate us from them. Contrary to the aforementioned delivery motto, "from anywhere in the world to anywhere in Cuba," the principle that "delivers" a national understanding of things "markets" a clear center: *from* Cuba *to* anywhere else. Juan experiences his birthplace from a position that resembles the secured scope of his fishing outing in the first sequence of the film: his raft floats off the coast without losing sight of Havana's seawall. Even when he used to live on the fringes of society, indifferent about his future, it was unthinkable for him to be uprooted from a Cuban physicality, and he only reacts when the ghoul threatens to take it away. To lose material ground is to lose an objective right, which explains his fear of the actual presence of a 'difference made flesh,' as well as his disdain for virtual reality. He fights for the nation on obvious terms: us (the living) versus them (the zombies), ignoring that the latter are Cuban living-dead; maybe they do not look the same but they *were* us, and the past, though not a *reality* anymore, is still an occurrence to be dealt with.

In comparison, the filmmakers' active virtual presence shows that unphysical spaces are used for their feasible impact on everyday practices, e.g., email communication was key to the May 4th gathering. Commenting and sharing ideas online are actions that people are getting used to, normalizing a culture of open debate that reflects what they want to do in a 'real' scenario but cannot, while simultaneously expanding the horizon of original proposals and aspirations. Another important aspect is that their initiative shows a center made up of different experiences of national filmmaking (institutional, foreign, independent), as if, in aforementioned delivery terms, a multifaceted practice was generated from anywhere *in* Cuba. Professional self-determination and self-differentiation are important parts of a national project such as the proposed Cuban Film Law, which is based on legal outsiders, or film laws from Colombia, Venezuela, Argentina, and Dominican Republic.

From this many-sided perspective the filmmakers still defend the principle of national cinema as the essential center of meaning for their profession, which avoids a 'monstrous' fragmentation in the form of every filmmaker for him/herself. It is revealing to place this in a context of restricted access in which Cubans, even the connected ones, still do not *feel* Internet as an indefinite reality where boundaries of time and space are permanently blurred by 24/7 mobile and home accessibility; even if Venegas rightly acknowledges that it is difficult to assess Cubans' real level of connectedness due to ever-increasing informal practices. The irony being that their appetite for digital media is the result of global *as well as* national influences, due to individuals' growing aspirations to be included as members of the local community of legitimate Internet users. Global and digital practices create 'holes' in the state's portrayal of Cuban culture, which until now (as seen in the case of ICAIC) connected what was possible and impossible to a clear official center. Besides the impact of digital technology in non-institutional production, it is now common for films with limited or no screen time in Cuban theaters to be broadcast on global channels such as YouTube and distributed in Cuba via flash memories or other portable devices. These 'bad' practices challenge the authority of the state to formalize how to produce and consume cinema.

What is promising about the filmmakers' project is a view of the global/digital ghoul as a weird rather than a good or bad presence; it cannot be absolutely feared or loved but engages people in a complex interrelation of "government policies, responses to these policies, and private initiatives" (Venegas, 2010, 3). The group's official access to digital media was used to challenge the state's plans to restructure ICAIC as a way of restructuring Cuban cinema—as if one meant the other—without consulting the filmmakers. This provoked the email calling for their initial meeting. But filmmaker, Enrique Álvarez had already urged for changes and professional involvement in matters of cultural policy in two letters that first circulated via email and were later posted online. Since the encounter on 4 May, the Internet has functioned as an active space of public participation through ideas on comment sections of digital magazines, official documents, open letters, blog posts, and updates in the *Cine Debate* webpage—all of which have shown an important aspect of their project: their common objectives go hand in hand with publicly accepted differences among themselves.

The webpage *Cine Debate* also illustrates a fruitful dialogue with foreign matter. It includes copies of film laws from Venezuela, Colombia, Dominican Republic, as well as other official documents from Argentina. They are used as references since there has never been a Cuban Film Law; hence the filmmakers' *vision* of a national project relates to foreign *versions* of the same project, in what could be recognized as a "relationality of transnational flows" (Venegas, 2010, 278). This practice gives flexibility to notions of authenticity by negotiating with other influences and proposals in order to provisionally stabilize a common ground in which *all* professionals can make films. This means at times supporting a foreign view that is thought to better represent local present practices and ideas about cinema. For instance, Cuban filmmakers posted their support for their European colleagues after the decision on 14 June 2013 that upheld the principle of cultural exception in Europe when negotiating a Free-Trade Agreement with the United States.

Although Cuban Law no. 169 is based on a similar principle that protects national cultural interests, current official practices privilege foreign films over *some* local ones. Based on this national programming strategy, in 2013, foreign films *Killing Them Softly* (Andrew Dominik, U.S., 2012) and *Sherlock Holmes* (Guy Ritchie, U.S., 2011) were released in 11 movie theaters while Cuban independent productions *Molasses* (Carlos Lechuga, 2012) and *The Swimming Pool* (Carlos Machado Quintela, 2011) were screened in only one theater of a multiplex complex. A principle of state cultural exception applies in the case of ICAIC's productions, which enjoy more screen time in an exhibition circuit that is state-owned. In light of this, the presence of certain foreign *and* national 'monsters' threatens a current order that is not designed as a level playing field for *all* films and filmmaking practices; with one exception, these ghouls have been invited.

Appetite, Fear, and Birthright: After Raúl

All of the above can be resituated in a context that Carmelo Mesa-Lago and Jorge Pérez-López have approached in their study *Cuba Under Raúl Castro: Assessing the Reforms*. The authors make a remarkably balanced and well-informed deconstruction of Cuban state of affairs since 2006, when Raúl Castro became leader. In one of Raúl's official speeches on 26 July 2007, he spoke of changes in "structural and conceptual reforms," however, since then things have only marginally shifted, moving a little or simply stalling (Mesa-Lago, 2013, 169). In debates on economic and social conditions, many past/present errors and a multitude of future aspirations have *emerged* (Mesa-Lago, 172–181). The filmmakers relate their project to this specific circumstance, a legitimate response to Raúl's political attempt to re-construct or reimagine Cuban communities, "calling for people to debate, question, look for ideas, get involved, feel that the Cuban project belongs to all and that it is not something engineered from a desk, no matter how good the intentions" (Cambiar todo lo que debe ser cambiado, 2013). In response, many Cubans have started to take creative liberties, only that to debate and question means different interpretations of what/how/when/why to do so. In the filmmakers' case, they connected it to a real "structural reform" in the way of making films in Cuba.

It is revealing to place the filmmakers' claims of a national legal framework, legalization of private production companies, involvement in cultural policies, decentralization, dialogue with valuable foreign models, and viable enterprises, in a socioeconomic sphere. Globally, financially viable methods from China and Vietnam are being acknowledged (Mesa-Lago, 2010, 173), people are demanding more participation in policymaking (180), changes in the productive role of the state (175), and a certain degree of self-employment has been legalized (228). The filmmakers' emphasis on a legal framework contrasts with the government's idea of simply "updating" a model that has never really been defined (Mesa-Lago, 225). They hope to recreate the law aimed towards embodying a well-delineated new concept of filmmaking. In relation to Juan and his collective, their efforts to work independently of the state are met with resistance in so much as the state demands an organizational role.

The present analysis has focused on a specific group and the audiovisual sphere at the center of its initiative. The filmmakers' project is not connected to a social movement, though they have challenged public practices and developed strategies for a group to autonomously negotiate with the state. The film professionals speak on behalf of themselves; they are a guild, a community with concrete problems and proposals to solve them in a specific socioeconomic and political conjuncture. While initially being independent was a leading strategy, they have now adapted means to legally effect change. Although Juan is never given the opportunity to fully engage with the Cuban State, his choice to remain behind, despite others' efforts to leave, implies a desire to overcome the country's hardships. This desire can only truly be realized in collaboration with others who share a similar vision. For the G-20, their acceptance and allegiance to other, less 'artistic' communities who share their philosophies will play a large part in their success. Their 'film' is still rolling, and perhaps by the end the filmmakers will think like Juan, who concludes that it is time to look for all others and start sharing his vision of a post-zombie Cuban society. What is important to address further in these situations is the strength of the individual and their role within the collective. As Gerard Delanty has suggested, communities are able to realize significant change, but they must remain inclusive of diverse visions, otherwise they risk transforming into the same exclusive institution that they seek to overcome. The monster may emerge in deceivingly paradisiacal waters.

While Juan starts the film inertly waiting for a fish to take his bait, he ends up discovering his own 'appetite' to willingly look for zombie ghouls—ironically so, due to the ghouls' own voracious cannibalism. An interesting dilemma is how to define the appropriate voracity of his appetite. *Juan of the Dead* is described on its web site as a "zombie revolution," and the presence of the monsters certainly causes radical changes in Cuban society. The filmmakers are betting on a more 'evolutionary' process with strategies of negotiation, although filmmaker Pável Giroud—who initially established the G-20—still considers that "important structural changes will come only with radical proposals such as ICAIC no longer functioning as a production company, which is thus far the State's will" (Pável Giroud, 2013). However, he does welcome an emerging appetite for questioning, "being in the [filmmakers'] debates have been a class on democracy that would be beneficial for other areas of the country" (Pável Giroud, 2013). Juan's approach to change is definitely more revolutionary, however, he seems to recognize that change does not happen instantaneously; it is a process of negotiation. Drawing similarities between Juan and the G-20 provides insight into the processes that lead to change; the importance of individual initiative, community-building, and adaptability.

What happens next? What is the scope of Juan's authority to slay his way into a post-zombie Cuban society? How does he form/find his new community? For Juan, the idea of turning into a monster is simply unbearable because it completely changes the personage; they forever lose any vestige of authentic will. While the traditional 'cultural zombie' could be free by eliminating the person or entity that controls his/her will, the modern ghoul's appetite is absolute and 'truthful:' monsters that only eat, as objective as that. When confronted with the zombie outbreak, Juan realizes the importance of free will and accesses his ability to become a community leader; working with other community members to renegotiate their place within society. This resembles an important question in the filmmaker's project. Who has an unequivocal right to envision Cuban cinema? What is a 'wrong cinematic body'? Despite state stipulations, the answer entails a process of negotiation, not fact. The filmmakers, having displayed an authentic willingness to accept co-productions, independent, and institutional productions as Cuban cinema, are helping to create a new/modern definition of collaboration. Similar to Juan's community, the group is able to defend themselves from the zombies through collaborative efforts and strong leadership. For both the filmmakers and film characters, effecting change was made possible only through the unity and collective strength of their communities—noting that neither group would have been able to achieve such feats without the support of their peers.

In the film, ghouls, zombies, and monsters embody situational fears and notions of threat that are felt from a difference of position. As a "cultural zombie," Juan's initial fear of a foreign ghoul transforms into horror towards nationalized flesh eaters. As such, the state's "monstrous" control of the digital sphere stems from "[f]ear of the characteristics of network digital technology (decentralized networks, one-to-one/many-to-many communication, and so on) [that] prompts centralized command of the Internet" (Venegas, 2010, 70). Giroud's fear is to

> fall in the usual trap of demanding via disciplined mechanisms. [He] always thought more effectual to start a revolution and behave a bit bad, but one learns to work in a group and with common claims, some more radical, others less drastic.
>
> (Pável Giroud, 2013)

Threat and fear, like proposals and influences, are mobile joints of a multi-part cultural body. However, this is repeatedly viewed in terms of a national space that people are expected to consider essential to their existence. Juan is represented as the nation's self-defense mechanism, and ICAIC and the filmmakers' ultimate legitimacy is their genuine bond to a national cinema.

After the 4 May meeting, the filmmakers released their first official document "Cuban Filmmakers for Cuban Cinema," and it is interesting in the way it 'naturalized' the survival of ICAIC, as a film institute, in terms of birthright: "It was born with the Revolution." Filmmaking in Cuba is hence the 'biological' offspring of Nation and State. As such it builds a factual center from which to advance other professional rights. To define a factual center by national and revolutionary birthrights not only naturalizes something that has been constructed, but, as Cohen has noted, it engenders monsters that keep coming back to remind us that meaning is a process (1996). Renowned filmmaker, Fernando Pérez, who is also a member of the G-20, was recently interviewed for a documentary about an independent music project in crisis with the state, and he spoke of an important anxiety: "I got used to speaking of the Revolution, [but] many young people in whom I truly believe speak of the Government, a word that I never used because I didn't see it separately." Younger generations do question:

> Who are those [in power]? Why? What for? What are they telling me? Does it coincide with me? That needs to be heard ... not only tolerated, we need ... to open [ourselves] to the complexity of life and the dynamic of a revolutionary process.
>
> (Ni rojo, ni verde ¡Azul!, 2013)

As is evident in the film, many Cubans seem unable to see beyond the state, however, given the right opportunity they are able to grow and change, overcoming whatever obstacles they encounter.

To envision filmmaking guided by a national principle in the form of a Film Law requires a mindset of inclusiveness and negotiation, understanding permanent and provisional elements, 'biological' and 'adopted' offspring. A similar predisposition is expected from a film institute and the state in the implementation of cultural and national policies that would help, as the filmmakers have acknowledged, to keep a balanced system without losing sight of cinema as a process that is constantly changing its economic, social, professional, and symbolic scope. An important shift has just occurred. A guild is expanding its professional competency into matters of social and legal policy to advance "a project of law in the [Cuban] National Assembly as an initiative of a social sector, in this case artists, something that, as far as we know, has never been done" (Actualizando las citas, 2013). This is significant given all the symbolic and *real* 'flesh' they have already amassed trying to piece together this new creature. Drawing a comparison between *Juan of the Dead* and the G-20 provides an opportunity to see how communities work together during times of hardship, finding strength and support amongst their peers. While in the film the community arises as a byproduct of a catastrophic event, this does not have to be the case, as the G-20 forms through a more natural progression of communication and development. Regardless of the circumstances, both groups display the power of individual and collective action, drawing attention to the fact that the people, citizens from all walks of life, can create change.

Notes

1 Two of "nine classifications of zombies" by Kevin Boon: "zombie ghouls" are a mix of undead and cannibal (57) and "cultural zombies" are zombie-like people in "real" scenarios (59).
2 Other *minor* official 'industries' are ECTVFAR (Armed Forces' TV and Cinema Studios), ECTV (TV's Cinema Studios), and EICTV (Film and TV International School) (Borrero, Guía crítica 11).
3 Juan A. García Borrero questions the "icaicentrismo" of studies of Cuban cinema that only focus on ICAIC films ("Sobre el 'icaicentrismo' "), though he minimizes the role in what's officially 'seen.' The *national* Institute's *national* production data for 2001–2004 states that 2004 only 'saw' three ICAIC films and none of the 12 local independent productions of that year, among other discrepancies (Getino, 191).
4 Foreign co-productions and services have been essential to ICAIC's survival, increasing from the 1960s (0.9–1.5%), 1970s (5–25.8%), to the 1990s (more than 75% of ICAIC's budget) (Getino, 2007, 190). The studies of García Borrero and Dean L. Reyes also show the decades-long contribution of independent productions to the development of Cuban filmmaking.

References

"Actualizando las citas ..." *Cine debate*. Uneac. 21 June 2013. Web. 10 September 2013.
Boon, Kevin. "And the Dead Shall Rise." In D. Christie & S.J. Lauro (Eds.). *Better off dead: the evolution of the zombie as post-human* (5–8). New York: Fordham University Press, 2011. Print.
Brugués, A. (Director). (2012). *Juan of the dead*. [DVD/Motion picture]. Perf. Alexis Días de Villegas & Jorge Molina. Entertainment One.
"Cambiar todo lo que debe ser cambiado." *Cine Debate*. Uneac. 15 July 2013. Web. 25 September 2013.

"Cineastas cubanos por el cine cubano." *Cine Debate.* Uneac. 5 June 2013. Web. 10 September 2013.

Cohen, Jeffrey Jerome. "Monster Culture (Seven Theses)." In J.J. Cohen (Ed.). *Monster theory: reading culture* (3–25). Minneapolis: University of Minnesota Press, 1996. Print.

Cohen, Jeffrey Jerome. Preface. *Monster theory.* vii–xi. Print.

Cordero, S., & Hanny Marín (Directors). (10 June 2013). *Ni rojo, ni verde ¡Azul!* YouTube. Web. 1 January 2014.

Delanty, Gerard. *Community.* London: Routledge, 2010. Print.

Douglas, María Eulalia. *La tienda negra: el cine en Cuba, 1897–1990.* La Habana: Cinemateca de Cuba, 1996. Print.

García Borrero, Juan Antonio. *Guía crítica del cine cubano de ficción.* La Habana: Editorial Arte y Literatura, 2001. Print.

García Borrero, Juan Antonio. "Sobre el 'icaicentrismo.' " *Cine cubano, la pupila insomne.* 28 June 2009. Web. 1 September 2013.

Getino, Octavio. *Cine iberoamericano: los desafíos del nuevo siglo.* Buenos Aires: Ediciones CICCUS, 2007. Print.

Giroud, Pável. "Pável Giroud: 'urge una ley de Cine en este país.' " *Cuba Contemporánea.* By Marianela González. 28 October 2013. Web. 20 January 2014.

Johnson, Mariana. "Spanish–Cuban Co-productions: Tourism, Transnational Romance and Anxieties of Authenticity." 279–296. Jay Beck & Vicente Rodríguez Ortega (Eds.). Manchester; New York: Manchester University Press, 2008. Print.

Mall Cubano. Agencia Exportadora Soy Cubano Artex. Web. 1 January 2014.

Mesa-Lago, Carmelo, & Jorge Pérez-López. *Cuba under Raúl Castro: assessing the reforms.* Boulder, Colorado: Lynne Rienner Publishers, 2013. Print.

"Otro intercambio con Fernando Rojas." *Cine Debate.* Uneac. 29 July 2013. Web. 25 September 2013.

"Palabras al Consejo Nacional." *Cuba Debate.* Uneac. 15 July 2013. Web. 1 October 2013.

Reyes, Dean Luis. "After ICAIC: The Three Categorical Imperatives of Current Cuban Cinema." In L. Duno-Gottberg & M.J. Horswell (Eds.). *Submerged: alternative Cuban cinema* (119–140). Houston: Literal Publishing: 2013. *Academia.* Web. 1 October 2013.

"Segunda cita … de cineastas cubanos." *Cine Debate.* Uneac. 5 June 2013. Web. 20 September 2013.

The Ghost Breakers. Dir. George Marshall. 1940. Perf. Bob Hope & Paulette Goddard. Universal Studios. 2012. DVD.

Venegas, Cristina. *Digital dilemmas: the state, the individual, and digital media in Cuba.* New Brunswick, NJ: Rutgers University Press, 2010. *Western Libraries.* Web. 1 October 2013.

Part III
Civil Society

8 Intercultural Democracy and Civil Society Participation in the New, Decolonized Bolivia

Roberta Rice

Indigenous movements have reinvigorated Latin America's democracies. The political exclusion of indigenous peoples, especially in countries with substantial indigenous populations, has undoubtedly contributed to the weakness of party systems and the lack of accountability, representation, and responsiveness of democracies in the region. In Bolivia, the election of the country's first indigenous president, Evo Morales (2006–present) of the Movement Toward Socialism (MAS), has resulted in new forms of political participation and governance that are, at least in part, inspired by indigenous communal traditions. The MAS emerged out of one of Bolivia's strongest social movements—the coca grower's movement of the Chapare region of the highland department of Cochabamba, led by Morales. As outlined by Oxhorn in this volume (Chapter 2), the MAS was able to capitalize on the political instability of the late 1990s and early 2000s that produced an atmosphere of confrontation between civil society and the state. Now that the MAS is the governing party, civil society actors are increasingly becoming a part of the state. To understand the implications of this new state–society relationship, the present chapter addresses the following question: What is the democratic contribution of indigenous and popular sector engagement with the state in contemporary Bolivia?

Civil society participation is crucial to inclusive democratic governance. Indigenous movements have played a decisive role in determining the extent and nature of democratic inclusion in Bolivia. The chapter argues that the incorporation of civil society actors into the structures of the state has produced a deeper, more meaningful form of democracy. Democracy in the 'new' Bolivia is being reimagined based on indigenous citizenship. Innovative features of the MAS administration include the introduction of elements of direct, participatory and communitarian democracy, policies to promote the decolonization and depatriarchalization of the state, and constitutional reforms to advance plurinationality and indigenous autonomy in the country. In keeping with Cameron, Hershberg, and Sharpe (2012), the chapter suggests that while the shift to intercultural democracy may have changed the character of Bolivia's representative democracy, it need not be seen as undermining it. The entrance of indigenous groups into the political arena has made a positive contribution to democracy in Bolivia, while greatly improving indigenous–state relations.

The chapter begins with an overview of Bolivia's tumultuous transition from a pacted democracy with little room for opposition groups to one in which formerly marginalized actors are front and center. Special attention is paid to the unintended consequences of the 1994 Law of Popular Participation in terms of the projection of a new generation of political movements onto the national political stage. The second section of the chapter highlights the state-led decolonization efforts of the Morales administration following the passage of the 2009 Constitution. The extension of the political sphere towards civil society is suggested to have strengthened state–society relations in the country. The final section of the chapter assesses the promise and limits of institutional change in the Bolivian case. This section reveals the challenges of reconciling representative democracy with indigenous peoples' demands and expectations.

From Pacted to Intercultural Democracy

Bolivia, like much of Latin America, has long suffered from exclusionary governing structures. Political parties in Bolivia have generally served more as vehicles for the capture and circulation of state patronage among political elites than as organizations expressing the interests of society (Gamarra & Malloy, 1995). Bolivia's neoliberal governments of the 1980s and 1990s relied heavily on political pacts between the major parties to impose draconian structural adjustment programs. Shortly after launching the neoliberal-inspired New Economic Policy (NEP) in 1985, President Víctor Paz Estenssoro of the National Revolutionary Movement (MNR) negotiated the so-called Pact for Democracy. The pact provided legislative support for the new policy in exchange for a share of state patronage for the main opposition party, the National Democratic Action (ADN), led by former dictator Hugo Bánzer Suárez, as well as a mechanism to ensure the rotation of the presidency between the two parties (Gamarra, 1994). Defenders of the pact argued that since the arrangement was between the top two finishers in the presidential election, then a majority of the electorate was duly represented. However, the opposition, headed by Jamie Paz Zamora of the Revolutionary Movement of the Left (MIR) charged the two leaders with attempting to establish a hegemonic party. In a round of political bargaining, the MIR's electoral reform proposal favoring minority parties was accepted in exchange for the official opposition's mild resistance to the NEP. Together, the MNR, ADN, and MIR coalitions came to dominate elections throughout the 1990s, rotating in and out of power. While the ability to form coalitions gave the party system a measure of stability, it also effectively shut out non-coalition parties from access to the state. As a result, Bolivia's pacted democracy generated the potential for frustrated opposition groups to resort to extra systemic means of affecting change (Rice, 2011).

In an attempt to draw in excluded sectors of the polity, the government of President Gonzalo Sánchez de Lozada of the MNR undertook a number of important electoral reforms in the mid-1990s. A key reform initiative was the 1994 Law of Popular Participation (LPP), which was one of several new pieces of legislation designed to incorporate increasingly mobilized indigenous peoples into the legal and political life of the country (Kohl, 2002; Postero, 2007). The reforms served the dual goal of cutting back on the central government's expenses and responsibilities by downloading them to the local level while co-opting resistance to neoliberalism by shifting the focus of popular struggles to local issues rather than national ones (Arce & Rice, 2009; Veltmeyer, 2007). The LPP instituted the first-ever direct municipal elections, significantly strengthened local governments, and provided indigenous organizations with key powers of municipal oversight. As detailed by Oxhorn (this volume), the newly created oversight committees (*comités de vigilancia*) sought to formalize traditional indigenous institutions and include them in the political system through a top-down process of controlled inclusion. Although the LPP failed to generate citizenship as agency, the reforms had a number of unanticipated effects. In addition to creating opportunities for the emergence of local political systems, the reforms aided in the development of new local leaders and movements, including Evo Morales and the MAS (Laserna, 2009). The more favorable set of institutional opportunities led to the shift in strategy of Bolivia's indigenous and popular movements from direct action tactics to electoral competition. The MAS managed to project itself onto the national political stage during a period of social mobilization in the early 2000s by moving the focus of resistance beyond the local level to a national critique of the neoliberal economic model and of a political system that produced strong barriers to genuine participation.

The national rise of the MAS took place within the context of a severe crisis of democratic representation. The victorious Water War of Cochabamba in 2000 against the privatization of that city's water supply marked the first in a series of massive civil uprisings that led to a rupture in the national political system and the dissolution of the neoliberal consensus (Kohl & Farthing, 2006; Olivera & Lewis, 2004). The period of social mobilization reached its peak with the Gas War in the capital city of La Paz in October 2003 that led to the ousting of President Sánchez de Lozada, who had been serving in office for a second time. The underlying factors in the mass mobilization included the social costs of economic restructuring, the control of strategic sectors of the economy by transnational capital, and the loss of legitimacy of the nation's democratic institutions (Bonifaz, 2004; Suárez, 2003). The crisis highlighted the complete disconnect between the state and society. The protest cycle ultimately opened the door to the presidential election of Morales. As Levitsky and Roberts (2011, 408) note, not only was Morales a political outsider, he was also a regime outsider who won on a pledge to abolish the established political order and refound the country along more inclusive, participatory lines.

The 2005 presidential win by Morales and the MAS marked a fundamental shift in state–society relations and in the composition and political orientation of the state.[1] In the bid to promote a more inclusive polity, Morales made indigenous rights the cornerstone of his administration. The 2009 Constitution became the tool used to transform the state. According to the new constitution's preamble, Bolivia has left behind the colonial, republican, and neoliberal state of the past.[2] In its place is a plurinational state that rests on indigenous autonomy. The constitutional recognition of plurinationality replaces, at least conceptually, the unidirectional relationship between the state and indigenous groups with a bilateral or government-to-government relationship based on mutual respect and consideration (Becker, 2011; Walsh, 2009). The new constitution goes further than any previous legislation in the country in securing representation and participation for the nation's indigenous peoples including, for example, the recognition of all 36 indigenous languages of Bolivia as official languages of the state (Art. 5) and the guaranteed right to proportional representation of indigenous peoples in the national legislature (Art. 147).[3] It also redefined Bolivian democracy as "intercultural." Intercultural democracy is a hybrid form of democracy that is direct and participatory, representative, and communitarian. Some of the new mechanisms for direct citizen participation include recall referendums, town councils, citizen-led legislative initiatives, and the legal–political recognition of citizen's associations and indigenous groups to contest elections. These democratic innovations presuppose that representation and participation occur beyond, and at times outside, the traditional channels of representative democracy (Exeni Rodríguez, 2012).

Indigenous and popular sector input was central to the democratic gains of the 2009 Constitution. The constituent assembly to draft the new constitution counted on the active participation of civil society organizations, political parties, and governing officials. In a concerted effort to influence the direction of the new constitution, Bolivia's main indigenous and peasant organizations came together as part of the so-called Unity Pact to draft their own proposal (Quispe et al., 2011; Tapia, 2011). The document put forward by the Unity Pact introduced the concepts of communitarian democracy, decolonization, plurinationality, and indigenous autonomy subsequently taken up by the MAS and incorporated in the new constitutional text, albeit in reduced form.[4] The Unity Pact member organizations envisioned a form of democracy in which indigenous communities would govern themselves at the local level while being actively involved in national decision-making processes, particularly with regard to the exploitation of natural resources within their territories (Hilborn, 2014). Tapia (2011) has suggested that the Unity Pact served as the space for imagining and designing a plurinational state while the MAS was tasked with narrowing it to fit within the confines of a liberal state.

Shifting State–Society Relations

The Morales administration has embarked on an ambitious project of state decolonization and societal transformation. Decolonization refers to the revalorization, recognition, and re-establishment of indigenous cultures, traditions, and values within the institutions, rules, and arrangements that govern society. According to Bolivia's Vice Minister of Decolonization (2013), the Bolivian state has not only historically excluded indigenous peoples; it was founded in opposition to them. The project of decolonization thus entails reimagining the nation-state as indigenous (García Linera, 2014). This means not only infusing the state with indigenous principles and practices, but an attempt to create a national indigenous culture with new political subjects and forms of citizenship. Racism and patriarchy have been identified by the Morales administration as two key underpinnings of the colonial state that need to be uprooted before the plurinational state can take hold (Viceministerio de Descolonización, 2013). Decolonization is considered to be the objective of the indigenous rights revolution, while depatriarchalization is viewed as part of the indigenous women's rights struggle (or the revolution within the revolution). The focus in Bolivia has been on redesigning governing institutions in more culturally relevant and locally accessible ways in an effort to meet these twin goals.

Bolivia is undergoing a dramatic shift from government to governance. New institutional arrangements are challenging traditional state-centric forms of policy-making and generating forms of governance-beyond-the-state. Whereas government centralizes power in the state, governance disperses political authority amongst governmental and nongovernmental actors in potentially democratizing ways (Krahmann, 2003; Swyngedouw, 2005). Indigenous governance innovation, such as indigenous self-rule, fosters inclusive development processes by linking formerly marginalized groups to the state. Previous attempts at linking indigenous populations to the state, including the 1994 Law of Popular Participation, sought to reshape society along the lines desired by governing elites while targeting indigenous peoples as the problem in need of change. In contrast, the project of decolonization calls for the meaningful incorporation of indigenous peoples into democratic nation-states with a focus on transforming the state to better serve and reflect the interests of society. This entails doing democracy differently. Representative democracy—with its reliance on elections and parties as the only available channels of communication between representatives and citizens—does not demand citizen deliberation on policy matters or collective engagement with the state. According to Cameron (2014, 5), "[w]ithout a voice in deliberations over the decisions that may affect them directly, many citizens become disengaged. This malaise may be especially acute in indigenous communities with strong traditions of collective decision making." Simply put, democracy without indigenous participation is insufficient. The emergence of new mechanisms for indigenous and popular participation in Bolivia has the potential to strengthen democracy by enhancing or stretching liberal conceptions of democracy.

Indigenous autonomy offers the best hope of bringing about a fundamental restructuring of state–society relations by the way in which it devolves power to local communities. Autonomy is the articulating claim of indigenous peoples around the world. The demand for autonomy centers on the call for greater self-determination and self-government within indigenous territories (Aparicio Wilhelmi, 2007; Díaz Polanco, 1998). Bolivia's new constitution provides for multiple pathways to indigenous self-government. Under current provisions, existing indigenous territories as well as municipalities with a substantial indigenous presence may convert themselves into self-governing entities. These autonomous areas would see the restoration of traditional forms of governance that are the lifeblood of communitarian democracy. While the indigenous autonomies would coordinate with departmental governments, they would not be directly subordinate to them (Centro de Investigación y Promoción del Campesinado, 2009). Indigenous autonomy could potentially deepen democracy by provoking much-needed changes to Bolivia's democratic system and to the vertical power structure of the state. If the experiment in intercultural democracy is to succeed, indigenous governments must function.

To advance the horizontal restructuring of the state, the Morales administration has created new institutional interfaces between the state and society. The introduction of a number of bold and innovative vice ministries has been the first step in generating strategic projects, programs, and policies to promote decolonization within the governing apparatus. Chief among them are the Vice Ministry of Indigenous Justice, Vice Ministry of Traditional Health, Vice Ministry of Intercultural Education, Vice Ministry of Decolonization, Vice Ministry of Indigenous Autonomy, and the Vice Ministry of Coordination with Social Movements and Civil Society. The MAS has cast itself as a "government of social movements" by incorporating social movement leaders into government posts as part of its effort to "lead by obeying" (Quispe et al., 2011, 243). Morales himself continues to serve as the general secretary of the coca growers' federation. Currently, more than two-thirds of the deputies in the national legislature come from social movement backgrounds (García Linera, 2014, 51). Since the passage of the 2009 Constitution, the MAS has also made gender parity a priority for its government. Following the 2009 presidential election, Morales assigned women to 50% of his cabinet positions, a vast improvement over the 6.7% of female cabinet ministers under the government that preceded Morales (Viceministerio de Descolonización, 2014, 142). The Vice Ministry of Decolonization is currently drafting a Law of Decolonization and Depatriarchalization that would require gender parity at all levels and in all departments of the government.[5] For the first time in Bolivian history, the government closely reflects and represents the interests of society.

The Morales administration has identified government bureaucracy as the main impediment to the implementation of its new policies and programs. According to the Vice Minister of Decolonization,

> much of our effort will be wasted if there are entities and public authorities within our system that are producing neo-colonization by way of the rules and norms of previous administrations, and so we must remedy this by issuing new standards that give life to the plurinational state.
>
> (2014, 116)

The government has passed a number of laws to enhance civil and political rights in the 'new' Bolivia. For example, the 2010 antiracism and antidiscrimination law (*Ley 045 Contra el Racismo y Toda Forma de Discriminación*) authorizes criminal sanctions against public and private sector institutions, including those of the media, that disseminate racist and biased ideas (Farthing & Kohl, 2014, 65). In 2012, a language rights law (*Ley General 269 de Derechos y Políticas Lingüísticas*) was passed, requiring all public and private institutions serving the public to have their staff trained in the official indigenous languages of use in the region in which they are located (*Gaceta Oficial del Estado Plurinacional de Bolivia*, 2012). A recent empirical study of the extent of bureaucratic decolonization in Bolivia compared the profiles of public servants from 2001 and 2013 and found the public administrative body of today to be younger, have a greater presence of women, and a record number of indigenous peoples. An impressive 48% of public employees now self-identify as indigenous (Soruco et al., 2014, 14). These findings suggest that broad-based changes are occurring in the polity.

The reimagining of democracy in Bolivia has gone hand in hand with new notions of citizenship. The 2009 Constitution explicitly identifies a new political subject: first peoples indigenous peasants (*indígena originario campesinos*). This hybrid term is inclusive of the first peoples of the highland plateau, the indigenous peasants of the highland valley region, and the indigenous peoples of the Bolivian lowlands. Canessa (2012) has suggested that Bolivia is witnessing a new form of indigenous citizenship, one that goes beyond the notion of citizenship for indigenous peoples. In Bolivia today, the model citizen is an indigenous person. Not only do indigenous peoples experience a privileged position before the state, the moral foundation of the nation-state is now rooted in indigenous culture. For example, the Morales government makes an explicit commitment to the indigenous principle of "living well" as an alternative model of development, one that is enshrined in the new constitution. The living well principle is based on the values of harmony, consensus, and respect, the redistribution of wealth, and the elimination of discrimination within a framework that values diversity, community, and the environment (Fischer & Fasol, 2013). The Morales government utilizes this nationalist indigenous discourse as an effective means to defend and protect the nation's natural resources against globalization and to forge ahead with its program of growth with equity (Larson, 2009). In an attempt to promote a new national indigenous culture, the government has 'invented' certain traditions, such as the Aymara New Year (June 21), that are now celebrated nationally. Indigeneity provides the Morales government with the legitimacy to rule. It has become the language of governance. In Canessa's words (2012, 18), "indigeneity is the foundation of a new nationalism."

The Promise and Limits of Institutional Change

The governance innovations of the MAS have brought about important changes to the structure of the state, the practice of democracy, and the national identity of Bolivia. The redesign of governing institutions to serve the needs and interests of indigenous peoples and the popular sectors has been a priority for the MAS administration. Institutions imposed by the dominant society have not historically served the interests of indigenous peoples (Eversole, 2010). The new constitution is the principal tool used by the Morales government to leverage the political influence of formerly marginalized groups and remake national institutions in a more indigenous mold. Yet, tensions and contradictions within the new constitution have limited the construction of the plurinational state in practice. According to constitutional scholar, Roberto Gargarella (2013), the concentration of executive power in Bolivia is at odds with the exercise of local power by self-governing indigenous bodies. While the 2009 Constitution represents the region's best effort at championing indigenous rights, it failed to address the concentrated organization of powers within the government. A commitment to popular participation requires serious attention to the existing distribution of powers. Instead, Bolivia's new constitution concentrates political powers while expanding indigenous rights. Stated differently, it pits governance against government. As we shall see, a highly centralized organization of power tends to work against the application of indigenous rights.

The Morales government's commitment to indigenous autonomy is at odds with its resource-dependent, state-led model of development. The constitutional provision that all non-renewable resources remain under state control places firm limits on the right to self-government and self-determination (Rice, 2014; Tockman & Cameron, 2014). Bolivia's Constitution (Article 30.15) establishes the right of indigenous peoples to free, prior and informed consultation, not consent, concerning planned measures affecting them, such as mining and oil or gas exploration. The constitution does stipulate that the prior consultation process by the state must be conducted in good faith and in a concerted fashion, and that it should respect local indigenous norms and procedures. Nevertheless, indigenous groups cannot veto state-sponsored development and resource extraction projects in their territories (Schilling-Vacaflor & Kuppe, 2012; Wolff,

2012). As it stands, the new constitution does not fully change power relations between the state and indigenous peoples. The consolidation of indigenous autonomies in Bolivia will be a long and difficult process marked by tension and conflict.

The practice of communitarian democracy is also heavily circumscribed, despite its equal standing in the new constitution. Communitarian democracy is based on indigenous customs and traditions. The constitutional recognition of communitarian democracy holds considerable promise as a means to strengthen democratic governance by constructively linking formal and "non-formal" institutions (Retolaza Eguren, 2008).[6] In other words, it institutionalizes indigenous forms of governance as part of the state. The creation of self-governing indigenous communities is the key to fostering communitarian democracy. According to Cameron and Sharpe (2012, 246), "[t]he cumulative effect of these innovations is to use direct institutionalized voice to transform and democratize the state as a whole— not by scaling up but by devolving more democratic power to small-scale self-governing communities everywhere." Under the current constitutional configuration, communitarian democracy is relegated to lower-level governments. Communitarian democracy is to be exercised within the indigenous autonomies through the election or selection of governing authorities using traditional methods. However, as Quispe et al. (2011) point out, the election methods and governance structures at the local level do not inform practices at the national level. Nonetheless, indigenous organizations view these constitutional gains as the first step to building an authentic intercultural democracy.

Indigenous governance innovation can enhance representation by including new voices in the political process and reorienting policy priorities toward vulnerable groups. The development of new sites of institutionalized participation can also open up potential conflicts (Peruzzotti & Selee, 2009). The governing agenda of the MAS has created new patterns of inclusion and exclusion. The political inclusion of indigenous peoples and popular sector groups has improved considerably under the Morales administration. However, this has produced something of a reversal of fortune for the country's political elites, who now find themselves excluded from the state. Opposition groups centered in the four eastern lowland departments have suggested that the MAS, in general, and the new constitution, in particular, discriminate against white and *mestizo* citizens by only representing the interests of indigenous and poor people (Eaton 2007; Fabricant 2009; Gustafson 2008). There is also a deepening divide between the Morales administration and the indigenous peoples of the lowland region. A significant degree of distrust and hostility has developed over the government's proposed plan to build a highway through the Isiboro-Sécure Indigenous Territory and National Park (TIPNIS) in the eastern department of Beni that would connect the central Andean highlands with the lowlands to the north. The MAS maintains that the road is essential for national development (Achtenberg, 2012; Picq, 2012). Opposition groups in TIPNIS have vowed to impede the highway's construction. The conflict has served to complicate indigenous–state relations in Bolivia.[7]

It is much too early to offer a definitive assessment of the democratic contributions of the MAS administration. Nevertheless, it is possible from the current vantage point to ascertain that important democratic gains have been made. First, the practice of citizenship as agency has clearly been enhanced in this case. Many of the governance proposals of the MAS originated within civil society. This has resulted in a profound transformation of both the state and civil society itself. Second, the new institutional interfaces and mechanisms to promote direct citizen participation have resulted in a dramatic improvement in state–society relations in Bolivia. The previous dynamic of 'civil society versus the state' has given way to an important degree of synergy between the state and civil society that is narrowing the gap between citizens and the political system. Third, if the strength of civil society is mirrored in the scope and depth of citizenship rights (see Oxhorn in this volume), then the governance innovations of the MAS administration have plainly served to strengthen civil society. The capacity of formerly disadvantaged and marginalized groups to catalyze meaningful improvements in government responsiveness and accountability has provoked a remarkable transformation in Bolivia's democratic system. It may be that the traditional institutions of representative democracy were simply insufficient to generate this series of democratic goods.

Conclusion

What happens when civil society actors capture state power? In the case of Bolivia, this chapter has found that the rise of MAS has had a mostly positive impact on democracy. While new forms of civil society participation, such as indigenous self-rule, may challenge traditional forms of political participation, they do not threaten democracy (De Munter & Salman, 2009). Instead, they broaden and deepen it by making democracy more inclusive and government more responsive and representative. New spaces of citizen engagement are not construed as an alternative to democracy, but are part of an effort by the Morales government to overcome the basic problems associated with representative democracy (Peruzzotti & Selee, 2009; Wampler, 2012). The previous model of pacted democracy served the narrow interests of political elites. Bolivia's new intercultural democracy is building and expanding upon representative democracy in novel ways. In short, intercultural democracy is "democratizing democracy" (De Sousa Santos, 2004). Although Bolivia's governance innovations may face many challenges and contradictions, in the long run they are likely to foster a powerful democratic culture and strengthen the country's democratic structures (Villarroel & Gargarella, 2014).

The conquest of democracy is one of the biggest victories of civil society organizations in contemporary Bolivia. There is much to celebrate here, just as there is much work left to do to bring about the plurinational state. The construction of the nation-state against pre-existing indigenous nations did not serve the interests of its citizens. Civil society participation and engagement have transformed Bolivia from a democratically dysfunctional state to one in which there is a degree of fusion between social movements, the governing party, and the state. Bolivia's bold experiment in indigenous governance and participatory democracy has led Brooke Larson (2009, 183) to label the country "the mouse that roared." The Bolivian case offers important instructional lessons in how to push the limits of representative democracy and work toward inclusive democratic governance even in the most difficult socioeconomic and institutional environments.

Notes

* Fieldwork for this chapter was carried out by the author in La Paz, Bolivia in August 2014 under the auspices of a standard research grant by the Social Sciences and Humanities Research Council of Canada (SSHRC).

1 The MAS won the 2005 election with 53.7% of the vote, the only party to win an absolute majority since the country's transition to democracy. In 2009, Morales was re-elected with 63.9% of the vote. In 2014, he was elected to a third term (technically a second term under the rules of the new constitution) with 61.4% of the vote.

2 The 2009 Bolivian Constitution is available for download at: http://pdba.george-town.edu/constitutions/bolivia/bolivia.html.

3 Indigenous peoples constitute a slight majority of Bolivia's total population. The Aymara and Quechua are the principal indigenous peoples in the highlands. The Bolivian lowlands are home to over thirty ethnic groups, including the Guaraní, Chiquitano, and Moxeño peoples.

4 The member organizations of the Unity Pact included: United Peasant Workers' Confederation of Bolivia (CSUTCB); Confederation of Indigenous Peoples of Bolivia (CIDOB); Bolivian Syndicalist Confederation of Colonizers (CSCB); Bolivian National Federation of Peasant Women, "Bartolina Sisa" (FNMCB-BS); and the National Council for *Ayllus* and *Markas* of Qullasuyu. The Unity Pact proposal is available for download at: www.cebem.org/cmsfiles/archivos/propuesta-organizaciones-indigenas.pdf.

5 Félix Cárdenas, Vice Minister of Decolonization. Author interview, La Paz, August 22, 2014.

6 Non-formal institutions refer to indigenous values and beliefs, customary laws and practices, and traditional authority and governance structures. They are neither informal institutions nor formally recognized by the state.

7 In the 2014 presidential election, the department of Beni was the only department in which the MAS failed to receive a majority of the votes.

References

Achtenberg, Emily. 2012. "Bolivia: End of the Road for TIPNIS Consulta." *NACLA Rebel Currents* (blog), 13 December.

Aparicio Wilhelmi, Marco. 2007. "La Construcción de la Autonomía Indígena: Hacia al Estado Intercultural como Nuevo Forma de Estado." In S. Martí-I-Puig (Ed.). *Pueblos indígenas y política en América Latina* (335–359). Barcelona: Fundación CIDOB.

Arce, Moisés, & Roberta Rice. 2009. "Societal Protest in Post-Stabilization Bolivia." *Latin American Research Review* 44(1), 88–101.

Becker, Marc. 2011. *Pachakutik: indigenous movements and electoral politics in Ecuador*. Lanham: Rowman & Littlefield.

Bonifaz, Carlos Romero. 2004. "Las Jornadas de Octubre: Levantamiento Popular en Bolivia." *Artículo Primero: Revista de Debate Social y Jurídico* 8(16), 13–38.

Cameron, Maxwell A. 2014. "New Mechanisms of Democratic Participation in Latin America." *LASA Forum* 45(1), 4–6.

Cameron, Maxwell A., Eric Hershberg, & Kenneth E. Sharpe. 2012. "Voice and Consequence: Direct Participation and Democracy in Latin America." In M.A. Cameron, E. Hershberg, & K.E. Sharpe (Eds.). *New institutions for participatory democracy in Latin America* (1–20). New York: Palgrave Macmillan.

Cameron, Maxwell A., & Kenneth E. Sharpe. 2012. "Institutionalized Voice in Latin American Democracies." In M.A. Cameron, E. Hershberg, & K.E. Sharpe (Eds.). *New institutions for participatory democracy in Latin America* (231–250). New York: Palgrave Macmillan.

Canessa, Andrew. 2012. "Conflict, Claim and Contradiction in the New Indigenous State of Bolivia." Desigualdades.net, Working Paper Series No. 22.

Centro de Investigación y Promoción del Campesinado. 2009. *Posibles Caminos Hacia las Autonomías Indígena Originario Campesinas*. La Paz: CIPCA.

De Munter, Koen & Ton Salman. 2009. "Extending Political Participation and Citizenship: Pluricultural Civil Practices in Contemporary Bolivia." *Journal of Latin American and Caribbean Anthropology* 14(2), 432–456.

De Sousa Santos, Boaventura. 2004. "Democracia de Alta Intensidad: Apuntes Para Democratizar la Democracia." Cuaderno de Diálogo y Deliberación No. 5. La Paz: Corte Nacional Electoral.

Díaz Polanco, Héctor. 1998. "La Autonomía, Demanda Central de los Pueblos Indígenas: Significados e Implicaciones." In V. Alta, D. Iturralde, & M.A. López-Bassols (Eds.). *Pueblos indígenas e estado en América Latina* (213–218). Quito: Editorial Abya-Yala.

Eaton, Kent. 2007. "Backlash in Bolivia: Regional Autonomy as a Reaction Against Indigenous Mobilization." *Politics and Society* 35(1), 71–102.

Eversole, Robyn. 2010. "Empowering Institutions: Indigenous Lessons and Policy Perils." *Development* 53(1), 77–82.

Exeni Rodríguez, José Luis. 2012. "Elusive Demodiversity in Bolivia: Between Representation, Participation and Self-Government." In M.A. Cameron, E. Hershberg, & K.E. Sharpe (Eds.). *New institutions for participatory democracy in Latin America* (207–300). New York: Palgrave Macmillan.

Fabricant, Nicole. 2009. "Performative Politics: The Camba Countermovement in Eastern Bolivia." *American Ethnologist* 36(4), 768–783.

Farthing, Linda C. & Benjamin H. Kohl. 2014. *Evo's Bolivia: continuity and change*. Austin: University of Texas Press.

Fischer, Valdi & Marc Fasol. 2013. *Las semillas de 'buen vivir': la respuesta de los pueblos indígenas del Abya-Yala a la deriva del modelo de desarrollo occidental*. Quito: Ediciones Fondo Indígena.

Gaceta Oficial del Estado Plurinacional de Bolivia. 2012. No. 0405. August 3.

Gamarra, Eduardo A. 1994. "Crafting Political Support for Stabilization: Political Pacts and the New Economic Policy in Bolivia." In W.C. Smith, C.H. Acuña, & E.A. Gamarra (Eds.). *Democracy, markets, and structural reform in Latin America* (105–127). Miami: University of Miami, North-South Center.

Gamarra, Eduardo A. & James M. Malloy. 1995. "The Patrimonial Dynamics of Party Politics in Bolivia." In S. Mainwaring & T.R. Scully (Eds.). *Building democratic institutions: party systems in Latin America* (399–433). Stanford: Stanford University Press.

García Linera, Alvaro. 2014. *Identidad Boliviana: nación, mestizaje y plurinacionalidad.* La Paz: Vicepresidencia del Estado Plurinacional.

Gargarella, Roberto. 2013. *Latin American constitutionalism 1810–2010: the engine room of the Constitution.* New York: Oxford University Press.

Gustafson, Bret. 2008. "By Means Legal and Otherwise: The Bolivian Right Regroups." *NACLA Report on the Americas* 41(1), 20–26.

Hilborn, Paul J. 2014. "Can a State Decolonize Itself? A Critical Analysis of Bolivia's State-Led Decolonization Process." Master's Thesis, Dalhousie University, Canada.

Kohl, Benjamin. 2002. "Stabilizing Neoliberalism in Bolivia: Popular Participation and Privatization. *Political Geography* 21(4), 449–472.

Kohl, Benjamin, & Linda Farthing. 2006. *Impasse in Bolivia: neoliberal hegemony and popular resistance.* London: Zed Books.

Krahmann, Elke. 2003. "National, Regional, and Global Governance: One Phenomenon or Many?" *Global Governance* 9(3), 323–346.

Larson, Brooke. 2009. "Democratic Progress or Peril? Indigenous and Popular Mobilization in Bolivia." In G. Bland & C.J. Arson (Eds.). *Democratic deficits: addressing challenges to sustainability and consolidation around the world* (183–194). Washington: Woodrow Wilson International Center for Scholars.

Levitsky, Steven, & Kenneth M. Roberts. 2011. "Conclusion: Democracy, Development, and the Left." In S. Levitsky & K.M. Roberts (Eds.). *The resurgence of the Latin American Left* (399–428). Baltimore: The Johns Hopkins University Press.

Olivera, Oscar, & Tom Lewis. 2004. *¡Cochabamba! Water war in Bolivia.* Cambridge: South End Press.

Peruzzotti, Enrique, & Andrew Selee. 2009. "Participatory Innovation and Representative Democracy in Latin America." In A. Selee & E. Peruzzotti (Eds.). *Participatory innovation and representative democracy in Latin America* (1–16). Washington, DC: Woodrow Wilson Center/The Johns Hopkins University Press.

Picq, Manuela. 2012. "The Failure to Consult Triggers Indigenous Creativity." *Aljazeera,* 22 December.

Postero, Nancy Grey. 2007. *Now we are citizens: indigenous politics in postmulticultural Bolivia.* Stanford: Stanford University Press.

Quispe, Alber, et al. 2011. *La democracia desde los márgenes: transformación en el campo político Boliviano.* La Paz: Muela del Diablo/CLACSO.

Retolaza Eguren, Iñigo. 2008. "Moving Up and Down the Ladder: Community-Based Participation in Public Dialogue and Deliberation in Bolivia and Guatemala." *Community Development Journal* 43(3), 312–328.

Rice, Roberta. 2011. "Bolivia: Ethnicity and Power." In K. Isbester (Ed.). *The paradox of democracy in Latin America: ten country studies of division and resilience* (277–298). Toronto: University of Toronto Press.

Rice, Roberta. 2014. "UNDRIP and the 2009 Bolivian Constitution: Lessons for Canada." Centre for International Governance Innovation Special Report: The Internationalization of Indigenous Rights, UNDRIP in the Canadian Context, 59–63.

Schilling-Vacaflor, Almut, & René Kuppe. 2012. "Plurinational Constitutionalism:

A New Era of Indigenous–State Relations?" In D. Nolte & A. Schilling-Vacaflor (Eds.). *New constitutionalism in Latin America: promises and practices* (347–370). Burlington: Ashgate.

Soruco, Ximena et al. 2014. *Composición social del estado plurinacional: hacia la descolonización de la burocracia*. La Paz: Vicepresidencia del Estado.

Suárez, Hugo José. 2003. *Una semana fundamental: 10–18 Octubre 2003*. La Paz: Muela del Diablo.

Swyngedouw, Erik. 2005. "Governance Innovation and the Citizen: The Janus Face of Governance-Beyond-the-State." *Urban Studies* 42(11), 1991–2006.

Tapia, Luís. 2011. "Consideraciones sobre el Estado Plurinacional." In *Descolonización en Bolivia: cuatro ejes para comprender el cambio* (135–168). La Paz: Vicepresidencia del Estado/Fundación Boliviana para la Democracia Multipartidaria.

Tockman, Jason, & John Cameron. 2014. "Indigenous Autonomy and the Contradictions of Plurinationalism in Bolivia." *Latin American Politics and Society* 56(3), 46–69.

Veltmeyer, Henry. 2007. *On the move: the politics of social change in Latin America*. Toronto: University of Toronto Press.

ViceMinisterio de Descolonización. 2013. *Resoluciones: 1ra cumbre internacional de descolonización, despatriarcalización, lucha contra el racismo y la discriminación*. La Paz: Ministerio de Culturas y Turismo.

ViceMinisterio de Descolonización. 2014. *Descolonizando el estado desde el estado*. La Paz: Ministerio de Culturas y Turismo.

Villarroel, Gratzia, & Roberto Gargarella. 2014. "Diversifying Democracy in Latin America in the 21st Century." *LASA Forum* 45(1), 2–3.

Walsh, Catherine. 2009. "Estado Plurinacional e Intercultural, Complementariedad y Complicidad Hacia el 'Buen Vivir.'" In A. Acosta & E. Martínez (Eds.). *Plurinacionalidad: democracia en la diversidad* (161–184). Quito: Ediciones Abya-Yala.

Wampler, Brian. 2012. "Participation, Representation, and Social Justice: Using Participatory Governance to Transform Representative Democracy." *Polity* 44(4), 666–682.

Wolff, Jonas. 2012. "New Constitutions and the Transformation of Democracy in Bolivia and Ecuador." In D. Nolte & A. Schilling-Vacaflor (Eds.). *New constitutionalism in Latin America: promises and practices* (183–202). Burlington: Ashgate.

9 Conceptualizing Transnational Civil Society in Guatemala

Candace Johnson

Approximately three million years ago, the continents of North and South America were physically distinct and separate. The geographical transformation known as the Great American Interchange resulted in the joining of the continents, and the isthmus that joined them became contemporary Central America. The joining allowed for the integration of ecological zones, including plant and animal species, such that in Guatemala there are pine trees and palm trees, maple groves and banana plantations, river otters and howler monkeys. There are also several distinct climatological and geographical zones, among them, highlands, sub-tropical areas, rainforest, and both Pacific (volcanic) and Caribbean coastlines. The environmental diversity of the country is impressive in both its range and beauty. The Great American Interchange might also serve as an appropriate metaphor for other geographical disruptions and integrations, in this case of the human and moral varieties. The social and political relationships between the countries of North America and Guatemala replicate colonial patterns of extraction and exploitation, which are also resisted by civil society actors with the same transnational pedigrees. Michael Flitner and Dietrich Soyez claim that these actors, both the perpetrators and resisters of colonial and post-colonial practices, create "new 'transnational geographies' in terms of both innovative constituting contexts and pervasive spatial impacts" (2000, 2). Therefore, this chapter makes the political/social science case for the humanities/literary argument advanced by Pablo Ramirez (Chapter 4, this volume). Both chapters contest the existence of and utility of fixed *borders* and demonstrate instead the conceptual superiority of *borderlands*, which are more complex, nuanced, vibrant analytical spaces. As such, they offer possibilities for understanding beyond the boundaries of oppression/resistance, tradition/progress, past/present, inside/outside, and national/international.

The continued patterns of extraction and exploitation include such practices and industries as mining, agro-export business, and garment factories (maquila). In 2014, there were over 100 metal mines operating in Guatemala, and "close to 350 active licenses for exploration or production, with nearly 600 pending" (Guest, 2014). Of these, a significant proportion is held by foreign-owned companies. And while the government promotes the sector as a way to raise revenues, Guatemalan legislation only requires that 1% of all mining royalties remain in the country, which results in a mere 2% of the country's GDP generated through mining (Guest, 2014). In December 2014, the Guatemalan Congress passed legislation that raised this proportion of royalties to 10%, but the matter of revenue-sharing is only one part of a very complex environmental and political set of problems (Jamasmie, 2014). Lack of respect for internal political processes (such as community *consultas*, see for instance Laplante & Nolin, 2014), depletion of freshwater resources, contamination of the environment, and physical violence as a means to ensure compliance, are also the unfortunate consequences of the mining industry in Guatemala (Rey Rosa, 2014).

A recent report by Oxfam makes the connection between pre-civil war economic exploitation and post-civil war extractive industrial imperialism:

> A US mining company is at the center of a contentious debate in Guatemala that has led to a government crackdown on communities and outbreaks of violence. This is happening 60 years after another American company, the United Fruit Company, together with the CIA, overthrew a democratically-elected government and installed a dictatorship to protect their interests in Guatemala. Although there are important differences, the parallels raise questions.
>
> (Blair, 2014)

Foreign and elite domestic political and economic interests are protected by a system that replicates patterns of internal and external colonialism. Indeed, the legacy and continued practice of extraction and export of profits is facilitated by a state that is riddled with weak political institutions and characterized by impunity at all levels. As the above quote indicates, a CIA-backed coup in 1954 destabilized Guatemala during a critical period of nation-building and progressive reform. A protracted civil war began in 1960 that would last until 1996, and leave a country deeply divided and fragile. Many of the bloodiest state-led massacres of the civil war were, suspiciously coincidentally, future sites of metal mines, agro-export plantations, and hydro-electric projects. As Michael L. Dougherty succinctly explains, "Guatemala's mix of lenient policies and appropriate geology has made it a world epicentre of low-cost gold production, facilitating an anti-mining social movement of unprecedented mass" (2011, 404).

Such a troubled (recent) history of colonialism also produces unique configurations of civil society actors. Roman Krznaric (1999) explains the importance of various civil and "uncivil" (groups focused on economic matters) actors in the negotiated peace process in the 1990s. Human rights groups and activists, from both inside and outside Guatemala, worked through an *Asamblea*, created to facilitate the peace accords and subsequent transition to a post-conflict democracy, to consolidate a framework for peace and reconciliation. While the *Asamblea* was contentious and, unsurprisingly, fraught with political divisions, its composition—transnational—is revealing of the landscape of Guatemalan civil society. As will be explained throughout this chapter, the transnational character of Guatemalan civil society is, for better or worse, a fact of its political reality. Transnational civil society actors have mobilized and supported resistance to mining projects, political impunity, and structural violence. They have also facilitated transition from civil war to peace through support for truth commissions and human rights prosecutions, and were instrumental in rescuing and operationalizing the decaying, forgotten national police archive (Weld, 2014). Further, transnational actors continue to engage in struggles toward post-conflict justice at both a societal level and in particular cases through court systems at various scales. Moreover, the transnational character of Guatemalan civil society is consistent with Mayan interpretations of the universe. As Dominga Vásquez explains, "solidarity is a characteristic of the Maya people. Our cosmovision enables us to be in solidarity with another department [region], another people who are suffering or who face unfortunate circumstances" (2011, 539).

Political Geographies of Civil Society

Citizens of Guatemala are promised much through constitutional and other political promises, but the state delivers very little. Key social rights, such as health care and education, are not realized in practice, as resources do not meet demand and political leaders tend to direct scarce resources toward other, less tangible, less practicable, objectives. The result is that the state (as provider of primary and other social goods) is largely absent from the lives of most Guatemalans. This is also true with regard to more minimalist political contractual obligations, like the provision of policing services and shared infrastructure. The gap between citizens' needs and state provision is frequently and regularly filled by nongovernmental organizations (NGOs) that are configured at both domestic and international levels. NGOs active in critical social areas, such as health care, education, gender equity, and community-building, provide the tangible benefits that are required for fully realized, meaningful lives (and sometimes for mere survival). But they also do much more. Provision of critical social goods by NGOs often serves to mediate the state–society relationship, and therefore has the potential to (a) build the social capital that is a necessary precursor to full(er) citizenship; and (b) represent the state's commitments to upholding or developing social rights.

The significance of the former (NGOs as generators of social capital, which is critical to civil society) is the focus of this chapter. NGOs in Guatemala are ubiquitous and fundamental to social development and political transition. The expectation that civil society could and should develop organically and authentically out of shared interests and proposed responses, without support from international NGOs and other extra-territorial agencies, completely misses the mark in a country like

Guatemala. In the post-conflict period (beginning with the signing of the peace accords in 1996), international agencies have been central to the ongoing project of transitional justice (Krznaric, 1999), in particular, international agencies, actors and venues have helped Guatemalans fight for justice in key human rights abuse cases. In addition, yet not unconnected to the broader struggle for peace and justice, NGOs are providers of infrastructure, education, health services, information, and funding for community projects and resistance efforts. To add to the complexity of work dedicated to transitional justice through the provision of social and political resources (which, I argue, leads to the development and/or strengthening of social capital), it must be acknowledged at the outset that much of this work is motivated by religion (current estimates suggest that approximately half of the 10,000 NGOs that have been active in Guatemala since 1996 are faith-based) (Beck, 2014, 147, 151).

Thus, if NGOs serve as proxies for the state, they also serve as proxies for civil society. NGOs deliver on the unfulfilled obligations of the state, at the same time that they generate social capital and build civil society. While the first seems to be well understood in the literature, the second is more complex and opaque, not to mention more controversial. In order to construct this argument, I will begin with a discussion of the conceptualization of civil society and its limitations. Then, I will demonstrate that the possibilities of transnational civil society have more analytical potential for assessing Latin American cases. I will conclude with some detailed examples to provide empirical support for the suggestion that transnational civil society is conceptually appropriate to the region and that NGO-generated social capital is critical for political transformation. In fact, unless conceived in this way, there is virtually no potential for civil society in Guatemala, and dismissal of the transnational character of civil society fails to recognize the complex avenues for political engagement that are available and operationalized on an ongoing basis.

Civil Society in Latin America?

According to Philip Oxhorn (Chapter 2, this volume), the "appropriate conceptualization of civil society" is "the social fabric formed by a multiplicity of self-constituted territorially and functionally based units which peacefully coexist and collectively resist subordination to the state, at the same time that they demand inclusion into national political structures" (from Oxhorn, 1995a, 251–252). The requirements of this definition are very ambitious, perhaps impossible to achieve, which lead Oxhorn to conclude that "...the weakness of civil society in Latin America is one reason for the region's notorious historical problems of inequality and socioeconomic exclusion" (5).

The alternative to the impossibility of civil society for Oxhorn is a collectivist interpretation of the conversion of social capital into civil society. He explains that, it is important to emphasize that while poverty and exclusion themselves can be important obstacles to the emergence of strong civil societies, it would be a mistake to assume that they are insurmountable. This is why a collectivist perspective is essential for understanding civil society's potential. Organization and collective action, by taking advantage of the sheer numbers of people who are disadvantaged and their shared interests, are the principal resources that are potentially at the disposal of poor, marginalized groups in order to seek redress for their exclusion.

(5)

It is quite clear that the case of Guatemala would not fulfill either of these visions of civil society. On the first definition, it fails at every lexical hurdle: there is no coherent social fabric; organization and resistance is not territorially based; co-existence is not often peaceful; and instances of collective resistance against the state are predictably few. Finally, the goals of collective resistance are more immediate (such as to demand the end to the environmental degradation and physical violence that result from government-supported extractive industries) than the democratic fantasy of formal political inclusion.

While Oxhorn does not cite the seminal work of Cohen and Arato on civil society, his own conceptualization, modified to speak directly to the historical contingencies and political realities of Latin America, does seem to be similarly driven by the *products* of liberal democracy. Cohen and Arato ask, rhetorically,

is not the revival of the discourse of civil society in the East and the South simply part of a project to attain what the advanced capitalist democracies already have: civil society guaranteed by the rule of law, civil rights, parliamentary democracy, and a market economy?

(2003, 282)

Moreover, Oxhorn's conceptualization is focused on the associationalist aspects of the myriad definitions of civil society. Such a conceptualization tends to romanticize the significance of the formation of groups that exist beyond politics and markets, and posits that this associationalist bent provides the foundation for robust democratic institutions. Individuals, families, and communities can participate in neighborhood associations, sports clubs, and other groups as a means of expressing and generating political and other ideas. This is also the essence of a pluralist society: voluntary, diverse, inclusive, and purposeful.

Michael Edwards describes this romanticization with associational life as tantamount to a "love affair" (2014, 19), and it is not difficult to understand why Oxhorn would want to extend the pluralistic imaginary to Latin America. Edwards warns of the "danger in expecting too much from associational life, as if it were a 'magic bullet' for resolving ... intractable social, economic and political problems..." (Edwards, 2014, 19). Indeed, the importance of associations and cooperative spirit to democratic trans-formation should be recognized. However, it is not the only conceptual option available, and might not be the most appropriate when considering newly formed and/or struggling democracies.

For example, Michael Walzer's treatment of the concept is much more robust, albeit messier, than those of Cohen and Arato (2003), Barber (2003), and Oxhorn (1995a). Walzer concludes his theoretical inquiry into the concept of civil society in the following way:

> Civil society itself is sustained by groups much smaller than the demos or the working class or the mass of consumers or the nation. All these are necessarily fragmented and localized as they are incorporated. They become part of the world of family, friends, comrades, and col-leagues, where people are connected to one another and made respons-ible for one another.
>
> (2003, 321)

This definition also focuses on associations, but in a less structural, less pluralist way. It is also a definition that is non-territorial, which is to say that it makes possible networks and associations beyond the borders of the nation-state. The main concern for Walzer seems to be realization of the Good Life (Walzer, 1995, 17; Edwards, 2014, 43–65), through multiple means and strategies. Walzer rejects standard approaches to civil society as the Good Life as "wrongheaded because of their singularity. They miss the complexity of human society, the inevitable conflicts of commitment and loyalty" (1995, 16). Moreover, community associations are not able to achieve the substantive ends of democracy, in fact "none of this can be accomplished without using political power to redistribute resources and to underwrite and subsidize the most desirable associational activities" (Walzer, 1995, 26). His suggested alternative is for a perspective of "crit-ical associationalism" (25). He explains that,

> I want to join, but I am somewhat uneasy with, the civil society argu-ment. It can't be said that nothing is lost when we give up the singlem-indedness of democratic citizenship or socialist cooperation or individual autonomy or national identity. There was a kind of heroism in those projects—a concentration of energy, a clear sense of direction, an unblinking recognition of friends and enemies. To make one of these one's own was a serious commitment. The defense of civil society doesn't seem quite comparable. Associational engagement is conceiv-ably as important a project as any of the others, but its greatest virtue lies in its inclusiveness, and inclusiveness doesn't make for heroism.
>
> (1995, 25)

The virtue of inclusivity is also incapable, on its own, of attending to the distributional problems that he mentions, and that are the responsibility of the state. Hence, his perspective of "critical associationalism," which requires attention to power and resource issues. Similarly, Evelina Dagnino asserts that "civil society and the state are always mutually constitutive" (2011, 124), and that "the State in Latin America has always been a mandatory interlocutor for social movements and other civil society organizations, even during the harsh times of authoritarianism" (125). She describes attempts to draw conceptual distinctions between civil society and the state in Latin America as "simplistic" (125), and in response calls for more critical, context- and historically specific approaches (125–126). However, it is also the case that in countries where the state is mostly absent from citizens' lives, the void is filled by NGOs who perform a number of both state-like and societal functions.

Toward a Transnational Civil Society

One such critical approach is captured under the conceptual banner of 'transnational civil society.' A transnational approach attends to the complexities of North–South distributional (in)equity, as well as to the potential for building the social capital (associational vibrancy, networks, critical expression, communal trust, collective organizing, and so on) that is fundamental to the development of civil society. Dagnino warns (if indirectly) of the dangers of putting too much faith in the potent promise of a conceptually weak construct, noting that civil society has a neo-liberal flavor that has cast attention away from states' obligations and citizens' rights, toward seemingly beneficent, yet highly problematic, solidarity projects. It might also be overwhelmingly American, with its tendency to focus on civil society's pluralistic and associationalist elements. She explains that "when social policies are transferred to civil society organizations, philanthropy, and volunteer work, citizenship is both identified with and reduced to solidarity with the poor and needy" (2011, 130). Notwithstanding this critique (primarily regarding domestic and international NGOs as proxies for the state), it is important to investigate the ways in which NGOs serve as proxies for civil society and thereby strengthen associational and collective political action. While it is undeniable that the role of the state is relevant to all discussions of individual agency and political action, and civil society as an analytical term can only be fully operationalized in relation to the state (see Oxhorn, 2007), there are other, equally significant forces and relationships that require attention. Alejandro Colás emphasizes this point in quoting Keohane and Nye: "a good deal of intersocietal intercourse with significant political importance takes place without governmental control" (2002, 2). This is the case not only because it is important to understand international and transnational political dynamics as political phenomena, but because these transnational political dynamics are significant in analyzing and understanding national and local level politics.

Much of what is written about transnational civil society focuses on global political activism that is not linked to particular national contexts (see Batliwala & Brown, 2006; Brysk & Jacquemin, 2006; Oxhorn, 2007; Jordan, 2011), and this activism is manifest in social movements that address the global problems of international trade, environmental degradation, human rights violations, and corporate (ir)responsibility. One recent example would be the Occupy Wall Street movement, which organized to collectively resist the injustice of unprecedented capitalist accumulation. From a Gramscian perspective, "civil society is associated with the capitalist market and the contest between hegemonic and counter-hegemonic forces that arise from this 'private' sphere of social relations" (Colás, 2002, 10). From an institutionalist perspective, such movements do not constitute civil society, as they do not have recognizable rights–responsibility relationships (i.e., citizenship) with states or other international institutions (Oxhorn, 2007). Either way, these conceptions reveal serious weaknesses in theoretical and practical political terms. Conceptually, transnational civil society is ephemeral, imprecise, and, quite expectedly, only sometimes produces concrete political results.

However, it is also possible to conceive of transnational political action that is, at least partially, territorially based at the level of one nation-state, or a collection of communities within a single nation-state. Joe Bandy's study of transnational activism aimed at addressing the problems of the maquiladora industry in Mexico is an excellent example of this possibility (2004). Bandy observes that "transnational civil societies are emerging, public spaces that span geographic, cultural, and political borders, and that are relatively autonomous from both government and market actors" (2004, 410). He then proceeds to quote Pasha and Blaney to clarify that "the democratic possibilities of transnational actors and networks ... must be judged ... in relation to specific institutions, groups, and networks, and specific problems, activities, and contexts" (Pasha & Blaney, 1998, 434; Bandy, 2004, 411). The importance of linking transnational organizing and activism to specific contexts and cases is demonstrated through Bandy's research on the Coalition for Justice in the Maquiladoras (CJM), as well as through Robert Smith's study of the impact of migration and migrant networks on Mexican politics (2003).

Although Bandy's conceptualization of civil society is Gramscian in orientation and thereby inherently critical, he does acknowledge and argue for the democratic potential of (transnational) civil society. He claims that transnational civil society is simultaneously generated by, and generative of, neoliberal forces of globalization, yet has enabled some significant advances in labor rights in contexts (in this case Mexico) where the state had been hitherto recalcitrant. He claims that "the CJM has achieved notable successes in supporting maquiladora unionization, limiting repressive abuses against workers, promoting environmental mediation, and mostly, educating and mobilizing workers to participate in transnational labor campaigns" (2004, 412). This was achieved through the creation of a "culture of solidarity," which is a much more amorphous strategy and result than those that are associated directly with institutional change. He explains that:

this culture of solidarity entails the alignment of workers' critiques of neoliberalism, the shared moral indictment of labor abuses, the political socialization of workers into unionism and international campaigns, the promotion of intercultural dialogue and interpersonal ties across borders, and the creation of a culture of hope among workers that a more just and democratic development is possible.

(2004, 412)

However, the CJM, which was a carefully formed, organizationally deliberate collaborative effort of labor unions and workers' rights organizations from Mexico, the United States, and Canada (rather than a mass movement of protestors), also achieved more tangible gains. Many of these, such as "toxic clean-up ... health/safety improvements ... severance or profit-sharing payments ... wage raises ... [and] financial payments for damages" were achieved through "CJM-supported litigation" (416).

The relationship between civil society and the market is also made by Robert Smith (2003). Through a detailed ethnographic study of the complexities of transnational citizenship inside and outside of Mexico (i.e., the relationships between Mexicans in various diaspora groups and the Mexican state), he demonstrates that the global dimensions of civil society are as intuitively integral and theoretically consistent, as are the global dimensions of capitalism. In assessing possible conceptualizations of global political communities, Smith notes that

> Mexico, the Dominican Republic, Colombia, Haiti, Ecuador, El Salvador, Guatemala, Italy and Portugal have all taken measures attempting to strategically incorporate their diasporic populations into their imagined political communities (Anderson, 1991)—their 'global nations'— and more selectively into their actual political, economic and social lives.
>
> (2003, 298)

Therefore, states themselves tend to understand the fluidity of territoriality and citizenship, at the very least for their own members. However, as Flitner and Soyez (2000) observe, much transnational political activity is undertaken by NGOs, who "act predominantly on behalf of people outside the active group or, more specifically in the present context, in favor of environmental changes the benefits of which will not accrue to NGO members exclusively" (2). Taken together, these relationships (between diasporic populations and states and between international NGOs and various territorially bound and spatially indeterminate entities) provide evidence of the existence of transnational civil societies.

Beyond mere examples of robust, transnational civil societies, Smith provides a compelling theoretical justification for their conceptual soundness. The genesis of this conceptualization is T.H. Marshall's essay on social rights as citizenship development. Smith states that, "the strand of

Marshall's thought treating citizenship as developing in a dialectic relationship with capitalism opens the door to membership practices that, like capitalism, extend substantively beyond borders" (2003, 300). Whereas Marshall argues that states ought to compensate members with social rights to mitigate inequality generated by the market, Smith extends this "juxtaposition of membership and markets" to transnational capitalism and its logical counterpart, transnational civil society (302). Indeed, it seems highly problematic that transnational and/or global dimensions of capitalism (such as the mining industry in Guatemala, for example) are simply taken for granted while the transnational/global dimensions of civil society are called into question. At best, the potential for transnational civil society is reduced to groups of global actors who fall outside of the conceptual parameters of territory- and institution-driven definitions of civil society (Oxhorn), and at worst, "global idiots" (Flitner & Soyez, 2000, 1), who mobilize for various causes without understanding the complexities of the problems on the agenda. But it is worth emphasizing this point: transnational flows of global capital are taken for granted, while other forms of transnational organizing are met with suspicion. Indeed, the relegation of political activity and resistance to the domestic realm (and within this, to organized, sustained politically agentive groups) is a significant conceptual and material constraint in the context of globalization. Why would it be the case, in either philosophical or political terms, that transnational civil society is illegitimate, ineffectual, while global capitalism is, for better or worse, accepted as a force of reality? This is the conceptual point of departure for Chandra Mohanty, whose research addresses the goal of solidarity within the context of anti-capitalist struggle:

> A transnational feminist practice depends on building feminist solidarities across the divisions of place, identity, class, work, belief, and so on. In these very fragmented times it is both very difficult to build these alliances and also never more important to do so. Global capitalism both destroys the possibilities and also offers up new ones.
>
> (2003, 250)

Presumably, this is the challenge and promise of transnational civil society.

Smith also provides conceptual clarification concerning the democratic requirements of citizenship and transnational civil society. He offers the following:

> Citizenship and membership can be stronger, or thicker, and weaker, or thinner, along two dimensions: a group's ability to command material, symbolic or political resources based in or controlled by the state (and hence be able to "deliver the goods," seen on the state institutional axis) or its ability to exercise its will autonomously from the state (the democratic autonomy axis), including its ability to "scale up" (Fox, 1996) and find outside support, for example, through relations with NGOs

and international human rights institutions which can affect how state power is used with respect to that group.

(2003, 303)

In a country like Guatemala, there is very little potential along the first, state institutional axis, but great potential along the second, democratic autonomy axis. To assess civil society, in both conceptual and empirical terms, exclusively on the first axis, is to fail to understand the realities and complexities of the membership–market nexus in Guatemala and to preclude the potential for alternate (yet consistent with accepted wisdom on global capitalism) conceptions of civil society development and mobilization. Further, the overemphasis on institutional configurations of citizen–state relationships obscures a diversity of important political goals. For example, in addition to "delivering the goods," which can be impossible in countries characterized by weak institutions, networks of national and transnational actors might aim to "destabilize given power settings and taken-for-granted framings of reality" (Flitner & Soyez, 2000, 2).

To return to Oxhorn's definition of civil society laid out in Chapter 2, it is evident that the conceptual integrity of the definition rests entirely on the first axis. A group's ability to get the state to "deliver the goods" is the marker of a robust civil society. Oxhorn provides concrete examples:

> …organized labor's demands contributed to the emergence of welfare states and democracy in both the North and Latin America (*sic*) … much in the same way that the emergence of women's movements across the globe have since the 1960s have (*sic*) led to the adoption of a myriad of policies promoting greater gender equality. Without sufficient pressure for change from society itself, at best reforms will be partial, creating new forms of inequality, and conditional at the discretion of those elites benefitting most from the existing structure of society…
>
> (5)

From here Oxhorn moves on to discuss the inevitability of social conflict, and the role of civil society in mitigating its consequences. This claim is what distinguishes his collectivist perspective from what he refers to as the "liberal" view of civil society (9); the former understands conflict and division to be unavoidable and the latter assumes conflict to have been eradicated by the introduction of individual rights. However, Oxhorn's interpretation of civil society is similarly 'liberal' in its emphasis on representation and associational inclusion. To be sure, it is more nuanced than naive Lockean visions of the social contract, but its main improvement is that it acknowledges what the canon ignores: the difficult reality of deep social conflict.

Therefore, the institutional, pluralist notion of civil society (whether labelled 'collectivist' or 'individualistic') is conceptually inconceivable for many countries in Latin America, certainly in Guatemala. But does this mean that civil society is inconceivable as well? The second axis, that of democratic autonomy, offers more possibilities. Many groups in Guatemala, vis-a-vis the mining sector, for example, do express a (collective) will that is autonomous from (and acrimonious to) the state. This expression is often 'scaled up' to benefit from the support of international actors, which results in a more powerful source of pressure to demand that the state 'delivers the goods.' Without this capacity for engaging with actors and developing civil society beyond borders, the promise of civil society in Guatemala might be entirely unfulfilled.

Transnational Civil Society and Political Action in Guatemala

In the introduction to this chapter, I mentioned the process of *consultas* for soliciting opinions concerning proposed mining operations in indigenous communities. While the main purpose of these is to engage local communities in decisions that will affect virtually every aspect of their lives, and therefore can be considered an example of grassroots level, participatory exercises, some community members explain that the *consultas* actually have much broader, more ambitious political goals. One participant explains that

> the popular consultation (*consulta*) is an expression, a manifestation, of not just the rejection of mining, but to tell the Government, the State: "we want to participate in the decisions of government, in the decisions of the state, that do not take us into account."
> (Laplante & Nolin, 2014, 240)

And another elaborates on this point:

> [the *consulta*] is an expression of resistance to everything about the situation in which we live. The desire to improve the conditions of life, the desire to have a more democratic country, not only in word but in substance, so that the people share in the power of decisions of the state.
> (Laplante & Nolin, 2014, 241)

The will expressed in these quotes serves as evidence for civil society as Oxhorn defines it, and the form and substance of the *consultas populares* provide examples of the "democratic autonomy" that is characteristic of the second axis as described above. However, the decisions rendered by the *consultas* (i.e., to deny mining companies access to community land for assessment or extraction) are routinely ignored or flouted by government officials and mining companies. Therefore, there is no capacity for community democratic practices, however conceived and organized, to affect politics and policy-making at municipal or national levels.

What are the consequences of this incapacity? If civil society organizing has virtually no chance of affecting political decision-making and resulting in more inclusive processes, then what is its value and why should continued organization and struggle be encouraged? In part, the response is found along the second axis, in the 'thinner' description of citizenship. While the *consultas* on their own cannot claim much success, their effects can be 'scaled up' to generate more political impact. The consultation processes, if not their decisions, have been the recent focus of legislative reform efforts. As Laplante and Nolin explain,

> ...the *consultas* have taken on a life of their own in Guatemala. Perhaps due to the creation of slightly safer spaces for protest and resistance afforded by the Peace Accords, these communities are acting in ways that would have been unimaginable 25 years ago. The recent announcement by Guatemalan legislators that they seek to "regulate" the *consultas* affirms the strength that the movement has gathered.
>
> (2014, 243)

On its own, the example of the *consultas* provides evidence of the sort of civil society that Oxhorn envisions, territorially bound, conflict-managing exercises, with distinct procedures and purposes. The *consultas* are perhaps most noteworthy for their ability to engage divisive perspectives, as many communities, even families, are deeply conflicted over mining issues. Local mines are often the only source of employment for community members, and workforce participation is important for subsistence and higher-order human needs. Therefore, there are often irreconcilable divisions between those community members who are willing to accept the employment offered by mining companies, and those who refuse to capitulate, deciding instead to defend livelihoods and the environment. In fact, the community *consultas* seem to be prototypical of Oxhorn's definition of civil society in Latin America. However, their ability to get the state to 'deliver the goods' is facilitated (although not ensured) by cooperation with transnational actors.

As Leire Urkidi notes, the *consultas* themselves were constituted with reference to the International Labour Organization "Convention 169 on Indigenous Peoples and the Guatemalan Municipal Code" (2011, 557). Concerning the proliferation of academic analysis on *consultas* in Guatemala, Urkidi states the following:

> In every study, the multiscalar character of the Marlin [gold mine] case is manifest. By multiscalar, I mean that the movement is composed of actors in different geographical locations, that it acts simultaneously in various political spheres, and that it is influenced by a combination of international, regional, national, municipal and communitarian social processes and regulations. The increased flows of information and resources between scales may be a novelty of the anti-mining and other

current social movements in Guatemala. However, there is another relevant process regarding the political innovation of this movement: the reconstruction and defence of community as the proper scale for decision-making on mining and natural resources management.

(557)

In this instance, the global dimensions of the mining industry are (somewhat) counterbalanced by transnational civil society that mobilizes to resist global capitalist incursions. Therefore, while the community-level elements of the *consultas* would pass as civil society exercises, their interpretation as such is incomplete. Even on a community level, participants are resisting multi-scalar violations. Yet it is also the case that the composition of the *consultas* has a transnational character. To further this point, Urkidi argues that it is important to rethink "community" itself, such that,

> …the strategic rescaling of the movement, resorting to transnational courts and to national and supra-national networks, is compatible with the claims of the local place. I argue that the defence of community should not be understood as its idealization and essentialization (Vayda & Walters, 1999), but as a historically contextualized political strategy.
>
> (2011, 558)

Urkidi refers to this, borrowing from Agnew, as "the territorial trap," namely that,

> …territorial conceptions of places and scales typically feed a politics of nostalgia rather than one of progressive change, and that they fuel 'localist or nationalist claims to place based on eternal, essential, and in consequence exclusive, characteristics of belonging' (Massey, 2004, 6).
>
> (Urkidi, 2011, 560)

Nevertheless, many local struggles, such as those associated with resistance to mining in Guatemala, are place-based, but this territorial character is mobilized to network and "…engage in broader scales in order to construct solidarities and political opportunities" (Urkidi, 2011, 560). Thus, the definitions of community and civil society are diverse and embody the sorts of transformations that are experienced at all levels of politics.

Conclusion

Conceptions of civil society that are linked exclusively to institutions, associations, and outcomes at domestic levels do not reflect the global dimensions of politics and economics. Nor are they appropriate to analysis of post-conflict, fragile democracies like Guatemala. In fact, given the limitations discussed throughout this chapter, they might not be applicable anywhere. The transnational character of global capitalism and community is a perennial fact of political reality, and the place-based fantasies of grassroots associational life and bowling leagues are relics of a romanticized past. Of course, this does not mean that the concept of civil society has no boundaries. Civil society is marked by its political nature (i.e., participants demand recognition and possibly inclusion in institutions of the state (Oxhorn, Laplante and Nolin), its inclusiveness (Walzer), its ability to demonstrate an autonomous (from the state) position (Smith), its ability to transform the potential for conflict into productive debate (Oxhorn), and its ultimate interest in pressuring the state to "deliver the goods" (Smith). However, in Guatemala, this conception is only fully realized through its transnational dimensions.

It is also important to emphasize that 'delivering the goods' ostensibly refers to tangible public goods, such as increased resources for education and health care, or investment in infrastructure. These are all important basic entitlements in any society, and finding ways to pressure states to deliver on them is of the utmost importance. However, in post-conflict societies, such as Guatemala, less tangible, more symbolic goods are also significant. The struggle for "truth, memory, and justice," is concretized in truth commission reports (such as the United Nations' CEH, Informe de la Comisión de Esclarecimiento Historico, and the REMHI, Informe Proyecto Interdiocesano de Recuperación de la Memoria Histórica), and numerous domestic and international court cases. Yet it also has a set of metaphysical qualities, manifest through conversations, debates, the process of bearing witness, and creating affective ties through the emotions of compassion, indignance, and rage (see Berlant, 2007; Ahmed, 2004a; 2004b; Hemmings, 2012). Transnational civil societies aim to procure both sets of goods, through a multi-scalar politics of engagement and resistance.

References

Ahmed, Sara. 2004a. "Affective Economies." *Social Text* 22(4), 117–139.

Ahmed, Sara. 2004b. "Feminist Attachments." In *The cultural politics of emotion* (168–190). Edinburgh: Edinburgh University Press.

Bandy, Joe. 2004. "Paradoxes of transnational civil societies under neoliberalism: the coalition for justice in the maquiladoras." *Social Problems*, 51(3), 410–431.

Barber, Benjamin. 2003. "Strong Democracy: Participatory Politics for a New Age." In V.A. Hodgkinson & M.W. Foley (Eds). *The civil society reader* (234–254). Hanover, NH: University Press of New England.

Batliwala, Srilatha, & L. David Brown. 2006. *Transnational civil society: an introduction*. Bloomfield, CT: Kumarian Press.

Beck, Erin. 2014. "Countering convergence: agency and diversity among Guatemalan NGOs." *Latin American Politics and Society*, 56(2), 141–162.

Berlant, Lauren. 2007. "Nearly Utopian, Nearly Normal: Post-Fordist Affect in La Promesse and Rosetta." *Public Culture* 19 (2), 273–301.

Blair, Alex. 2014. "Corporate greed and human rights: is history repeating itself in

Guatemala?" *The Politics of Poverty: Ideas and Analysis from Oxfam America's Policy Experts* (http://politicsofpoverty.oxfamamerica.org/2014/11/corporate-greed-and-human-rights-is-history-repeating-itself-in-guatemala/), accessed 14 December 2014.

Brysk, Alison, & Céline Jacquemin. 2006. "Bridging borders for human rights." In S. Batliwala & L. David Brown (Eds.). *Transnational civil society: an introduction* (159–180). Bloomfield, CT: Kumarian Press.

Cohen, Jean L., & Andrew Arato. 2003. From "Civil Society and Political Theory." In V.A. Hodgkinson & M.W. Foley (Eds). *The civil society reader* (270–291). Hanover, NH: University Press of New England.

Colás, Alejandro. 2002. *International civil society*. Cambridge, MA: Polity Press.

Dagnino, Evelina. 2011. "Civil society in Latin America." In M. Edwards (Ed.). *The Oxford handbook of civil society* (122–133). Oxford: Oxford University Press.

Dougherty, Michael. 2011. "The global mining industry, junior firms, and civil society resistance in Guatemala." *Bulletin of Latin American Research*, 30(4), 403–418.

Edwards, Michael. 2014. *Civil Society* (3rd ed.). Cambridge, MA: Polity Press.

Flitner, Michael, & Dietrich Soyez. 2000. "Geographical perspectives in transnational civil society actors." *GeoJournal*, 52(1), 1–4.

Guest, Pete. 2014. "Dubbed terrorists, Mayans fight back against Guatemalan mining projects." *Newsweek*, 29 August (www.newsweek.com/2014/09/05/dubbed-terrorists-mayans-fight-back-against-mining-projects-266962.html), accessed 14 December 2014.

Hemmings, Clare. 2012. "Affective solidarity: feminist reflexivity and political transformation." *Feminist Theory*, 13(2), 147–161.

Jamasmie, Cecilia. 2014. "Miners in Guatemala to pay ten times more royalties." *Mining.com* (www.mining.com/miners-in-guatemala-to-pay-ten-times-more-royalties-75059), accessed 14 December 2014.

Jordan, Lisa. 2011. "Global Civil Society." In M. Edwards (Ed.). *The Oxford handbook of civil society* (93–108). Oxford: Oxford University Press.

Krznaric, Roman. 1999. "Civil and uncivil actors in the Guatemalan peace process." *Bulletin of Latin American Research*. 18(1), 1–16.

Laplante, J.P., & Catherine Nolin. 2014. "*Consultas* and socially responsible investing in Guatemala: a case study examining Maya perspectives in the Indigenous right to free, prior, and informed consent. *Society and Natural Resources*, 27, 231–248.

Mohanty, Chandra. 2003. *Feminism without borders: decolonizing theory, practicing solidarity*. Durham and London: Duke University Press.

Oxhorn, Philip. 1995. "From controlled inclusion to coerced marginalization: the struggle for civil society in Latin America." In J. Hall (Ed.). *Civil society: theory, history and comparison* (250–277). Cambridge, MA: Polity Press.

Oxhorn, Philip. 2007. "Civil society without a state? Transnational civil society and the challenge of democracy in a globalizing world." *World Futures*, 63, 324–339.

Rey Rosa, Magalí. 2014. "Ahorremos Q192 millones." *Prensa Libre*, 6 June (www.prensalibre.com/opinion/ahorremos-q192-millones_0_1151884822.html), accessed 14 December 2014.

Smith, Robert. 2003. "Migrant membership as an instituted process: transnationalization, the state and the extra-territorial conduct of Mexican politics." *International Migration Review*, 37(2), 297–343.

Urkidi, Leire. 2011. "The Defence of Community in the Anti-Mining Movement of Guatemala." *Journal of Agrarian Change*, 11(4), 556–580.

Vásquez, Dominga. 2011. "Solidarity is a characteristic of the Maya people." In G. Grandin, D.T. Levenson, & E. Oglesby (Eds.). *The Guatemala reader* (537–540). Durham: Duke University Press.

Walzer, Michael. 1995. "The concept of civil society." In M. Walzer (Ed.). *Toward a global civil society* (7–28). Providence and Oxford: Berghahn Books.

Walzer, Michael. 2003. "A better vision: the idea of civil society." In V.A. Hodgkinson & M.W. Foley (Eds). *The civil society reader* (306–321). Hanover, NH: University Press of New England.

Weld, Kirsten. 2014. *Paper cadavers: the archives of dictatorship in Guatemala*. Durham and London: Duke University Press.

10 Collective Banks and Counter-Acts

Building Civil Society from within in Jamaica and Guyana

Caroline Shenaz Hossein

In the 1990s, Britain's Prime Minister, Margaret Thatcher, coined the idea of TINA; that "there is no alternative" to free markets and neoliberal politics for the world. TINA sparked protests by people against market fundamentalism very much like the ones in the 1800s by the Rochdale weavers of England who organized from the ground up a cooperative movement to resist efforts to construct a market society that privileged business over people. The banker ladies in this chapter also confirm that alternatives can be sustained and counter mainstream ideas of business. In his chapter (this volume), Philip Oxhorn highlights the tensions and conflicts inherent within communities as people find their voice. Building a strong civil society is a messy process, and it is in the seeming debates among people where ideas flow from within that emphasizes that there are alternatives.

As Oxhorn rightly cautions, we should avoid the temptation in much of the civil society literature to glorify or romanticize life in marginalized communities. Life in such environments can be difficult and dangerous, especially when people are testing alternatives. In *Collective Courage* (2014), Jessica Gordon Nembhard posits that group organizing by African Americans was viewed as dangerous because it meant going against individualized capitalism by a historically oppressed community. Oxhorn's point is that there is an inevitable tension between the ideal and local conflicts within marginalized communities as people search for a new system.

In the Caribbean region, many social economy programs which try to build civil society have gone awry in certain contexts because of their failure to understand the historical and intersectional oppressions within poor communities. For instance, Verrest (2013, 68) has found that subsidized business development programs which aimed to help nurture positive social development in the slums of Trinidad and Tobago and Surinam were unable to do so because the managers were detached from the real-life realities on the ground. Far too often there is a disconnect between the business managers charged with helping marginalized people and their clients because they are not aware of their lived realities in a way to bring about positive change. In fact, many of these subsidized economic programs are viewed with suspicion from the targeted communities. Change has to come from within.

The idea that microbanking can contribute to strong civil societies warrants further attention. In 2006, the Nobel Peace Prize went to Bangladesh's Grameen Bank and its founder, Dr. Mohammed Yunus, because of the role that microfinance has played in cultivating peaceful civil societies. While formal microfinance lending schemes may serve to strengthen community ties in some instances, in this study, I argue that informal banks are better placed to create positive social change in slum environments. Informal banks are an example of functionally based civil society organizations that may develop the collective action of excluded people.

At first glance, the low-income urban communities of Kingston, Jamaica and Georgetown, Guyana demonstrate high levels of group division and low levels of interpersonal trust. However, people within these same communities have overcome some of these challenges by collectively organizing informal banks when they are excluded from accessing credit for their activities. The people who run these informal banks, the 'banker ladies,' are attuned to the fact that formalized business programs to reach excluded groups do not work. Instead, banker ladies have crafted their own informal collectives that rework mainstream financial systems. The mainstream experts and practitioners paid to manage pro-poor financial programs assume that there is no wealth or underestimate the degree of internal conflict in these communities; whereas the banker ladies embedded in these societies understand complex social relations among people who have been routinely denied opportunities. It is not that civil society is lacking, rather the way in which it is to be constructed needs to happen from within and this will mean that tensions and conflicts will inevitably arise in the search for an alternative social and economic system (or 'ideal' as Oxhorn speaks to). Excluded groups in Jamaica and Guyana are skeptical of pro-poor targeted financial programs, and will counteract these formalized economic programs with informal collective institutions they know and trust.

The central question addressed in this study is: In what ways do community-based banks contribute to strong communities and civil society? My findings are based on empirical qualitative data derived from individual interviews and focus groups with 398 small-business people, civil society activists, government officials, leading businessmen and women, and bankers in the capital cities of Kingston, Jamaica and Georgetown, Guyana.[1] I hold that the informal banks operating in the slums are premeditated counter-acts organized by marginalized people. Their goal is to build functional institutions that strengthen civil society on its own terms.[2] I ground the informal banking systems in their regional context to show that Jamaican 'hustlas' (business people) opt for 'Partner banks' (informal banks) to avoid being co-opted by politicians and gangsters. In Kingston, Jamaica where many microfinance lenders (and commercial banks) exist, informal banks are hugely popular. Handa and Kirton (1996) argue that Jamaican women are able to do business on their own terms through the Partner banks. Unlike the Jamaican case, Afro-Guyanese 'hucksters' (business people) participate in 'Box hand' (informal banks) to restore their personal pride and choose systems they trust when a racialized class politics has berated persons of Afro-Guyanese descent for the past two decades.

Informal banks permit marginalized Caribbean entrepreneurs, who value their independence, to interact with one another and to engage in politics on their own terms, and not in ways required of them in structured banking programs for the poor. What is more, people are organizing in a collective manner that is peaceful, despite the hostility against them. By incorporating indigenous systems of collectivity, financial services reach excluded groups and can be viewed as subversive acts because people are developing business lives that fit their social needs (Polanyi, 1944).

Most people have a strong desire to improve their living conditions on their own terms, and they will organize activities in a way that does not undermine their social lives. In a concerted effort to reclaim local economic resources and to meet the social needs of each other, the Caribbean region has what are called community bankers, or 'banker ladies,' who institute a program of social connectedness and social justice to agitate against external, profit-driven forms of economic development. Caribbean banker ladies mobilize funds from within the slums to financially support the projects of the residents. It is important to note that these bankers are not only reorganizing money markets in their communities, as well as increasing voice, but they are managing local tensions in a non-violent manner.

Caribbean banker ladies in Jamaica and Guyana are building social action within oppressed slum communities by supporting local livelihood activities. The findings show that in both case studies, persons of African descent, especially women, turn to ancestral savings and lending plans as a way to cope emotionally and financially when society's banks and formal economic programs reject them. Informal banks work mainly because they are outside of the state's purview and control of economic elites, thus allowing ordinary people the right to assert their own ideas and autonomy within their own communities.

ROSCAs: A Worldwide Phenomenon

Informal banks are unregulated financial systems that provide quick access to savings and credit systems for people, mostly women, who are excluded from formal banking channels (Ardener & Burman, 1996; Geertz, 1962; Rogaly, 1996; Rutherford, 2000). Informal banks are known globally as Rotating Savings and Credit Associations (ROSCAs). Informal banks have spread to many parts of the world, including advanced industrialized democracies like the U.S. and Canada with large diaspora populations. Immigrant women who have a hard time accessing financial services bring these informal banking systems to their new homelands (Ardener & Burman, 1996).

Informal banks run by poor women are a massive global phenomenon, with hundreds of millions of people engaged in informal financial services.

Stuart Rutherford's *The Poor and Their Money* (2000) found that ROSCAs are in high demand among the poor because they function efficiently, offer both low defaults and low transaction costs, and require fewer formalities. The informality of informal banks is what makes them distinctive in their own right, and attractive to people. The practical aspect of making money accessible in the community for a low cost has resonated with entrepreneurs around the world.

Poor people pooling money is one of the most studied phenomena in highly diverse cultural settings, as in the Caribbean, with important political implications. The informal banks in the Caribbean are a valued African tradition, rooted in the local saving systems *susus* (term known in English-speaking Caribbean) and *tontines* (term used in French-speaking countries) brought by slaves to the Americas (Wong, 1996; Witter, 1989; Mintz, 1955). Guyanese scholar, Maurice St. Pierre (1999) explains that informal banks were in existence in Guyana when African slaves rotated funds among each other, as they did in the *susu*, or Box hand groups. Harrison's work (1988) showed that since slave times, Jamaican higglers have long struggled to make a livelihood in precarious economic and political environments and used Partner banks to meet their financial needs. During slavery and colonization in the new lands, African slaves had rotational credit groups in their markets (Heinel & Heinel, 2005; St. Pierre, 1999). In Haiti, poor women have earned the title of *poto mitan* (meaning 'pillar of the family' in Kreyol) because of their ability to provide sustenance for their families under extreme hardship. Haitian women have organized *sols* (informal banks) under the brutal Duvaliers' dictatorships (1957–1971 and 1971–1986) when people were banned from forming associations (N'Zengou-Tayo, 1998, 118). Under colonialism, British banks in Jamaica and Guyana did not lend to the local people so women turned to their own local savings systems handed down to them by the generations before them. Even after emancipation, indentured servants from India also relied on their indigenous systems of sharing economic resources through a 'buddy' system. In the documentary *Poto Mitan: Haitian Women, Pillars of a Global Economy* (2009), Haitian women in Cité Soleil (the largest slum in Port-au-Prince) are shown borrowing on the African traditions of sol (informal banks) to manage their financial lives.

Social inequality in the Caribbean explains why informal banks are vital to the region. Stigma against Black businesspersons in the slums has mobilized these entrepreneurs as a group. Hustlas and higglers (small entrepreneurs) in the downtown slums of Kingston, Jamaica have developed a strong social consciousness that sets them apart from outsiders or people who are not from the area (Gray, 2004). The banker ladies are fully aware of this distinct identity, they know the context, and are able to organize people in such a way that benefits the collective group. Banker ladies are well respected because of the fact that they manage their own business affairs and do not rely on handouts. Krishna (2002) has found that high levels of community mobilization in India can be turned into active capital to resist oppressive forms of social capital embedded in a culture with forms that are locally nurtured. Informal banks in the Caribbean demonstrate that people participate in these community banks and opt out of formalized, pro-poor financial programs as a way to resist unfair economic systems.

Community-led Banks and the Spirit of Collectivity

Informal banks, usually run by women, are well documented (Rutherford, 2000; Collins et al., 2009; Ardener & Burman, 1996). In *Portfolios of the Poor*, Collins, Murdoch, Rutherford, and Ruthven (2009, 26), trace 250 financial diaries of hundreds of poor people in the developing world, and find that informal banks are an important financial device for poor entrepreneurs who cannot access sufficient levels of financing. Yet few scholars, if any, have studied the political practice of the members in informal banks to build a strong civil society. In fact, the work of the banker ladies benefits the community as a whole because the concept of reciprocity and helping one another is ingrained into these banking systems. In *Money-Go-Rounds*, Ardener and Burman (1996) show that women rely on informal banks mainly for supporting social networks. The banker ladies in this study can also be viewed as a subversive group in that they are collective groups firmly rooted in civil society. Their objective is quite different from commercial financial programs in that the banker ladies are precisely focused on sharing community resources amongst each other in an equitable manner, in contrast to mainstream ideas of economic development of the conventional banks.

Commercial banks have long excluded poor women from financial programs. Now the microfinance lenders, charged with reaching the poor, are also alienating a segment of the urban poor who do not meet their rigid requirements (Hossein, 2014a; 2012). Microfinance programs are not trusted by the very target group they are designed for, and at times are perceived by the people to be politically motivated. And while informal banks are important for meeting people's cash flow needs, they are deeply embedded in the political action of the women who create alternative financial systems. People in marginalized communities have local resources that they organize through mutual aid to reduce dependence on corrupt local leaders, politicians, and corporations. They turn to informal banks created locally to avoid being manipulated by outside managers and politicians who target them. Despite the odds against them, banker ladies persevere under difficult conditions to incorporate fair systems. In this way, banker ladies reflect Karl Polanyi's (1944) double movement as they rearrange financial systems to bring social life back to the fore, ahead of business.

We have seen a growth of scholarship detailing how female entrepreneurs take it upon themselves to organize community banks to ensure people have access to non-politicized funds. For example, Rutherford (2000) found that poor people deemed "unbankable" will fill the gap of commercial banks by creating and participating in locally based financial programs that collect deposits on and lend money to each other. Throughout the Global South, citizens viewed as "unbankable" now have a place where they are listened to and can partake in financial transactions as needed. These informal community banks are grounded in self-help ideas that are grassroots and outside of the control of local elites (Hossein, 2014). Informal banks are unregistered institutions, and based on people-to-people agreements. Throughout the scholarship, we see that while this informal aspect of the banks can lead to misunderstandings (Collins et al., 2009; Rutherford, 2000), there are many people who prefer to deal with them (Hossein, 2014b).

Informal institutions have been in use during enslavement and colonization as well as under authoritarian dictatorships when people were banned from organizing. It is important to examine the banker ladies and their informal banks, not only as a means to correct current financial systems but to understand that they are experimenting with collective financial systems that are culturally adapted for people's everyday needs and not the other way around. It is the ancestral and cultural connection that I found reduces any danger to banker ladies in these two countries, unless they were to abscond with the bank's funds (Hossein, 2012). Local people respect and value the community engagement in these banks and protect them because they recognize that their African ancestors have authored their creation. The default rate (people who do not repay) is also minuscule in these personal arrangements because the possibility of ostracism is so real that people would never default on their payments, as it would mean denying a friend access to these resources (Hossein, 2012; Handa & Kirton, 1999). In fact, participants have admitted they would rather default on a formal bank loan and not the community bank; one main reason being that members trust the very people managing their local banks, as well as the other members in the group bank.

Informal banks in the Caribbean are grounded in business and society, and are intermeshed with human compassion and values. The social economy literature has demonstrated that organizations such as self-help groups and informal banks, rooted in civil society, are reaching people's needs when states and the private sector fail to do so. When the private and public sectors are limited in their capacity to reach an entrepreneur's needs, it appears that informal banks can fill the gap. Haynes and Nembhard (1999) find that cooperative enterprises in American ghettos provide alternative livelihood options for African Americans. Through collectivity, African Americans can move toward sustainable economic self-reliance as well as community activism. Yet, the social economy literature often does not capture the various ways such organizing of alternative financial services to contest oppression in a society is a way of nurturing a strong and thriving civil society from within. Banker ladies in the Caribbean draw on their African traditions of collectivity to build an inclusive economy.

Clientelism in Economic Development Programs

The deliberate social exclusion of people in the Caribbean slums drives the urban poor's determination to organize informal banks. This is what makes the organization of banks simply more than a system to meet basic needs. Quite understandably, the social tensions that exist in society diminish a small-business owner's desire to take loans from potentially biased micro-lenders—loans that would increase ties to political elites or unrecognized leaders. Informal banks help people to access monies from trusted sources. Scott (1977) argued that resistance from below is not new and peasants seek out ways to make life livable under clientelist systems. Much of what banker ladies do today is rooted in slave times when Africans used earnings from market days to pool money amongst themselves (Ulysse, 2007; Katzin, 1959). Similarly, one can effectively argue that informal banks in today's Caribbean continue the quiet forms of protest against the exclusionary economic environment of the slums. Jamaican political scientist, Obika Gray (2004; 2003) points to widespread urban resistance and "social power" among the urban poor, including very small businesses. In both Jamaica and Guyana, marginalized people turn to local financial devices as a way to harness their own power and to resist the partisan, class, or racial politics dominating their lives.

In practice, however, most business people in my study have never set foot in a formal bank (Besson, 1996, 269; Harrison, 1988, 113). For example, "Miss Paddy," a cookshop owner in Kingston, Jamaica who serves fried chicken, rice, and peas, has never held a bank account at a formal bank. Miss Paddy, who requires a bank account, is one of thousands of Jamaican hustlas living in tenement yards in the downtown slums who do not have birth certificates or tax revenue numbers. That is why people like Miss Paddy turn to the local bank in their community. Miss Paddy's story represents the hundreds of business people included in this study who prefer informal banks. Entrepreneurs like Miss Paddy do not want so-called "Big Men" (discussed in the next section) ruling their lives (Interview, Miss Paddy, 27 March, 2009).

Informal banks strive to create effective forms of social capital where people are a part of the process to decide how things occur. Social capital in slums is often characterized as non-existent or limited because of clientelist politics. However, in this study, both of my cases demonstrate that the urban poor, mostly women, who feel rejected by society's educated and economic elites, are pushing forward a new form of financial independence (Hossein, 2014b). Women of little educational training are mobilizing groups of people to pool their money to permit others to achieve their goals and to have options to avoid political patronage. Banker ladies have amassed social capital in a positive way to increase the assets of local communities and to reduce dependence on formal and political actors.

Informal banks are an example of Oxhorn's functionally based organizations because they weave cohesion amongst excluded groups by providing them with access to financial services. Bridge, Murtagh, and O'Neill (2009, 8) posit that social economy organizations with a people focus build the collective spirit. Informal banks are doing exactly this because the banker ladies build active social capital from within, based on local knowledge and the collective (Krishna, 2002). These self-help initiatives should not be viewed as bootstrap responses but rather through the lens of people of African descent who are drawing on systems that they know and trust.

Resistance to Big Man Politics through Partner Banks in Jamaica

Women bankers, not trained as bankers per se, are organizing financial programs and creating alternative financing devices throughout Jamaica. Partner banks are made up of groups of people who know each other (often related) and who make the decision to join the group and then to pool their money. Several variants of the Partner bank exist, and although all offer savings plans, many offer lending plans as well. This will vary from bank to bank, as it is the members who decide the structure and rules of their local banks. Historically, women have run Partner banks (Klak & Hey, 1992), because they tend to have lower-paying jobs and (some) experience greater difficulty in accessing credit relative to men (Handa & Kirton, 1999). Business people downtown seldom have access to large sums of money, nor do they have easy access to credit cards or lines of credit when they require expensive items, such as a refrigerator, sewing machine, or deep freezer. In Figure 1, 233 community people in six different slums seemed to value Partner banks (57%) over other financial institutions.

The banker lady decides who gets access to the lump sum first, and she assesses the person's risks for defaulting, just as a trained loans officer would. Each person's contribution to the Partner is called a 'hand' and it is 'thrown' (deposited) for a designated period; the pooled money is called a 'draw.' In some Partner banks, people draw lots to determine the order for obtaining a loan (Three Banker Ladies Interview, March–July, 2009; Rutherford, 2000; Handa & Kirton, 1999). Peer dynamics ensure people comply with payment rules, and social sanctions are applied in the case of default.

People engage in Partner banks because they know and trust the women who run them (Besson, 1996). In his work on Jamaica, Benson Honig (1998) explains that, in his interpretation, community banks stimulate social capital, and also ensure access to capital for business people. So-called 'Partner' is socially embedded in the traditions and emotions of the urban poor and it allows people to launch their enterprises through access to a lump sum of cash needed for their big-ticket purchases. Women come together to chat and discuss issues and the informal bank creates a space for them to do this. Partner is cost-efficient, easy to access, and trusted by hustlas.

The basic organizing principle of the Partner bank is that it generally involves a group of people who know each other well and who agree to pool their money together (Three Banker Ladies Interviews, March–July 2009; Klak & Hey, 1992; Katzin, 1959, 439). The banker ladies interviewed for this study were three single mothers with limited schooling who managed these banks with at least 100 clients. In Handa and Kirton's (1999) survey of 1000 people in Kingston, they found that 75% of the banker ladies were women between the ages of 26 and 35 who organized Partner for an average of nine years.

People want financial systems that enable them to do what they need to do without restricting their freedoms. At least 82% (191 out of 233) of the entrepreneurs I interviewed "throw partna," that is, they participate in Partner (see Figure 10.1). Gray (2004, 83) asserts that people in the slums are very close and intent on helping one another. Entrepreneurs preferred Partner banks because there was "no rigmarole" (such as increased paperwork), it is trustworthy, and is easily accessible. The banker ladies interviewed claim that repayment rates are high (usually 100%) because people trust these systems. While the formalized microfinance programs lack a social embeddedness with people, Partner is deeply rooted in people relationships and is there to help people when nobody else is.

Jamaican Partner (also referred to as 'Pardna') is very much part of the country's African heritage. Following years of biased financial systems, local women have emerged as trusted leaders, reverting to a cultural practice of organizing money systems and offering a way for people who do not go to formal banks to save safely. These banker ladies reach possibly one million people through Partner banks. Yet, the implications of these informal banks are seldom analyzed as a way to grow strong communities (Hossein, 2014b; Handa & Kirton, 1999; Katzin, 1959).

To understand why Partner banks are so relevant in Jamaican society one needs to situate the cultural context. Politics in Kingston, the country's

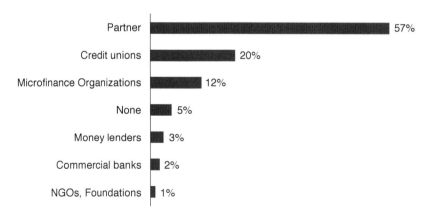

Figure 10.1 What Kind of Financial Provider/Model Meets the Needs of Small-Business Owners in the Slums?

main urban center, is marred at election time by violence. Whitened political elites, usually those who have power, make promises of money, lodgings, and jobs to their political activists who, if they fail to deliver the vote for their candidate, will lose the political handouts. Academics have written extensively on the entrenched mechanism wherein elites use uneducated masses in the ghettos to carry out heinous crimes to assure votes and political victory (Sives, 2010; Tafari-Ama, 2006). Poverty, endemic in the urban areas of Kingston, has enabled political elites to misuse resources to secure votes for their party, and this trend continues into present-day politics (Henry-Lee, 2005, 84). Years of politicians using residents in the slums to carry out their dirty work has led residents in the slums to distrust the political and business elites.

While Jamaican political elites continue to exert control over the slums, another local actor called 'Dons' (gangsters) has emerged as a consequence of the structural adjustment programs that limited the capacity of politicians to disburse benefits to party followers. Dons are informal leaders in the community who run lucrative illegal activities (e.g., drugs and weapons trafficking) and provide security, jobs, and welfare services for slum residents in exchange for complete control of the community. The local connotation 'Big Man' in Jamaica can refer to either a politician or one of these informal leaders. Indeed, the collusion between politicians and Dons is a common theme in popular film, theater, music, and media.[3] The widespread practice of political gift-giving, kickbacks, and handouts from the politicians or Dons is deeply entrenched in downtown Kingston communities (Keith & Keith, 1992, 160).

Political slums in Kingston are defined by an area's affiliation to one of the two political parties: the People's National Party (PNP) or the Jamaica Labour Party (JLP). These slums, also called 'garrisons,' take on a 'political tribe' persona: residents are either PNP or JLP depending on which political party controls the area. An entire community votes one particular way and there is no tolerance for opposition. Some garrison communities have an established structure, referred to as "one order," in which the Don controls all of the community's affairs (Rapley, 2006, 95–97). In this context, some could argue that social capital is limited or exists in a negative form. Once we examine the slums closely, however, it becomes evident that banker ladies embedded in this politicized environment are bringing about positive forms of social capital. Banker ladies understand this environment and create financial programs that meet the needs of people living under informal politics.

The fact that people's lives downtown are entangled in informal politics is not new. But when informal politics emerges in banks and other formal financial programs for the urban poor, tensions may arise. Dons, tied to the political elites by guaranteeing votes in exchange for government contracts, must ensure that residents vote for the "correct" party (Sives, 2010). In the 1980s, structural adjustment programs (SAPs) imposed by the International Monetary Fund (IMF) scaled back welfare functions, leaving

Dons to fill the gaps and provide basic welfare services and policing in certain ghettos (as well as the banker ladies). Because of increasing profits from the extortion of business elites and from the drug and weapons trade, Dons now often have more financial resources and power than elected leaders. The people who live in the slums are aware of the shift in power from political elites to Dons. In this context, it is understandable why banker ladies' banking terms are viewed as a safe bet for social action as opposed to borrowing money from Big Men.

Most people create and use informal banks to meet their cash flow needs. However, in the Jamaican case, people also use Partner banks to help each other to build wealth and rotate funds, as well as resist political co-optation. In my study, 41% (96) of the Jamaican entrepreneurs interviewed self-exclude or opt out of formal micro-loan programs that they view as political. Certain microfinance programs are perceived by micro-entrepreneurs as attempts to exercise political control over borrowers—that is, taking the loan involves a commitment to actively support a particular political party. Jamaicans, refusing to become involved in politics through business loans, exercise *political resistance* by participating in informal community-owned banks. These community banks therefore become centers of resistance.

Jamaican business people gravitate toward Partner banks to avoid supporting the established political parties, which attempt to co-opt and control them through conventional microfinance programs. The data in this case show that business people in the slums avoid manipulation by microfinance managers, politicians, and Dons and many of these business people exclude themselves if they perceive that these loans are linked to partisan politics. Scott (1977; 1972) suggests that compliance within a patron–client relationship depends on how important the patron's services are to the client. I see this as a form of political resistance because these business people, with the full knowledge that a loan can leverage a higher return, make a conscious decision to opt out of microfinance programs to avoid being what they refer to as "binded by a Big Man politics;" that is, controlled by politicians or gangsters. Banker ladies demonstrate leadership when they organize community resources and build trust that opposes partisanship in all aspects of their lives.

Small-business owners interviewed stated that "Partna is fi wi, and bank is fi di big man uptown"—that is, the Partner bank is for the poor (us) and formal banks are for the rich. "Yuh don't have to be rich or educated to throw partna." Partner bank is a locally owned, homegrown institution for the *small man*. Hustlas repeatedly made comments in support of Partner, something that was completely missing in microfinance. Hustlas would say repeatedly: "Mi luv mi partna." By way of an example, "Millie"—an elderly slum-dweller who owns a cookshop that serves soup and chicken—has never held a bank account at a commercial bank or credit union. She is one of the thousands of Jamaicans living in tenement yards downtown who do not have a birth certificate required to open a bank account.

People like Miss Millie turn to the local banker lady where unbankable business people like her can get a loan. Banker ladies go against the rules of formal finance and in this defiance create systems to reach those defined as "unbankable" or unworthy of accessing credit. For Miss Millie, Partner banks are people's finance.

Many Jamaicans are quick to say, "politics is in almost every aspect of Jamaican life." If politics is embedded in everyday life, and it is assumed to be prevalent in political strongholds, how can commercial banks catering to elites or a public resource such as microfinance, remain free from clientelist politics, as the managers would like to argue they are? Jamaican micro-entrepreneurs resist being controlled by politicized lenders, where party affiliations seemingly influence where microfinance operates and who gets it. The truth is that most independent-minded business people in the downtown markets do not want charity from the Big Men.

Banker ladies and their clients favor Partner banks not only for organizing their financial arrangements while avoiding the manipulative component of loan programs, but also as a political act of defying the grasp of Big Men. When ordinary people perceive mainstream bankers (including some microfinance lenders) to be in collusion with politicians or informal leaders, it violates the supposed role of microfinance in helping poor entrepreneurs self-develop—not only economically but also socially (Hossein, 2012). Politicians find a way to implicate themselves in formal funding programs for the poor. The citizens know who is at work 'behind the scenes.' Banks and pro-poor financial programs that collaborate with Dons to implement projects also inform hustlas that their financial growth is within the purview of the local strongmen.

Business people who want no part of violent and clientelist financial programs turn to informal lending, which has aspects of social capital they know and trust. These independent business people in slum communities make a pragmatic decision to exclude themselves from financial programs perceived to be intertwined with partisan politics and that can cause significant harm to their social and economic interests. Banker ladies are aware of this sentiment and fill the gap by offering functional services people can trust. These informal bankers are trusted because they live with and belong to the same social class as the very people with whom they work. This act of resistance against corrupt banks and targeted economic programs is a political act because the banker ladies knowingly subvert financing schemes that try to control them, and offer up alternative options that are in the best interests of the community.

Box Hand as a Refuge for Marginalized Afro-Guyanese

A pervasive cultural narrative denigrates the Afro-Guyanese entrepreneurial experience. Indo-Guyanese managers engaged in poverty alleviation programs such as microfinance do not construct programs to react against the class and racialized discourse prevalent in the society (Hossein, 2014a).

Indo-Guyanese microfinance managers refuse to recognize that class-based racism unfairly affects the allocation of resources. Indo-Guyanese managers in microfinance institutions focus instead on 'help my own kind.' Because institutions led by Indo-Guyanese prefer clients who resemble their cultural backgrounds, they are more likely to hire Indo-Guyanese. A lack of Afro-Guyanese at senior management levels decreases the likelihood that Blacks will be hired on the frontline to target clients of African descent.

Poor economic growth and biased state politics have forced many poor people to become entrepreneurial. The current government of Donald Ramotar (2011–present), which is supported by the Indo-Guyanese, ensures that this cultural group accesses loans (and is able to obtain large loan amounts) to develop their businesses. Bankers in the country are guided by their own inherent biases, such as class and race, and do not hire staff drawn from the urban areas where many Afro-Guyanese reside in order to counteract perceived (or real) discriminatory practices. As a result, banker ladies, also called 'boxers,' are the ones to retaliate against systems of oppression by offering excluded people access to credit and savings services.

In a small city like Georgetown all of the specialized microfinance lenders are in close proximity; yet, hucksters surprisingly turn to Box hand to meet their needs. As highlighted earlier, Guyana has a long history of informal mobilization of money. In slave times, Africans brought with them West African traditions of *susus* (group saving plans), where they mobilized savings on a weekly basis (St. Pierre, 1999; Mintz, 1955). Since slave times, Afro-Guyanese (and some Indo-Guyanese) have organized financial groups. These traditions have led Black hucksters to use informal credit facilities in response to their exclusion from formal microfinance. Indeed, the political and racial bias against Afro-Guyanese of the last 20 years has reinforced the importance of informal banking systems for marginalized Black people. However, in spite of the entrenched history of these informal banking systems, Box hand, a phenomenon widely used among the poor since slavery, has received little scholarly attention.

Indo-Guyanese microfinance managers are aware of the class and race discrimination against Afro-Guyanese but feel it is justified because of the many non-entrepreneurial characteristics they attribute to Blacks, as they view them as inferior in business. Afro-Guyanese are made to feel inferior because of their race, and microfinance does not aid this group of people. The exclusion of Blacks from banks and microfinance agencies, which makes Afro-Guyanese hucksters feel alienated by micro banks, has led them to become entrepreneurs. Many people rejected by lending institutions turn to informal ways of managing their money, such as hiding money at home in old chip tins or under beds. Afro-Guyanese business people, especially single mothers, often have no alternative but to use informal banks such as Box hand or Penny Bank (St. Pierre, 1999, 69; Besson, 1996, 264). These informal banks serve not only as a necessity for economic survival, but also as a way to preserve their dignity, when politicians deny this group access to basic resources.

Box hand provides a morale boost when people are denied access to economic resources. Box hand is very much part of the local financing system, and most of the hucksters interviewed (95%, 27) highly valued these banking systems. Most subjects (39) told me that Box hand restores personal pride to Black-owned businesses excluded from banks. "Nee," a 28-year-old mixed-race female who owns a hair and nail salon, stated, "Box help[ed] me start my business [...] [It has been] passed down from generation to generation, from grandmother's time and it [Box hand] helps me" (Interview, 26 April, 2010). Much like Jamaicans, Guyanese people are emotionally attached to these programs.

Box hand is a daily or weekly plan where the 'boxer' or 'box lady' (person in charge), usually a Black woman, manages the money collected from participants, and usually charges a small flat fee each cycle, usually six to twelve weeks. Box hand, like Jamaican Partner, enables poor business people to access a lump sum of cash after saving for a few weeks. Acceptance by the group is based on the person's capacity to repay and not on their race or color. In fact, Box hand members are open about their difficulty in getting loans from the banks, and the 'boxer' makes efforts to include them. Box hand gives poor Afro-Guyanese business people a safe place to lodge their savings. In my study, I found that at least 65% (29) of business people interviewed participate in Box hand or penny bank, and 95% (29) reported that they are highly valued. What is more is that these banks restore the dignity of a people who have been routinely denied access to basic services because of their culture and class background. Box ladies, in providing a local option, help people to save face and to access money when they need it.

Business people subjected to class and racial indignities every day are beaten down by the system. Box hand is an integral part of forming a civil society, to give people a choice to engage in an activity that is positive and supportive of what they do. These excluded people are able to come together as a group to do business and also discuss politics. These banks are revealed as being not merely coping mechanisms to build lump sums of cash, but forms of social collectivity to bring together people left out of the system in a way that is constructive and helpful to building social action from within. Ultimately, the work of Box hand validates the important businesses of Afro-Guyanese hucksters but it also helps them to engage collectively and to resist oppression as a group.

Conclusion

Millions of people across the Caribbean know about and engage in informal banking practices. Political interference in banking programs for the poor forces many small entrepreneurs to retreat towards self-financing options like informal banks. The literature on informal banks is extensive, and while this literature examines people's ingenuity in creating local banking programs to cope with financial and social exclusion, it does not discuss the way in which these informal collective banks may serve as building blocks for a strong civil society in oppressed communities. This chapter has found that banker ladies not only rework conventional lending systems, they are also restoring the notion of community first. This form of organizing may produce tensions, but it is being done in a peaceful manner as people work to grow a vibrant civil society from within.

Jamaican Partner banks are now so popular that the large retailers such as Bank of Nova Scotia of Jamaica and Jamaica National Building Society imitate informal banks and offer a "partner plan." However, these commercial banks that copycat indigenous banking programs do not offer the same kind of refuge for local poor people. Traditional bankers may copy informal banks because they understand the interconnectedness people have with their local banker ladies, however ordinary people perceive that formal banks exclude them, based on identities and partisan politics, and are not genuine 'Partners.' Agency in informal banks is cultivated because women organize local economic resources and give business people options to remain independent through enterprise. This creation of funds among people who now have the option to reject mainstream banking, in turn produces a form of resistance from below.

Informal banks are not only about economic survival; they are a testimony to people's perseverance to organize their financial lives in a way that is not manipulated by partisan politics. An agency emerges from within when poor Jamaicans create Partner banks to counteract clientelist politics through managed financial programs. Partner banks are trusted more than other programs run by elite intermediaries. Similarly, Afro-Guyanese hucksters, rejected by bankers because of their class and race, turn to Box hand for its reliability and to nurture each other in a hostile environment. When these entrepreneurs witness financial resources being squandered or whose provenance is perceived to be political in some way, they become skeptical about the intention of local economic development programs. For them, the banker ladies running informal banks represent a system that involves them in a meaningful way. As a well-respected system that started long before micro-banking became a policy focus for poverty alleviation in the region, informal banks will most likely outlast financial fads to help the urban poor.

Community-driven banks are self-managed and democratically controlled institutions. In communities where there is no supposed wealth, local people mobilize economic resources from within to meet their own needs. Community-based banks, energized by the banker ladies, operate under the radar deliberately in order to create collectivity, and to remake a financial system that builds social power and puts people first. The work of the banker ladies is at the core of civil society and this is surely political because they are intent in showing that alternative banks are possible. Banker ladies use cooperative economics as a means to build up local resources so that excluded people eventually move to a place where they can voice their opinions and actively participate in civil society.

Notes

1 The fieldwork was conducted from 2008–2009 in Kingston, Jamaica and 2008–2010 in Georgetown, Guyana. More details on methodology can be found in my dissertation (Hossein, 2012).
2 Informal banks are also referred to as rotating credit and savings associations (ROSCAs), institutions owned by local people (Rutherford, 2000).
3 Perry Henzell and Trevor Rhone's *The Harder They Come* (1973) shows the ties between criminals from the ghettos and political and business elites.

References

Ardener, Shirley, & Sandra Burman (Eds). 1996. *Money-go-rounds: the importance of rotating savings and credit associations for women.* Oxford, UK: Berg.

Besson, Jean. 1996. "Women's Use of ROSCAs in the Caribbean: Reassessing the Literature." In Ardener & Burman (Eds.). *Money-go-rounds: the importance of rotating savings and credit associations for women* (263–289). Oxford, UK: Berg.

Bridge, Simon, Brendan Murtagh & Ken O'Neill. *Understanding the social economy and the third sector.* Palgrave Macmillan, UK, 2009.

Collins, Daryl, Jonathan Morduch, Stuart Rutherford, & Orlanda Ruthven. 2009. *Portfolios of the poor: how the world's poor live on $2 a day.* Princeton, NJ: Princeton University Press.

Geertz, Clifford. 1962. "The Rotating Credit Association: A Middle Rung in Development." *Economic Development and Cultural Change*, 10(3) (April), 241–263.

Gordon Nembhard, Jessica. 2014. *Collective courage: a history of African American cooperative economic thought and practice.* University Park, PA: Penn State University Press.

Gray, Obika. 2003. "Baddness-Honour." In A. Harriott (Ed.). *Understanding crime in Jamaica: new challenges for public policy.* Kingston, Jamaica: UWIP.

Gray, Obika. 2004. *Demeaned but empowered: the social power of the urban poor in Jamaica.* Kingston, Jamaica: UWIP.

Handa, Sudhanshu, & Claremont Kirton. 1999. "The Economies of Rotating Savings and Credit Associations: Evidence from the Jamaican 'Partner.'" *Journal of Development Economics*, 60, 173–194.

The Harder They Come. 1973. Film. Dir. Perry Henzell & Trevor Rhone. Kingston, Jamaica: Island Records.

Harrison, Faye V. 1988. "Women in Jamaica's Informal Economy: Insights from a Kingston Slum." *New West Indian Guide*, 3(4), 103–128.

Haynes, Curtis, & Jessica Gordon Nembhard. 1999. "Cooperative Economics: A Community Revitalization Strategy." *The Review of Black Political Economy*, 47–71.

Heinl, Robert Debs, & Nancy Gordon Heinl. 2005. *Written in blood: the story of the Haitian people 1492–1995.* Expanded version by Michael Heinl. Laham, MD: University Press of America.

Henry-Lee, Aldrie. 2005. "The Nature of Poverty in the Garrison Constituencies in Jamaica." *Environment and Urbanization*, 17(2), 83–99.

Holden, Paul. 2005. *Implementing secured transactions reform in Jamaica: issues and policy options.* Kingston, Jamaica: Enterprise Research Institute.

Honig, Benson. 1998. "What Determines Success? Examining the Human, Financial and Social Capital of Jamaican Microentrepreneurs." *Journal of Business Venturing*, 13 (September), 371–394.

Hossein, Caroline Shenaz. 2012. *The politics of microfinance: A comparative study of Jamaica, Guyana and Haiti* (Unpublished doctoral dissertation). University of Toronto, Toronto, ON.

Hossein, Caroline Shenaz. April 2014a. "The exclusion of Afro-Guyanese in micro-banking." *The European Review of Latin American and Caribbean Studies*, 96, 75–98. Netherlands: CEDLA.

Hossein, Caroline Shenaz. 2014b. "The politics of resistance: Informal banks in the Caribbean." *The Review of Black Political Economy*, 41 (1), 85–100. US: Springer.

Interview with an academic, O'Neil Greaves, Georgetown, Guyana, 17 November, 2008.

Interview with "Miss Paddy," Kingston, Jamaica, 27 March, 2009.

Interview with "Millie," Kingston, Jamaica, 6 May, 2009.

Interview with "Nana," Kingston, Jamaica, 12 May, 2009.

Interview with three banker ladies, Kingston, Jamaica, March–July, 2009.

Interview with huckster "Nee", 26 April, 2010.

Interview with a senior banker at RBTT, Guyana, 22 April, 2010.

Interview with "Lam," a banker at Demerara Bank, Guyana, 4 May, 2010.

Katzin, Margaret Fisher. 1959. "The Jamaican Country Higgler." *Social and Economic Studies*, 8(4), 421–440.

Keith, Nelson W., & Novella Z. Keith. 1992. *The social origins of democratic socialism in Jamaica.* Philadelphia, PA: Temple University Press.

Klak, Thomas H., & Jeanne K. Hey. 1992. "Gender and State Bias in Jamaican Housing Programs." *World Development*, 20(2) (February), 213–227.

Krishna, Anirudh. 2002. *Active social capital. Tracing the roots of development and democracy.* New York, NY: Columbia University Press.

Mintz, Sidney. 1955. "The Jamaican Internal Marketing Pattern: Some Notes and Hypotheses." *Social and Economic Studies*, 4(1), 95–103.

Polanyi, Karl. 1944. *The great transformation.* Boston, MA: Beacon Press.

Poto Mitan: Haitian Women, Pillars of the Global Economy. 2008. Film; 60 minutes. Prod. Tet Ansanm. www.potomitan.net/.

Rapley, John. 2006. "The New Middle Ages." *Foreign Affairs* 85.3 (May/June): 95–103.

Rogaly, Ben. 1996 "Microfinance Evangelism, Destitute Women and the Hard Selling of a New Anti-poverty Formula." *Development in Practice*, 6(2) (May), 100–112.

Rutherford, Stuart. 2000. *The poor and their money.* New Delhi: DFID/Oxford University Press.

St. Pierre, Maurice. 1999. *Anatomy of resistance: anticolonialism in Guyana 1823–1966.* London: MacMillan Education.

Scott, James. 1972. "Patron–Client Politics and Political Change in Southeast Asia." *American Political Science Review*, 66, 91–113.

Scott, James. 1977. *The moral economy of the peasant: rebellion and subsistence in southeast Asia.* New Haven, CO: Yale University Press.

Sives, Amanda. 2010. *Elections, violence and the democratic process in Jamaica: 1994–2007.* Kingston, Jamaica: Ian Randle.

Tafari-Ama, Imani. 2006. *Blood, bullets and bodies: sexual politics below Jamaica's poverty line.* USA: Multi-Media Communications.

Ulysse, Gina A. 2007. *Downtown ladies: informal commercial importers, a Haitian anthropologist, and self-making in Jamaica.* Chicago, IL: Chicago University Press.

Verrest, Hebe. 2013. "Rethinking Micro-entrepreneurship and Business Development Programs: Vulnerability and Ambition in Low-income Urban Caribbean Households." *World Development*, 47, 58–70.

Witter, Michael. 1989. "Higglering/Sidewalk Vending/Informal Commercial Trading in Jamaican Economy." Department of Economics occasional paper series No. 4 (June).

Wong, David. 1996. "A Theory of Petty Trading: The Jamaican Higgler." *Economic Journal* 106 (March), 507–518.

11 War on Civil Society in Vargas Llosa's *The War of the End of the World*

Olga Nedvyga

> ...and soldiers were about to enter Canudos to destroy people who had gathered together there to live in the love of God and help each other since no one else had ever helped them.
>
> Even though the Counselor preached against gambling, tobacco, and alcohol, there were those who gambled, smoked, and drank cane brandy, and when Canudos began to grow, there were fights over women, thefts, drinking bouts, and even knifings. But these things were much less of a problem here than elsewhere and happened on the periphery of the active, fraternal, fervent, ascetic center constituted by the Counselor and his disciples.
>
> The War of the End of the World

Mario Vargas Llosa's *The War of the End of the World* is a unique project in the field of Latin American fiction and essays on associational life. Set in late 19th-century Brazil, the novel tells a story of four military campaigns (1893–1897) waged against an ever-growing religious group with Antônio Vicente Mendes Maciel (a.k.a. Antônio Conselheiro) at its head. Three of the war campaigns were infamously lost by the weak and decentralized Brazilian Republic in the years immediately following its formation in 1889. The fourth campaign was won only after being backed by civic rallies and the active voluntary participation of the inhabitants of São Paulo and Rio de Janeiro. The two interconnected outcomes of the fourth campaign were the violent destruction of Canudos—the settlement of Conselheiro's followers—and the consolidation of the nation-state around the two major cities.

This representation of the war of Canudos is historically credible, at least within the plausible range of postmodernism. The novel established multiple connections to historic evidence and brought together conflicting memories about the war.[1] However, Vargas Llosa's story is unsettling for those familiar with the first narrative account of the war given by the Brazilian journalist, Euclides da Cunha, a first-person witness of the events. Da Cunha went to Canudos for the first time in 1893 and was a war correspondent for *O Estado de S. Paulo* during the military expedition of 1897, during which time he actively defended the republic. Like the vast majority of educated Brazilians indoctrinated in the positivist notion of progress, da

Cunha first believed that "in this war combat, on one side, the Republic—that is to say, civilization, science, culture, progress—and, on the other side, the Empire [supposedly represented by Conselheiro's group], that is to say, prejudice, inequalities, obscurantism, barbarism" (Vargas Llosa, 1986, 246).[2] Da Cunha's view changed radically after the end of the fourth campaign. The resistance offered by the *jagunços*,[3] as well as the scope of violence unleashed by the regular army after the seizure of Canudos, a posteriori turned this war into a sort of enigma for da Cunha. He wrote his masterpiece, the documentary novel *Os Sertões*, in an attempt to illuminate what had been misunderstood and to explain—to himself initially—the war of Canudos. To accomplish this task, da Cunha did not limit himself anymore to positivist conceptual framework, primarily responsible for designating the backlands as barbaric. He resorted instead to the eclectic array of scientific, theoretical, and poetical knowledge available by the beginning of the 20th century. Vargas Llosa picked up where da Cunha had stopped and broadened the critique of the positivist ideology that upheld a paternalistic state, meant to protect the allegedly threatened urban civility. On the other hand, Vargas Llosa introduced a new and, for many, unexpected political player that had been absent from any previous theorizing of the war of Canudos: civil society. Not only did Vargas Llosa introduce civil society, but he successfully challenged the conventional assumption as to where in Latin America civil society is to be found and what social forces block its development.

For the purposes of this chapter, by civil society I understand a form of associational life organized around a "multiplicity of self-constituted territorially and functionally based units" (see Oxhorn, this volume) that negotiates their particular interests with the state. In the case that the state is not able to meet the needs of civil society units, they put forward political demands that propose changes to the economic, social, and cultural fabric of the society. Such an understanding of civil society belongs to a collectivist perspective advocated by Oxhorn and brought to critical examination by the present volume. This perspective allocates some elements that have been seen as an indispensable part of civil society (e.g., strong public sphere, nonviolence, etc.) to the domain of historical variables that, although present in most Western democracies nowadays, may be absent in other geo-temporal contexts. Instead, the emphasis is laid on the intensity and extent of associational and cooperative interactions between the constitutive units and the state as well as on the society's efforts to participate in self-government and local policy-making. Non-violent interactions do not constitute a defining feature: they signal the functionality of civil society since, either way, violence introduces the rule of force and cancels mutual gains-bargaining.

The eruption of violence thus should not automatically divert critical attention from the theorizing of civil society. Often the proposition of civil society in less democratic contexts is dismissed at the first sign of bloodshed. As a result, a civil society under attack is abandoned due to the excess of decorum while its challenges and proponents are ridiculed by pointing out the discrepancy of goals and means. In this context, Hegel provides a sort of methodological bridge: in the aftermath of the Jacobin Terror and without discarding the complexity of ill-fitting historical phenomena, he theorized—simultaneously rationalized and imagined, articulated and perpetuated—the theological–political landscape that would balance divergent social forces. He maintained that a modern state must be both conceptually and procedurally differentiated from civil society, thus confirming the possibility of confusion arising after the transition of sovereignty from the monarch to the French people. In *Elements of the Philosophy of Right*, Hegel proposed a seemingly weird reconfiguration, suggesting that what had been taken for the state in this emerging context should be thought of instead as civil society. The tone behind this move is prescriptive: in order to grant equal consideration to different individuals and groups, modern state, unlike civil society, should not be able to promote any particular interests. It is civil society that advocates for individual needs after those get abstracted to a collectively meaningful level:

> If the state is represented as a unity of different persons, as a unity which is merely a community [of interests], this applies only to the determination of civil society.... In civil society, each individual is his own end, and all else means nothing to him. But he cannot accomplish the full extent of his ends without reference to others; these others are therefore means to the end of the particular [person]. But through its reference to others, the particular end takes on the form of universality, and gains satisfaction by simultaneously satisfying the welfare of others. Since particularity is tied to the condition of universality, the whole [of civil society] is the sphere [Boden] of mediation in which all individual characteristics [Einzelheiten], all aptitudes, and all accidents of birth and fortune are liberated, and where the waves of all passions surge forth, governed only by the reason which shines through them.
>
> (1820/1991, 220)

The accomplished partition of rationality into the lawful abstract domain of the state and the situation-specific, although partially abstracted ("universal" in Hegel's idiom), domain of civil society allows for a historical critique of a particular correlation of forces between the two. The proposed reconfiguration inverts the loci of power accumulation. It is this inversion that allowed Herbert Marcuse, struggling to dissociate Hegel from the far right, to claim that Italian Fascism served as an extreme case of a weak rather than a strong state understood in Hegelian terms:

> Hegel's deified state by no means parallels the Fascist one. The latter represents the very level of social development that Hegel's state is supposed to avoid, namely the direct totalitarian rule of special interests

over the whole. Civil society under Fascism rules the state; Hegel's state rules civil society.

(Marcuse, 1963, 216)

It should be kept in mind at all times that the Hegelian impartial state, completely exterior to all singularity (1820/1991, 275–276), has never existed either in or outside of Europe. It was imagined as a regulative horizon of ongoing political struggles and as such can be a legitimate tool for theorizing the Brazilian and, more broadly, Latin American political modernity.

From this perspective, *The War* reads as a critique of the weak Brazilian state which cannot prevent certain groups (Epaminondas Gonçalves' Progressivist Republican Party, the middle-class reading public of the *Jornal de Notícias* and *A República*) within it from ruling, instead of governing them on equal terms alongside other groups integrative of that society. In the passage from the empire to the republic, the state de facto failed to grant equal rights to its subjects and thus mobilized the model of co-opt citizenship. According to Oxhorn (this volume), from the 19th century onward, state–civil society interactions in Latin America have resulted in the predominance of the model of co-opt citizenship based on the "process of controlled inclusion." The war between Canudos and the allied São Paulo and Rio de Janeiro commenced because the illiterate inhabitants of the rural Bahia had been consistently excluded from public debates.

According to Robert Fine, the Hegelian model of civil society eventually attempted to integrate contextual (free market economy) interests of civil society units with the state's policing over potential rights violations:

As the sphere of 'difference' between the family and the state in the formation of ethical life, civil society was a complex social and historical phenomenon, irreducible to any one of its aspects ... Hegel sought to grasp it as a differentiated whole: *the sphere of conflicting relations between needs and rights, policing and association.*

(Fine, 1997, 20–21)

In the novel, the Hegelian equilibrium "between needs and rights, policing and association" is disturbed in favor of excessive policing that is not nonetheless identified with a strong state in the sense of a disinterested normative institution. On the contrary, competing political parties recur to old-fashioned intrigues to usurp power while emerging media technologies make use of populist ideology to manipulate public opinion. By bringing together Hegel's political theory and the collectivist approach to civil society, this chapter explores civil war as a collapse of a dynamic, differentiated whole of conflicting relations between civil society and the state into a homogenous institution of selective citizenry.

The dissidence of Conselheiro's group, which I consider an act of civil disobedience, is a *vox clamantis* in *sertão* and as such is found incompatible with the ideal of modernization, a self-legitimating project of the Brazilian Republic. In the end, their spontaneous attempts at self-organization flounder due to direct violent intervention on the part of the state. Falsely accusing the aristocratic elites of collaboration with Conselheiro's group and on the grounds of the old elites' incompatibility with liberal values, the state redistributes their land, political influence, and monetary capital among the emergent political players. These contradictory processes marked the onset of political modernity in Brazil. Once violently severed from the wider social body, Conselheiro's group cannot function as an efficient civil organization and therefore entertains the utopia of an independent, self-governed commune.

The Canudos commune stages a divergent junction between the Hegelian and Marxist models of society, transported beyond their time and place of origin. Marx criticized the Hegelian idea of the conflictive equilibrium as anti-revolutionary since it constituted a sort of theoretical competitor to Marx's own proposition of the proletarian class struggle. Both Hegel's civil society and Marx's proletariat claimed to advocate for people's rights, freedoms, and social justice. In a footnote to the "Critique of Hegel's Doctrine of the State," Marx first discarded the model of civil society (1843/1975, 59). Only a few months later in "A Contribution to the Critique of Hegel's *Philosophy of Right*: Introduction," Marx offered a construct of the proletariat that "fraternizes and fuses with society in general," full of "enthusiasm" (1844/1975, 254). The proletariat was meant to redeem the unjust antagonistic past, end up with particular interests of different classes, and engage in the pursuit of universal well-being at the expense of group/class social heterogeneity. In other words, Marx advocated for the annihilation of inequalities and for the subsequent homogeneity of social structures.

The novel sympathizes with the Hegelian model of civil society. Through its heavy investment in Utopia, the Canudos commune conjures up the uncanny—never quite coinciding with itself—specter of communism. While a sober and detached narrative voice chronicles how communal life suppresses people's immediate interests and puts the individual under erasure, the critique of the Canudos commune extends metonymically to that of the Latin American political left. However, Vargas Llosa did not stop short on communism: all of the novel's principal structural elements, such as religious fanaticism, communism, and the ideology of statism, get in dangerous proximity with narcotics and operate as if under the sign of intoxication. Since traditional political players fall under the suspicion of intoxication, the text fails to provide an unequivocal answer to the question of what forces, logic, and discourses cut short civil society on the continent. In this situation, the reader is compelled to generate political ideals beyond unsatisfying, repetitive historical experiences. Another effect of the figure of narcotic intoxication is due to the fact that narcotics substitute for the magic which has been routinely attributed to traditional communities. Narcotics, instead, are placed in between rural areas of production and urban centers of consumption, ancient methods of extraction and scientific advances of chemistry and pharmacology. The substitution, thus, destabilizes the habitual distribution of the modern and the archaic, the rational and the irrational between the capital cities and the countryside. This is significant because the easy dismissal of the local initiatives of territorially marginalized populations has constituted one of the basic challenges that civil societies face in Latin America. Nonetheless, the substitution does not assign any positive quality to the modern being, destabilizing the very opposition rather than redistributing its specific content. All of the above allowed Vargas Llosa to tackle civil society as a theoretical model in search of some alternative imagery, political ideals, and horizons for Latin America beyond communism and populism.

Last but not least, this chapter will consider how *The War* may be reread if the historical circumstances of its writing are taken into consideration. It will ask what parallels may be drawn between the Brazilian *sertão* and the Peruvian *sierra*, on the one hand, and the act of civil disobedience of Conselheiro's group and insurgent guerrillas of the self-proclaimed Communist Party of Peru (Shining Path), on the other. This way, the novel articulates the guerrilla warfare of the 20th century as the "side effect" of long-lasting political exclusions.

Errant "Third Place"

The adopted approach automatically evades the issue of what is closer to the civil society model—the Canudos resistance or citizens' voluntary participation in the fratricidal war. The preliminary answer is neither of them. What could have constituted a sort of cornerstone for the formation of civil society is Conselheiro's group before any repressive actions against it were taken on behalf of the state. That is why I argue that the Canudos commune is not relevant per se for the authorial voice of *The War*. For Vargas Llosa, the settlement of Conselheiro's group is not the opening of space for a future community. It is rather the reduction of free agency, civil incentives and "functionally based community" which form part of a live social fabric, to the enclosed place of a self-governing and self-sufficient commune, albeit totally excluded from local and national politics.

From this perspective, the beginning of the story is highly suggestive. Conselheiro's group originates amid the arid *sertão* of Bahia as an errant "third place" (Ray Oldenburg) in the sense that it provides the poor populace, involved in exhausting work and family duties on a daily basis, with voluntary communal activities and recreation. First alone and later accompanied by his followers, Antônio Conselheiro shifts back and forth from town to town and engages locals in church restorations and cemetery reformations. Sometimes he preaches from the pulpit, but more often than not he is denied access to the congregation because his extravagant prophecies do not fit seamlessly into the official teachings of the Catholic Church. Instead, at dusk, when the work is finished and the children are asleep, he entertains *sertanejos* with his counsel at what vaguely resembles public squares (Vargas Llosa, 1984, 4). His counsel literally centers the world and history in a metaphysical apocalyptic sense around everyday local experiences.[4]

Having accumulated some symbolic power, Conselheiro starts seeking political participation. First, he gains his moral authority over the gangs of *cangaceiros* (Vargas Llosa, 1984, 16–17). With the establishment of the republic, he finally finds the edge for his critical platform. It is favored by the fact that peons and cowherds do not appear emotionally moved by grand political battles over the displacement of zones of economic and political influence from the first Brazilian capital of Salvador of Bahia in the north, to São Paulo and Rio de Janeiro in the south. The turning point comes when the republic, which so far had not contributed anything to the region, implements changes in local governance without consulting the people's opinion. Following the separation of church and state, cemeteries become municipal, weddings become civil, and a census and the metric system are introduced. At this stage, the public finds itself farther removed from any meaningful social participation because they do not understand these modern institutions.

A new taxation system provokes a different sort of reaction. Instinctively, people are enraged that money and produce will be taken away for purposes unknown to them. Moreover, to enforce the new policies, there will be tax collectors, and public opinion pronounces that they will become a bigger problem for the region than the brigands and police brigades combatting them. Conselheiro joins the indignant crowd that is as if at a prepolitical stage: its demands have not yet been articulated but there is already a sense of common interests involved. That is why Conselheiro compares the crowd to a "speechless" colony of insects: for him, people gathered at Natuba's main square emit "a sound like angry wasps buzzing" (Vargas Llosa, 1984, 21). At this crucial moment, he articulates their protests in an extravagant monarchist jargon and pulls down the decrees from the walls of the town hall.

However conservative, Conselheiro's stance against the republic can be seen as a political technology of self-empowerment. By defending the Emperor Dom Pedro and his daughter, Isabel, the *jagunços* claim that they do not break the law but rather restore and protect it from the illegitimate usurpers. According to Hannah Arendt, "[t]he law can indeed stabilize and legalize change once it has occurred but the change itself is always the result of extralegal action" (Arendt, 1972, 80). The passage from the monarchy to the republic in 1889 was this extralegal action which brought to power a new majority, claiming to represent a homogenous whole of the consolidated nation. Such a fraudulent representation concealed the exclusion of the poor rural inhabitants of Bahia and other northern regions, meanwhile the pro-government groups from São Paulo and Rio de Janeiro monopolized the law. In this situation, a position from which the inhabitants of Bahia can speak is that of rhetorically returning in time to the moment when the passage of sovereignty occurred and questioning its legitimacy. Their inverted act of civil disobedience, a sort of empty signifier, sets off the first military expedition against the errant group. Pushed to settle down in the backlands town of Canudos, Conselheiro's group finds itself in an ambiguous situation. On the one hand, it is being gradually severed from the wider social body, while on the other, it is continuously growing in number as those excluded from the nation find their place in the commune.

Political Sympathies in Context

The intradiegetic, political part of the story—in the sense of the potential participation of *sertanejos* in decision-making on local and national levels—ends with the seclusion of Conselheiro's group in Canudos. It may look like the history of civil society in 19th-century Brazil ended before it had properly begun. Still, the mood of *The War* does not degrade easily into melancholy—the story is brimming with effort, hectic activity, ecstatic petty individual and communal triumphs, and symbolic victories of Canudos. I claim that the remainder of the story is there to praise the commune as the only available 'outlet valve.' Given the circumstances, when the state denies any meaningful form of interaction to its population, all of the latter's energy and free will are invested in the sociopolitical forms that are "handy."[5]

From the start, it may look like an improbable development that, at the time when the Shining Path violently entered the Peruvian political horizon,[6] Vargas Llosa wrote a novel in which he sympathized with the fanatic commune of Canudos and positioned himself politically against the supposedly liberal Brazilian Republic.[7] Now, the situation is further aggravated since Vargas Llosa's literary career is usually envisioned in periods, according to his political preferences: socialist; pro-Cuban, as opposed to neo/liberal; and pro-Western. In this case, does it mean that *The War* still, anachronistically, belongs to the first period? The answer is, as I argue, a definite 'no;' however, to arrive at this conclusion, several points should be taken into consideration.

First, scholars cannot agree on whether Vargas Llosa's political divorce from the socialist platform in the 1970s produced a simultaneous narrative rupture in his treatment of social interactions.[8] According to Juan De Castro and Nicholas Birns, *The War* marked the paradigmatic shift in Vargas Llosa's poetical sensitivity (2010, 5). In *The Time of the Hero*, *The Green House*, and *Conversation in the Cathedral* his poetics are identified with leftist politics, supportive of the Cuban Revolution. Then, there is a transitory "humoristic" passage in *Captain Pantoja and the Special Service* and *Aunt Julia and the Scriptwriter*, followed by an eventual anchor in the "democratic Right" and neoliberal ethos from *The War* onward (2010, 6). However convincing this tripartite personal chronology looks like, it is notable that Vargas Llosa's interest in a self-organizing and conflictive society, persistently interrupted by the direct or indirect intervention of external authority, has been consistent throughout his writing career; it can be traced as far back as *The Time of the Hero*. Already in his first novel, the Leoncio Prado Military Academy is not a precarious contingent cadet community. Instead, the military academy presented a conflicting array of personal and group affiliations, their constant groupings and regroupings meant to better facilitate the pursuit of situation-dependent interests. In other words, Vargas Llosa's first novel can be read as an inquiry into social relations not based on 'thick' attachments (e.g., class, race, gender, religion, profession, etc.) but rather constituted in relation and in response to the presence of an institutional and pedagogic authority. Set in a different geo-temporal context, differing in ultimate consequences and in scope, *The War* nonetheless shares with the first Vargas Llosa novel a preoccupation for conflictive social interactions.

Second, on numerous occasions Vargas Llosa considered the accommodation of interests in a broad sense a principal mobilizing political agent. For instance, this premise underlies his foreword to Hernando de Soto's economic treatise *The Other Path*.[9] Written in defense of free market economy, the foreword asserts that in Peru the black market is less of a problem than the state for it simply signals malfunctions of the latter (Vargas Llosa, 1989, xiv). The foreword invites parallels between the unchecked enthusiasm for the "path taken by the black-marketeers" (1989, xix) and the sympathy aroused by the Canudos commune. Hastily equating the black-marketeers to the poor, Vargas Llosa writes:

> The system invents laws to frustrate the legitimate desires of the people to hold jobs and have a roof over their heads. What should the masses do? Stop living, in the name of a legality which in many ways is unreal and unjust? No. They have simply renounced legality. They go out on the streets to sell whatever they can, they set up their shops, and they build their houses on the hillsides or in vacant lots.
>
> (1989, xviii–xix)

As the black-marketeers in this account respond to bare economic necessities, *jagunços* similarly act in accordance to their needs and interests.[10] Vargas Llosa regards the Canudos commune as a forced and doomed form of civil organization because, as books III and IV reveal, the people's creative capacities are misled.

Despite the resonances, it is worth noting that the scenario that Vargas Llosa envisioned in the novel is far less simplistic than the one offered by de Soto and embraced by the author of *The War* just some five years later. In the foreword the black-marketeers are not complex human beings since they function in complete accordance with commercial expediency. This explains their absolute political opportunism. An easy prey to populism, the black-marketeers allegedly supported practically anything on the political spectrum from military dictators to the democratic Right to the revolutionary Left (de

Soto, 1989, xix). By means of this discursive gesture, Vargas Llosa homogenized any differences among the black-marketeers (why should they form a single voting bloc in the first place?) and presented them as a completely regulable, apolitical group. At this level, no negotiations with the state are sought, which in a way frees the hands of the political elites and allows them to quietly govern the populations of informal entrepreneurs. It is in this sense that the foreword is more neoliberal while *The War* keeps considerable links to the liberal humanism of the 19th century.[11]

Traditional liberal humanism concurrently conflicts with Vargas Llosa's sympathy for the Canudos commune. In a deconstructive demeanor, at the same time as the text generates the sympathy, it undoes its own operations. *The War* leaves an aftertaste of dislike for communal values and their degrading effects on the individual. Birns claims that *The War*'s radical difference from da Cunha's 'original' consists in the narrative treatment of a character. For da Cunha, "the vantage point is abstract, unindividuated – the 'him' is not Conselheiro but the *jagunço as a combatant and, even more, as a sociological phenomenon*" (2010, 76). Meanwhile, Vargas Llosa "is both repelled by and admires the rebels of Canudos" as individuals capable of improvement and moral growth (Birns, 2010, 76). I agree that from the onset of *The War*, the backlands characters are much more differentiated than da Cunha's prototypical *jagunço*. At the same time, the transformative effects of the Canudos commune on its members should not pass unnoticed: in the course of the book, *jagunços* rather "un-become" individuals. In Vargas Llosa's account, the commune is granted huge potential to reshape subjectivities in accord with their life stories and internal necessities. Still, the undergone transformations often resemble symbolic erasure. This process is doubled in the narration itself. On the one hand, at the end of the novel there is almost a literal erasure of Canudos from the surface of modern Brazil. The erasure will continue up until the 1970s when the settlement of Canudos will be inundated and, therefore, its elaborate underground architecture finally effaced.[12] On the other hand, the often repulsive "previous" selves of many *sertanejos* (e.g., Satan/Abbot João, Big João, Pajeú, Pedrão, the Vilanovas, Maria Quadrado, the Lion of Natuba) patently exceed the virtuous but are ultimately dull replicas of each other that appear in Canudos. A lot of work, which goes beyond the moment of conscious conversion, is required in order to supersede their old personalities. The traces of their previous selves—emblematized by Pajeú's scar—often prove insurmountable: they only fade away over time as the jagunços "un-become" themselves, often losing their family or sexual proximities for the benefit of a common cause. Controversially, they become heroes in the epic sense but also an identitarian community, a mere place, Canudos.

Utopianism and Intoxications

The middle-class inhabitants of São Paulo and Rio de Janeiro portray the enemy image of the *jagunços* as fanatic, obsolete, and unskillful; therefore, unable to use the proper technology of warfare and in need of external help (Vargas Llosa, 1984, 24, 129, 380). The narrator of *The War* attenuates the charges of obsoleteness and unskillfulness (Vargas Llosa, 1984, 216, 376). However, the same does not occur with fanaticism: under the benevolent gaze, the latter mutates into utopianism. Utopianism is different from fanaticism inasmuch as it is not the question of whether one's critical abilities are extremely limited by the excess of pre-fixed ideas or beliefs that totally determines one's line of conduct. Utopianism cancels immediate interests and needs in favor of common shared ideals whose realization is infinitely postponed. That is to say ideals, although more situation-dependent and flexible than in the case of fanaticism, contaminate and ultimately suppress the sphere of immediate interests. In turn, this suppression provokes unchecked enthusiasm leading to political activism.

In *The Archaic Utopia: José María Arguedas and the Fictions of Indigenism*, Vargas Llosa cited a revealing point from José Carlos Mariátegui's foreword to *Tempest in the Andes*: "It is not civilization, not the alphabet of white people that arouses the soul of the Indian. It is the myth, the idea of the socialist revolution. The indigenous hope is absolutely revolutionary" (cit. in Vargas Llosa, 1996, 68). That is to say, the hypothetical indigenous revolution needs an unchecked, mythical amount of belief that would "arouse the soul" in order to level any immediacy and mobilize people as a consolidated rather than a conflictive whole. This way, there can be traced a sort of precarious agreement between Mariátegui and Vargas Llosa on the nature of communism in Latin America: the radical schism between the two consists of where they position themselves in relation to it (inside or out, in favor or against).

The uneasy association between the Canudos commune and communism is staged and subsequently mocked in the novel's plot. This association is dismissed at the very moment of being established since it comes from an unreliable source. It is proposed and readily exported to Europe by one of the most tragicomic characters, the Scottish militant anarchist, communist, and devoted phrenologist, Galileo Gall. Despite never having been to Canudos, Gall writes laudatory "chronicles" about the commune for the Lyons leftist periodical *L'Etincelle de la Révolte*. In the beginning, Gall relies solely on his conversation with a Capuchin friar. The latter, upon his visit to Canudos, concludes that: "They [jagunços] are irreconcilable enemies of society. They are agitated, all excited. They shout, they interrupt each other in order to utter what strikes the ears of a Christian as the most egregious nonsense" (Vargas Llosa, 1984, 47). On the other hand, this allegedly revolutionary excitement of the people is exactly what attracts Gall, who seeks direct political participation by any means. Extremely biased, he believes that "Canudos has instituted the regime of communal property" and "marriage and money have been done away with" there (Vargas Llosa, 1984, 48). This is far removed from the socioeconomic structure of the religious commune to which the reader—unlike Gall—gets close access. Paradoxically, on the poetical level, it is precisely

Gall's grotesque enthusiasm, which—despite the escalating absurdities—draws even closer association between the religious commune of Canudos and communism in Latin America and beyond. It is at this point in the text that communism comes into dangerous proximity with Christian millennialism through the construct of intoxication.

Here the term intoxication is used in a broad sense, understood beyond "the religious ecstasies or the ecstasies of drugs" (Benjamin, 1999, 209); as a bodily experience that leads to the "loosening of the self" (Benjamin, 1999, 208). According to Walter Benjamin, the loosening of the self, suggested by the Greek etymology of *ek-stasis*, creates a very specific political collectivity, driven in its actions by a trance-like experience of freedom. In Vargas Llosa's account, the situation is more complex than the one theorized by Benjamin. Benjamin relied more on one, so to say, emancipatory side of intoxication. But what, asks *The War*, if intoxication is induced purposefully? What if ideals that make people forget their immediate interests are sold under one wrap with the designed experience of freedom that on any occasion should be confused with the freedom of choice? There is never time for an informed decision to be taken for just as readily as one is "thrown into the world" (Martin Heidegger), one finds oneself already intoxicated.

In late 19th-century Latin America, besides communism and Christian millennialism, there was another player that tried "to win the energies of intoxication" (Benjamin, 1999, 215–216): the modern nation-state. Not the Hegelian normative state but the extremely protean formation which, through education and propaganda, positivist science and populist rhetoric pretended to annihilate the mediating capacity of civil society and equate the ruling majority interests with those of the imagined nation. In *The War*, intoxication is disputed among bohemian artistic circles—represented by the nearsighted journalist (whose prototype was da Cunha), heretical commune, and the modern state. However, they are not totally commensurable. In the two former cases, it seems as though intoxication emerged from the inside and was closer to Benjamin's emancipatory version. Meanwhile the idiom of statism intrudes from the outside. To shroud nascent institution of co-opt citizenship, it resorts to the extremely rampant populist rhetoric. On the other hand, it relied on the institution of positivist science that by definition is sober but creates a huge intoxicating utopia of progress, injected into urban masses.

The storyline of Jurema is the most literal example that covers all of the above main competitors over the energies of intoxication. In *The War*, Jurema is the female character that is the implicit hub of the narration. Raised at the *hacienda* in Calumbi and secretly loved by the wife of the head of the Bahia Autonomist Party, Baron de Canabrava (Vargas Llosa, 1984, 502), she is first married to Rufino, Gall's guide to the *sertão*. Gall's seemingly firm beliefs about the need to sacrifice his sexual energy for the cause of the imminent revolution succumb in the presence of Jurema. Raped by the Scotsman, she becomes his involuntary companion for some time, until she ends up in Canudos—secretly desired and at the same time reverently worshipped by Pajeú and in passionate love with the nearsighted journalist. When the Baron de Canabrava learns that due to Jurema the nearsighted journalist discovered happiness in Canudos in the midst of massacre (Vargas Llosa, 1984, 501–504), her pivotal role in the narration is exposed:

> He [the Baron] suddenly had the absurd feeling that the former maid-servant of Calumbi was the only woman in the *sertão*, a female under whose fateful spell all the men with any sort of connection to Canudos unconsciously fell sooner or later.
>
> (Vargas Llosa, 1984, 506)

Vargas Llosa reminds his readers that the proper name of Jurema is also that of the tree, *Acacia jurema*, whose bark is notorious for its psychedelic effects (Vargas Llosa, 1984, 329). Like the tree bark, the woman's irresistible spells lead to a state of intoxication.

This ambivalence of Jurema is all the more compelling if it is recalled that the *jurema* tree initially appeared in *Os Sertões* where it implicitly opposed the positivist science. In *Os Sertões*, narcotics already breached open a political domain that Vargas Llosa would take over and rearticulate in *The War*. According to Adriana Johnson, narcotics largely inebriated da Cunha's narrative style (2004, 232–233). His scientific journalistic style collapsed in response to the narcotic discourse in the process of the poetic exploration of the *sertão*. In a proto-phenomenological move, the narcotic discourse urged da Cunha to abandon the bulk of positivist knowledge about the region. For him, magic and narcotics distort the logic of the *sertão*; they transform the desert into a paradise (da Cunha, 1902/1980, 32–33). Far from a simple fraudulent effect on the minds of the *sertanejos*, narcotics radically change power dynamics in the region. They become an indelible inscription on the bodies of those who experience the *jurema* but also—through a metonymical displacement—of those who experience the *sertão*. As a result, narcotics suspend any rigid political affiliations in the backlands.

Despite Efraín Kristal's influential reading, it is not as if in *The War* Jurema had stopped functioning as an idiosyncratic narcotic from the *sertão* to fully metamorphose into a mobile narrative femme fatale. Kristal sustains that:

> Vargas Llosa utilized *Rebellion in the Backlands* and other sources in crafting a work of fiction but with no intention to be faithful to Brazilian history or any of his research materials…. An instructive example is his transmutation of the sections in *Rebellion in the Backlands* in which da Cunha mentions the "Jurema," a plant the natives of the backlands use as a narcotic to relieve fatigue. Da Cunha describes the plant as "yielding but impenetrable." Its thickets slow the movement

of people through the backlands. Vargas Llosa used the name of the plant and transforms the botanical description into a female character: the woman of golden skin for whom the circumlocution "yielding but impenetrable" is aptly suited for Vargas Llosa's purposes.

(1998, 129)

Although Kristal mentioned both fanaticism and Jurema in the same paragraph (a few lines above the cited excerpt, fanaticism is identified as the main cause of the war of Canudos), he did not pursue any connections between the two. Paraphrasing, Kristal does not consider fanaticism/utopianism in *The War* to be the effect of intoxication. Such a reading may owe to the essential discrepancy between da Cunha's enthusiastic and Vargas Llosa's skeptical treatment of narcotics.

Vargas Llosa had to dissociate narcotics from the magic. The latter is generally perceived as archaic while narcotics easily transgress the "two Brazils" (urban and rural). Since the positivist Brazilian nation-state sought "disenchantment" (Max Weber) and literally expelled the sorcerers into the last redoubt of Canudos (Vargas Llosa, 1984, 87), any recourse to magical realism would have reiterated the logic of this symbolic partition. In contrast, the modern state relied on the pharmaceutical industry for its own legitimation: in the novel, this motive emerges when the Brazilian Republic fails to treat and soothe the pain of its injured subjects (Vargas Llosa, 1984, 447–453). Prior to his trip to Canudos, the nearsighted journalist had already been initiated into opium (prescribed by the science), ether (routinely abused by the artists), and *candomblé* rituals (preserving the mythical archive). While it may be seen as an inebriating habit, the journalist actually faithfully followed the letter of science that prescribed opium to relieve his excessive sneezing (Vargas Llosa, 1984, 288). Running out of opium amidst the war, the nearsighted journalist fell in love with Jurema. Depending on the preferred reading strategy, the love story of Jurema and the nearsighted journalist can be interpreted as a simple switch from opium to another, more powerful and socially acceptable drug. Their very relationship oscillates among emancipatory, elusive, and normalizing: it protects the couple from surrounding atrocities only to eventually inscribe them into a new symbolic family of the nation. *The War* figuratively demonstrates that in all three cases (Christian millennialism, communism, and the modern state), the liberated and deposited elsewhere psychic energy disguises the economy of sacrifice.

In Conclusion: What Emerges from the "Fog of War?"

The War constitutes an extremely paradoxical narrative due to its unwieldy apparatus of 'happy ending.' In the beginning, the reader encounters Brazil torn apart between antagonistic impulses of unification and decentralization, republicanism and monarchism, semi-presidential and military systems of government.[13] As the story unfolds, Brazil becomes a consolidated nation-state while separatism, monarchy, and the threat of military dictatorship fade into the dark of history, yielding place to their allegedly progressive counterparts (Vargas Llosa, 1984, 283, 345–349, 533–534, 541).[14] The economic prosperity of the former slave-owning aristocracy shrinks considerably and the freedom of expression goes as if uncontested. On the micro level, this unexpectedly happy ending is doubled by two accounts. First, by the sexual gratification that Baron de Canabrava eventually achieves after many years of repressed desires, and second, by the emotional accord that the nearsighted journalist enjoys with Jurema. As if unwillingly, the war of Canudos also finishes off with gangs of *cangaceiros* and subsequent police raids that both used to impoverish the region alongside natural plagues (Vargas Llosa, 1984, 57). In the end, the two belligerent parties achieve their ultimate goals. Symbolism suggests that some 30,000 massacred people—women and children among them (Vargas Llosa, 1984, 562)—appear even more victorious than the Brazilian army. The book ends with a symbolic victory of Abbot João over Colonel Macedo, who had been hunting the former leader of *cangaceiros* for decades. From the perspective of demolished Canudos and that of the army, Abbot João finally escapes the commanding officer of the Bahia Police Volunteer Battalion. An old surviving woman, "encircled by the eyes of the women prisoners," affirms that "[a]rchangels took him up to heaven" (Vargas Llosa, 1984, 568). Although there is a sense of ecstatic triumph on both sides, it is not quite the same. It is meant to be read with a grain of common sense which gradually disappears in the narrative, to the point that the implied reader cannot easily take sides. Besides the "barbaric" unnecessary hecatomb in Canudos, the problem with the supposedly progressive Brazil is that it is an antecedent of the contemporary situation on the continent where the model of citizenship as co-optation has precluded non-violent development of state–society interactions.

The civility of the creole society, consisting of the inhabitants of São Paulo and Rio de Janeiro, is questionable. One of the most intriguing moments of the novel is that the war of Canudos was never won by the regular army. Instead, the intoxicating ideology, the cause of the Bahian *sertões*, mobilizes masses of supposedly free and conscious citizens:

> …the vast national mobilization to punish the *jagunços*, the sending of battalions from all the states, the forming of corps of volunteers, the fairs and the public raffles at which ladies auctioned off their jewels and locks of their hair to raise money to outfit new companies about to march to defend the Republic.
>
> (Vargas Llosa, 1984, 382–383)

The foundational event of this modern society, apart from the 'barbaric' Canudos, are violent acts directed at members of the Monarchist Party, in particular those owning newspaper offices. The event is claimed as 'foundational' due to the appearance on the scene of an urban crowd. A series of images of this crowd seeks to be called revolutionary: a crowd of demonstrators who "parade down the Rua Marquês ... carrying posters calling for his [the Viscount of Ouro Preto's] head as the person responsible for the defeat of the republic at Canudos" (Vargas Llosa, 1984, 380). In addition, there are images of "[t]he demonstrations, the closing of stores and theaters, the flags at half-staff and the black crepe on the balconies, the attacks on newspaper offices, the assaults" (Vargas Llosa, 1984, 382). However, this crowd does not constitute a sort of civil society at which Conselheiro's group aimed before its seclusion in Canudos, since the crowd's interests completely oppose the public opinion dictated by propaganda.

In the full swing of propaganda, and due to unrestricted belief in the print word, the crowd is unable to see that its actions and fury do not serve the interests of the republic (which, in turn, are hardly those of city inhabitants). Public interests are not threatened by Canudos while demonstrations only suit interests of particular political parties. Active public participation results in putting Epaminondas Gonçalves' Progressivist Republican Party at the forefront, while defeating the Baron de Canabrava's Autonomist Party in the Province of Bahia. It also contributes to the commercial success of certain periodicals. The irony becomes bitter when the defenders of republican values, claiming to be emancipated and open-minded, find themselves among soldiers of the regular army and are forced into severe physical and mental discipline, as seen in the episode in which the First Brigade, consisting not only of professional soldiers but of regiments of enthusiastic volunteers, leaves for Canudos. Its departure is preceded by floggings of Private Queluz whose punishment is suggestively provoked by his undisciplined homosexuality (Vargas Llosa, 1984, 376–378).

The War takes us on a circular detour. Four times along the routes vanishing in the desert, the readers follow the restless Brazilian army in its quest for civil society, belonging, freedom, and justice. The irony reaches its zenith when we realize that what emerges from the fog of war is the present day Latin America; its own quest for civil society, belonging, freedom, and justice being superimposed on the triumphant military parade and wars of exclusion. All roads lead to Canudos, a non-place under erasure that encompasses the dynamic structure and main pitfalls of associational life. By bringing together Vargas Llosa and Hegel, this chapter calls for dissociating civil society in Latin America from necessarily urban centers and political vanguards. Without Vargas Llosa, Conselheiro's errant group would be another religious millennial commune—anthropologically distant, bizarre, and exotic. Without Hegel, there would persist a false opposition between the individual and the collective. For Hegel, the associational dimension is fundamental to modern life; however, by regarding it as partially abstracted and negotiable, he claimed that it is preceded by particular interests. It is this little gap between singularity and commonality where the novel closely checks for any signs of intoxication to ensure that the operative society does not annul the singularity.

Notes

1 For primary reference sources of *The War*, see Leopoldo Bernucci's detailed study (1989, 7–16).

2 Unless otherwise indicated, translations of Spanish originals are my own.

3 Nicholas Birns provides some basic glossary, useful for reading *Os Sertões* as well as *The War*:

> Its Portuguese title, *Os Sertões*, refers to the geographical terrain around the town of Canudos, in Bahia. The *sertanejos* are the inhabitants of the *sertão* in general; the jagunços are those inhabitants constituted into bands in armed rebellion supporting the utopian visions of Conselheiro.
>
> (2010, 83)

Additionally, the term *cangaceiros* is used to refer to the bands of poor peasants who plundered the *sertões* since the early 19th century; during the war of Canudos many former *cangaceiros* identified with Conselheiro's cause and joined the ranks of *jagunços*.

4 This effect is achieved by the constant switch from a solemn grandiloquent to a familiar, colloquial register (Vargas Llosa, 1984, 4–5).

5 It is the freewill, in Spanish, '*libre albedrío*,' whose loss, according to Estrella Sadhalá in *The Feast of the Goat*, is the major consequence of Rafael Trujillo's dictatorship (Vargas Llosa, 2000, 190–191).

6 It should be acknowledged that *The War* project precedes chronologically the guerrilla war waged by the Shining Path. The outbreak of the guerrilla war dates to May, 1980 but it is not until the end of 1981 that the government declared an emergency zone in the departments controlled by the Shining Path. However, the leftist revolutionary groups have been active in Peru since the 1960s and from the very beginning Vargas Llosa was aware of their agendas and proposed violent methods of struggle (Vargas Llosa, 2004, 143).

7 Fanaticism is announced from the preliminaries of the Spanish edition which include a full-length male portrait entitled *O Fanatico Antonio Conselheiro*.

8 For the nuanced analysis of Vargas Llosa's political alliances, see Efraín Kristal (1998, 99–123).

9 Another example is Vargas Llosa's celebration of the chichi culture that rose in response to economic challenges in the liminal space of shanty towns (1996, 327–336).

10 In this sense, Conselheiro does not confront Antônio Vilanova's merchant calculations and reasoning with transcendent values but rather insists that Antônio has not "learnt to count" properly (Vargas Llosa, 1984, 79, 81, 329).

11 Juan De Castro's is a useful distinction in this case. He writes that "neoliberalism – while still nominally supportive of individual rights and representative democracy – is weighed in favour of free markets, frequently even to the detriment of individual rights and democracy" (2011, 7).

12 This moment is of extreme importance in the novel given the fact that Conselheiro's preaching at the beginning of the novel (Vargas Llosa, 1984, 5) seems completely incongruous to today's reader. Since all the dates have already expired, the reader distances herself from the events in Canudos on the grounds of being better informed. However, Vargas Llosa reserved one last ironic smile for himself and for the inaccessible history of the region. As he discovered during his journey to the state of Bahia, "the reason for the war was also still much alive" (1991, 136). This reason finds its legitimacy in the fact that everyone can see with their eyes that Conselheiro's prophesies—among them the inundation of the desert Canudos—have become true (1991, 136).

13 For instance, Colonel Moreira Cesar dreams of establishing "a Dictatorial

Republic." The text puns his desire for unlimited power as he seeks a transition of power from Church to Army; more precisely into Caesar's—that is his own, Moreira Cesar's—hands (1984, 145–146).

14 Not necessarily in reality as none of the above-mentioned antagonistic impulses disappeared during the First Brazilian Republic and many have had repercussions in the political scene to date.

References

Arendt, Hannah. 1972. *Crises of the Republic: lying in politics; civil disobedience; on violence; thoughts on politics and revolution.* New York: Harcourt Brace Jovanovich.

Benjamin, Walter. 1999. "Surrealism: The Last Snapshot of the European Intelligentsia." In *Selected writings: Volume 2, 1927–1934.* Cambridge, Mass: Belknap Press. (Original Publication 1929.)

Bernucci, Leopoldo M. 1989. *Historia de un malentendido: un estudio transtextual de la guerra del fin del mundo de Mario Vargas Llosa.* New York: Peter Lang.

Birns, Nicholas. 2010. "Appropriation in the Backlands: Is Mario Vargas Llosa at War with Euclides da Cunha?" In N. Birns & J. De Castro (Eds.). *Vargas Llosa and Latin American politics.* New York: Palgrave Macmillan.

Da Cunha, Euclides. 1980. *Los sertones.* (W.N. Galvão, Trans.). Caracas, Venezuela: Biblioteca Ayacucho. (Original publication 1902.)

De Castro, Juan. 2011. *Mario Vargas Llosa: public intellectual in neoliberal Latin America.* Tucson: University of Arizona Press.

De Castro, Juan, & Nicholas Birns. 2010. "Introduction." In N. Birns & J. De Castro (Eds.). *Vargas Llosa and Latin American politics.* New York: Palgrave Macmillan.

Fine, Robert. 1997. "Civil Society Theory, Enlightment and Critique." In R. Fine & S. Rai (Eds.). *Civil society: democratic perspectives.* London: Frank Cass.

Hegel, G.W.F. 1991. *Elements of the philosophy of right.* Allen W. Wood (Ed.). (H.B. Nisbet, Trans.). Cambridge: Cambridge University Press. (Original publication 1820.)

Johnson, Adriana. 2004. "*The War of the End of the World* or the End of Ideology." *Journal of Latin American Cultural Studies*, 13 (2), 221–241.

Kristal, Efraín. 1998. *Temptation of the word: the Novels of Mario Vargas Llosa.* Nashville: Vanderbilt University Press.

Marcuse, Herbert. 1963. *Reason and revolution: Hegel and the rise of social theory.* New York: Humanities Press.

Marx, Karl. 1975. *Early writings.* New York: Vintage Books. (Works written 1843–1844.)

Vargas Llosa, Mario. 1984. *The war of the end of the world.* New York: Farrar Straus Giroux. (Original publication 1981.)

Vargas Llosa, Mario. 1986. *Contra viento y marea.* Vol. 2. Barcelona: Seix Barral.

Vargas Llosa, Mario. 1989. "Foreword." In Hernando de Soto and Instituto Libertad y Democracia (Lima, Peru). *The other path: the invisible revolution in the third world.* New York: Harper & Row.

Vargas Llosa, Mario. 1991. "The Author's Favorite of His Novels." In *A writer's reality.* Syracuse, NY: Syracuse University Press.

Vargas Llosa, Mario. 1994. *A fish in the water: a memoir.* New York: Farrar, Straus, Giroux.

Vargas Llosa, Mario. 1996. *La utopía arcaica: José María Arguedas y las ficciones del indigenismo*. México: Fondo de Cultura Económica.
Vargas Llosa, Mario. 2000. *La fiesta del chivo*. Madrid: Alfaguara.
Vargas Llosa, Mario. 2004. *Entrevistas escogidas*. Interviews by J. Coaguila. Peru: Fondo Editorial Cultura Peruana.

12 "Radical" Participatory Democracy Institutions in Venezuela and Ecuador

Strengthening Civil Society or Mechanisms for Controlled Inclusion?

Pascal Lupien

In the past decade, Latin America has witnessed a sudden increase in the formation of institutions designed to encourage and channel popular engagement in the political arena. Various types of participatory mechanisms have been embraced by actors across the political spectrum. Some of the governments behind these initiatives seek enhanced representation and more efficient governance, while certain left-leaning regimes have challenged the liberal representative model of democracy. In particular, those governments associated with the Bolivarian Alliance for the Americas (*Alianza Bolivariana para los Pueblos de Nuestra América*, ABLA)[1] have claimed a strong ideological commitment to "radical" participatory democracy. In order to implement this vision, these administrations have created local participatory mechanisms designed to be a space for civil society–state interaction. In contrast to the more 'liberal' participatory initiatives such as Bolivia's Popular Participation Law (LPP) and Brazil's participatory budgeting (PB) process (see Oxhorn, this volume), these new structures are not framed as instances of co-management between the state and civil society. Rather, they are presented as the centerpiece of a new political model in which "the people" play a leading role in the democratic process by participating through institutions that are simultaneously connected to the state yet independent from "traditional" authorities (see Venezuela, 2006, 2010; Ecuador, 2010). They draw on a collectivist definition of civil society and are promoted as having the capacity to enhance citizenship as agency. These mechanisms also lie at the intersection of civil society and community, as they provide a formal space for civil society to engage in local politics but are also deeply rooted in values of solidarity and mutual support between neighbors.

Not surprisingly, these initiatives have generated considerable debate. While seen as a move toward a more inclusive democracy by proponents, opposing groups and many academics argue that they are in fact a threat to established democratic institutions and to an independent civil society.

These criticisms are generally based on a liberal interpretation of democracy and reflect the aversion of many Western-influenced thinkers to models that emphasize collective over individual rights. As a result, analyses of these mechanisms often produce binary, normative interpretations that fail to recognize that some initiatives that diverge from the dominant liberal conception may be more appropriate to a particular time and place.

This chapter strives for a more balanced approach to assessing the positive and negative implications of "radical" participatory institutions for civil society and for citizenship as agency. It asks important questions that have not been adequately addressed in the literature: In what ways do participatory mechanisms in the context of "radical" participatory democracy affect civil society? To what extent do they encourage citizenship as agency as their proponents argue, or citizenship as cooptation as their critics charge? In order to strengthen civil society by providing participants with real powers and encourage citizenship as agency, participatory mechanisms must strike a delicate balance between autonomy and inclusion into political structures. If the latter is taken too far, it can lead to cooptation yet without direct links to the state civil society will likely be excluded from decision-making.

By focusing on Venezuela and Ecuador, two countries whose governments have expressed a commitment to "radical" participatory democracy, this analysis finds a mixed bag. Participatory institutions in these two countries provide significant opportunities for actors—particularly those from traditionally marginalized sectors—to engage in meaningful decision-making to an extent that is rarely seen elsewhere, including in more developed democracies. They allow these actors to exercise a degree of agency that was denied to them under traditional political structures. The danger is that design of these institutions creates relationships with the state that may simultaneously promote more inclusive decision-making while establishing parameters around democratic participation. Civil society organizations (as well as individuals) may only effectively exercise this newfound agency through state-sanctioned channels. The intention of "radical" participatory mechanisms may be to strengthen civil society and citizenship as agency, but the design of these mechanisms appears to be tipping the balance toward controlled inclusion.

Literature

An important current of the political science literature has emphasized the essential role that civil society must play in the construction and maintenance of democratic institutions. In the tradition of Tocqueville, these scholars argue that civil society fosters democratic norms among citizens and helps to establish the conditions for strong, effective representative institutions (Almond & Verba, 1963; Cohen & Arato, 1992; Diamond, 1992; Putnam, 1993; Cohen & Rogers, 1995). In contrast, others argue that certain elements of civil society may undermine rather than strengthen democracy. These authors point to inherent dangers of large numbers of people engaged in political activity outside of established procedures and rules (Kornhauser, 1959) or to the rise of fascism and more recent extremist movements from civil society (Berman, 1997; Booth & Richard, 1998; Chambers & Kopstein, 2001). It is therefore possible, then, that civil society can be used to undermine democratic governments, particularly when groups develop particularist notions that exclude members outside the group (Foley & Edwards, 1996; Chambers & Kopstein, 2001). Others worry that civil society may be incorporated into corporatist structures, thus reducing its autonomy and resulting in cooptation of individual activists and groups (Piven & Cloward, 1977; Rueschemeyer, Stephens, & Stephens, 1992; Diamond, 1999).

Much of this debate is related to the tension between popular participation in politics and more representative arrangements that can be traced back as far as Ancient Greece.[2] Throughout much of the 20th century, the mainstream literature advanced a 'minimalist' view of democracy in which mass participation is not a necessary criterion for democracy and is in fact undesirable and dangerous (Schumpeter, 1950; Crozier & Huntington, 1976). A number of theorists have rejected this minimalist framework, tracing the origins of this counter-hegemonic perspective to the "radical" democracy of Jean-Jacques Rousseau, for whom participation is not only about equitable decision-making but is the only legitimate means of exercising power (Rousseau, 1994 [1762]). More recently, critics of representative democracy have attempted to revive some of these ideas in a contemporary context. Carol Pateman (1974) stresses that the more an individual participates in decision-making (at home, the workplace, or in the political arena), the greater his or her sense of political efficacy. Involvement at the local level is seen as a good place to begin; participation in local decision-making is a means of "learning democracy", as it fosters "psychological qualities" required for participation at the national level as well as the development and practice of "democratic skills." Others emphasize participation as a means of achieving a more equitable distribution of public goods and services (Avritzer, 2002; Baiocchi, 2003; Fung, 2007; Goldfrank, 2011). A common criticism is that while the minimalist or 'low intensity' representative model leads to a disengaged citizenry and cynical perceptions of democracy itself, direct involvement in decision-making fosters an improved perception of the legitimacy of democracy and an increased sense of empowerment among participants, which should foster agency (Macpherson, 1977; Barber, 1984; Santos & Avritzer, 2005; Held, 2006; Smith, 2009).

The recent literature on participatory experiences in Venezuela and Ecuador reflects these tensions. When the people, or 'demos', like the supporters of leaders such as Hugo Chávez, are considered at all, it is assumed that they are emotional, easily manipulated, and poorly informed (Weyland, 2003; Petkoff, 2005; Castañeda, 2006; Castañeda & Morales, 2008; Rodríguez, 2008; Hausmann, 2013). The assumption is, therefore, that participatory mechanisms are mere instruments of the governing party by which it can control "friendly" civil society and weaken opposing groups (García-Guadilla, 2008). A handful of authors view the situation in Venezuela as more complex, and focus on experiences of participatory democracy at the local level. They tend to draw different conclusions from those who focus on central institutions of the state, often stressing the inclusion of actors who had never before been provided with opportunities to have their voices heard (Motta, 2009; Ellner, 2010; Smilde & Hellinger, 2011; Ponniah & Eastwood, 2011; McCarthy, 2012). However, little empirical research has been conducted to consider what is actually taking place at this level and the impact it has on citizenship.

Background and Institutional Design

Despite the growth of civil society organizations in Venezuela and Ecuador in the final decades of the 20th century, rigid political systems often prevented these actors from directly and effectively engaging in decision-making. Criticisms of the elitist nature of these systems allowed Hugo Chávez and Rafael Correa to gain mass support by portraying themselves as outsiders who would expand participation beyond the traditional circles of power. In both Venezuela and Ecuador, the participatory initiatives promoted by the Chávez and Correa administrations are more ambitious than the 'liberal' experiments in Bolivia and Brazil and are presented as a radical break with the past.

This chapter focuses on a particular type of participatory mechanism created by these governments: communal councils in Venezuela and local citizens' assemblies in Ecuador. The design of these mechanisms is similar: they are intended to be local deliberative bodies set up through citizens' own initiative and connected through regional organizations. They have local social and economic development, infrastructure, and neighborhood improvement as central to their functions and are intended to be spaces for citizens to engage in deliberation and decision-making about the issues that affect their lives (see Venezuela, 2006, 2010; Ecuador, 2010, 2010b). These "radical" participatory democracy mechanisms can be distinguished from the 'liberal' initiatives such as PB and the LPP in that they seek to institutionalize certain aspects of communities (mutual support, solidarity, communication) and state discourse emphasizes communitarian values over more efficient governance.

Venezuela

With the ascension to power of Chávez, the concept of popular democracy was enshrined in the 1999 constitution as a first step in the 'refounding' of the country's democracy. The opening Articles mention that the people's sovereignty must be exercised directly (Article 5), but Article 62 establishes a clearer definition of this 'new' democracy. It states that "the participation of the people in the elaboration, implementation and control of public matters is necessary to guarantee their complete development as individuals and collectively." The language used promotes active, participatory citizenship, with multiple references to solidarity, social equality, and communitarian values. The constitution also calls for the creation of institutions to channel this citizen participation, stating that communities will be incorporated into decision-making bodies that must be respected by elected authorities (Article 70) (Venezuela, 1999).

The first attempt to establish participatory mechanisms was launched in 2002, with the creation of Local Public Planning Councils (CLPPs). Based on PB initiatives in Brazil, the CLPPs were intended to integrate popular participation into decision-making at the municipal level, but participants complained that powerful local officials resisted citizen involvement. Communal councils (*consejos comunales*), a new mechanism designed to address these issues by providing greater autonomy from local governments, were formally established by a 2006 law that clearly establishes these mechanisms as the centerpiece of citizen participation in Venezuela (Venezuela, 2006). The councils operate at the intersection of civil society and the state. They have the power to establish and manage programs in local social and economic development, infrastructure, health, education, housing, sports, and other areas, and their decisions are not subordinated to the control of municipalities or other levels of government (Venezuela, 2006).

The councils are divided into a Citizens' Assembly, comprised of all members of the represented community, an Executive consisting of elected spokespeople, as well as financial management, community oversight and community engagement units, members of which are also elected by the Assembly. In addition to these organs, councils may elect to form work committees based on local needs (education, housing, electricity, sanitation, etc.) as well as cooperatives and even small businesses. While elected spokespeople drive the meeting agendas, all members of the council (generally 200–400 families in an urban setting) are eligible to participate in setting priorities and making decisions (UBV, 2007). Communal councils are expected to function according to a process known as the 'Cycle of Communal Power,' which includes agenda-setting, decision-making, funding, and implementation phases (see *Ministerio del Poder Popular para las Comunas y los Movimientos Sociales* [MPComunas]). The Assembly is supposed to be actively involved at all stages. Funding is complex: a portion of the national budget is allotted to funding communal council development plans but councils may also seek money from local governments and through fundraising or business activities. With respect to central government funding, proposed projects are evaluated and funding is allocated through a process that involves working groups made up of participants from various communal councils in a given territory working in collaboration with technical experts from agencies such as *Fundacomunal* and the *Consejo Federal de Gobierno* (a body charged with decentralization). Delegates review all project submissions, categorize them into areas (health, infrastructure, etc.) and assign priorities based on most pressing needs according to a defined methodology.[3] In order to ensure popular input at higher levels of government in Venezuela, elected spokespeople are able to participate in regional and national assemblies created for this purpose. The entire system of communal councils is framed as moving forward from the limitations of the past system of representative democracy.

Ecuador

Following the election of President Rafael Correa in 2007, popular participation has been promoted as part of a broader movement dubbed the Citizen's Revolution. The new constitution, adopted in 2008 by referendum, declares that citizen participation in decision-making is a fundamental right and states that citizens, as individuals or as part of a group, may exercise this right through various mechanisms (Ecuador, 2008). In 2010, the government followed up on these constitutional provisions with the adoption of the *Ley Orgánica de Participación Ciudadana* (Law of Citizen Participation) which creates various types of mechanisms through which citizens may exercise these rights at every level of the state. These include sectoral citizen councils corresponding to each government ministry and major policy area to promote dialogue, deliberation, and follow-up; citizen oversight bodies to provide 'social control' and monitoring of policy implementation and public administration; participatory budgeting; and a *silla vacía* (empty seat) on local government bodies for one or more citizen representatives (Ecuador, 2010b). In both the constitutional and legislative contexts, then, participation is presented in a framework of citizenship as agency.

Of all the newly created institutions, those that most closely resemble Venezuela's communal council model are the *asambleas ciudadanas locales* (local citizen assemblies). Citizens can form an assembly on their own initiative and, once established, put forward development plans and local policy initiatives, administer service and infrastructure improvements, promote education with respect to citizen rights, and exercise oversight over decisions made (Ecuador, 2010, Articles 56–60). A founding group of citizens must first elicit interest among fellow citizens, convoke a meeting of those interested in forming an assembly, and elect spokespeople to guide the institution. The process they are expected to follow mirrors that of Venezuelan communal councils: needs assessment (diagnostic); prioritization and budgeting (in collaboration with municipal and regional-level participatory mechanisms convened by the corresponding level of government); the elaboration of a development plan; implementation of selected projects (described as "participatory management"); and an evaluation stage which involves citizen oversight and accountability to the local assemblies involved in the project (see *Consejo de Participación Ciudadana y Control Social* [CPCCS]).[4] The process demonstrates more involvement from elected officials than in Venezuela, and decisions about funding are made in fora that include both citizen and local government representatives. As in Venezuela, the local assemblies can 'feed up' by sending representatives to provincial and regional assemblies and there are seats reserved for local assembly representatives on other participatory bodies, such as the National Planning Council and relevant sectoral councils.

Institutional Design: Control or Empowerment?

Arnstein's (1969) ladder of participation provides a frequently cited scale for evaluating participatory mechanisms according to the nature of the relationship between citizen participants and state actors. The levels range from manipulation (authorities allow members of the public to sit on "rubber-stamp" committees for the purpose of "educating" them) to citizen-control in which citizens have final decision-making power (also see IAP2, 2007; Nabatchi, 2012). The design of Venezuelan communal councils and Ecuadorian citizens' assembly incorporates elements of various levels of participation. We have seen from the discussion above that these mechanisms are designed to provide citizens with decision-making power (at least at the local level) and to allow for inclusion and deliberation among all members of the community. They are presented as fostering a new and fundamentally different (and superior) form of democracy. Yet while autonomous in their ability to debate and decide on local issues, they are also closely integrated into state institutions. The entire system of communal councils is under the oversight of a central government ministry, the MPComunas. Once a council is officially established (they must apply for and receive recognition from the central government, although legally this permission is only a formality if the members have proceeded according to the law), it must hold a meeting to assess community needs and to begin establishing priorities and considering how to obtain resources. Oversight for the system of popular participation in Ecuador is provided by a central government ministry, the *Secretaría Nacional de Gestión de la Política* which is charged with ensuring that central and local government departments fulfill their obligations. The CPCCS, a body made up of citizen and state representatives, serves as the interface between the central government and the various participatory institutions, but here too local assemblies must be recognized by these central institutions. Furthermore, participatory training in both countries is provided by central government agencies, which have developed pedagogy and related training materials. As we shall see, the inherent contradictions in the design of these participatory mechanisms results in a system that demonstrates both empowerment and controlled inclusion.

Data

The discussion presented here is based on a review of the relevant literature, various texts produced by state agencies, and on fieldwork conducted in

Venezuela and Ecuador from September, 2012 to February, 2013. Three participatory mechanisms were selected in each country according to a diverse case study method.[5] In Venezuela, interviews were conducted with participants in communal councils in Caracas (Libertador Municipality, Sucre parish), Guacara (Carabobo State) and Mérida. In Ecuador, cases include local assemblies from the outskirts of Quito (Calderón parish), Montúfar, Carchi province, and Manta, Manabí province. A total of 95 semi-structured interview transcripts conducted with individuals involved in these six participatory mechanisms were analyzed (49 in Venezuela, 46 in Ecuador). Over half of respondents (53% Venezuela, 55% Ecuador) were women and the largest number of respondents in both countries (31% Venezuela, 26% Ecuador) can be identified as precarious/unskilled workers (generally in the informal sector). This category included many informal sector construction workers and domestic workers. Other common categories include education (teachers), tradespeople, retail workers, and homemakers. A strong majority in both countries earned at or below the monthly minimum wage.[6]

Interviews were also conducted with state officials in both countries (26 in Venezuela, 38 in Ecuador). Texts produced by departments and agencies charged with oversight of public participation were also analyzed in order to identify linguistic and rhetorical mechanisms that could shed light on the questions discussed above.[7] A total of 27 texts were analyzed from Venezuela and 18 from Ecuador; these include relevant legislation and administrative documents, promotional material, websites, and training manuals provided to individuals involved in participatory mechanisms.[8]

Strengths and Weaknesses of the "Radical" Participatory Model

This section considers some of the potential strengths and the dangers of "radical" participatory mechanisms in terms of generating citizenship as agency and empowering civil society. It demonstrates that these types of mechanisms both create important opportunities for including marginalized groups in decision-making while simultaneously channeling this participation into state-sanctioned patterns and standards. The results are thus mixed, yet the balance between autonomy and inclusion is in constant danger of tipping toward the latter.

"Radical" Participatory Mechanisms and Agency: Empowerment and Voice

Previous studies have found mixed results with respect to the tangible outcomes of participatory democracy initiatives, as in the contrasting cases of the Bolivian LPP and PB in Porto Alegre (Oxhorn, this volume; also see Avritzer, 2009; Nylen, 2011; Postero, 2006). The present research finds variable results across the six cases studied. In general, however, communities were able to achieve more equitable access to public goods and services than in the past. Residents, local officials, and available documentation link these gains to the participatory mechanisms, and individuals interviewed almost unanimously feel that such benefits are more equitably distributed than in the past. Projects initiated and implemented through these mechanisms by citizens and civil society organization representatives include reconstruction of sewage and water systems (Sucre, Guacara, Manta), housing improvements (Sucre, Guacara, Mérida), electrification (Guacara, Calderón), street paving (Guacara, Calderón), distribution of natural gas (Montúfar), construction of sports and school facilities (Manta, Mérida), and various other types of community improvements. Some participatory mechanisms have established initiatives such as bursaries for local students, after-school programs, and community crime prevention strategies. While there was variation in the processes across the six cases, there are also general patterns. The projects were identified based on a needs assessment conducted by the community and voted on by participants in what most respondents describe as a deliberative and inclusive process. Hundreds of families benefited in most of the cases studied and representatives of local organizations as well as members of families living in the targeted areas were involved.

Participants pointed to a strong link between participatory mechanisms and what they believe to be more equitable outcomes than those provided by local representative institutions.[9] They claim that municipal and regional governments of the past only devoted resources to middle-class and wealthy neighborhoods, and most believe that the communal councils and citizens' assemblies have allowed inhabitants of poorer neighborhoods and rural areas access to public goods they were denied in the past by providing structures through which to exercise agency in local policy. Typical of the responses provided is the following comment by a homemaker from Caracas:

> I remember years ago, every house in this neighborhood was falling apart; our roofs were leaking a lot. Nobody did anything about it, nobody cared, it was up to us to fix it they said. But how could we make expensive repairs with the salaries they want to pay us? Now … every roof on this street has been repaired in the last five years and on top of that, we were able to take charge of this ourselves through our communal council.

Community members insist that citizens have a deeper and fuller knowledge of local needs than politicians in a centralized government and many of the responses linked concrete outcomes, such as improvements to housing and infrastructure, directly to the ability of citizens to engage in decisions that affect their lives, arguing that the people are in the best position to evaluate the fulfillment of their own needs and to monitor the use of funds. As expressed by a respondent from Guacara:

We know and understand our own needs better than any politician or any technician because we live with them every day, so we are the best ones to evaluate them. With these projects our council has implemented, we have all worked together to ensure that everything was done according to how the community wanted it.

Beyond improved distribution of public goods and services, respondents develop more positive perceptions of democracy and a belief in their own capacity to exercise agency, thus supporting a common claim of the participatory theory literature. A strong majority (78%) of respondents are either satisfied or very satisfied with the quality of democracy in Venezuela. This compares with 45% of Venezuelans as a whole.[10] A smaller but still significant 62% of respondents from Ecuador's local citizen assemblies are either satisfied or very satisfied with the quality of democracy in their country, as opposed to 49% of the general population. A strong majority of respondents in Venezuela and Ecuador (79% and 69%) felt they had considerable freedom of choice and control over their lives (compared to 37% and 23% respectively in the national survey).[11] Similarly high numbers of respondents felt they are able to have significant or moderate political influence. When asked whether they believe that they and their neighbors are able to be heard and to influence political decisions, 72% of Venezuelan respondents and 60% of Ecuadorians strongly agree that they are. An open-ended question was asked in order to assess why participants do (or do not) feel that participation has provided them with a heightened sense of political efficacy. Recognition, having a voice and a say in decisions that affect one's life was most frequently cited, with an overwhelming percentage of those who did claim to feel a sense of empowerment providing some variation on this theme (84% in Venezuela, 76% in Ecuador).

Like Bolivia's Territorial Base Organizations (OTBs), the institutional design of the mechanisms in both countries was developed by the state with relatively little input from civil society (although in the Venezuelan case, communal councils were designed based on complaints from civil society actors surrounding previously existing mechanisms). In contrast to the Bolivian case, however, the councils and assemblies themselves are initiated at the local level by members of the community and not by state officials. Any adult citizen can set up a communal council/citizens' assembly and no resources are required to do so. Interested citizens must begin by calling a first meeting. If they are able to achieve quorum (10% of community members aged 15 and older in Venezuela), they can proceed to elect members and spokespeople who will establish the participatory institution.

In the case of OTBs, Oxhorn (this volume) argues that participation was limited to identifying spending priorities and expressing demands. The Venezuelan communal councils studied here do demonstrate a meaningful devolution of decision-making to citizens that moves beyond consultation. There is alignment between citizens and state officials with respect to the powers that these mechanisms have; both groups agree that these are considerable, at least within the scope of local affairs. Legally, politicians and government officials (central or local) are not permitted to intervene in the decision-making process of communal councils and the evidence from these case studies suggests that this is respected. Officials themselves stressed that they cannot control councils. Representatives of state agencies charged with overseeing popular participation unanimously contend that it is the government's intention to devolve decision-making powers to citizens, and that the institutional design of communal councils reflects this goal. Perhaps more surprisingly, most elected officials interviewed also recognize the powers delegated to citizens (although officials representing opposition parties were more likely to express concerns about delegation of power and majority domination).

On the question of devolution of power, the views of state officials and citizen participants were closely aligned in the Venezuelan cases. Almost all participants agree that councils are autonomous vis à vis the state and/or local government, at least with respect to their defined scope of influence. Interviews suggest that communal council participants are generally pleased with the relationship they have with both the state and with the community. Over two-thirds (82%) of participants across the three cases agreed that they have real powers to make decisions about local affairs through their communal council. A total of 74% of participants surveyed said that the relationship between their council and state institutions that support and fund participation is good, while 71% believe they have a good relationship with their community. Most (68%) also believe that their council has sufficient mechanisms in place to ensure a permanent dialogue with the community in order to ensure that as many people as possible are represented when issues are discussed and decisions are made. In all three cases, participants were unanimous in recalling that the initiative to form a communal council originated with community members and not with state representatives. A similar number (69%) agree that the active council members are the ones who participate in the elaboration of community projects; less than 3% claim that state institutions have made final decisions on approved projects. The notion that power has devolved from the hands of a few (usually framed as elite groups) to 'the people' was the most common theme in response to interview questions on this topic, as exemplified by this statement from a participant from Caracas:

> Before, they were all linked, those who held power and made decisions. The national government, the mayor's office here in Caracas, all of them. Different faces, but all from the same elite groups, all representing the same interests. Not anymore, now we participate in decisions that affect our lives.

Ecuadorian participants were somewhat less enthusiastic with respect to autonomy and citizen control of their assemblies, which is likely reflected

in the relatively less positive perceptions they express. Many complained
that while participatory democracy is enshrined in the constitutions and
subsequent legislation, in reality it is not yet being fully implemented.
While autonomous in that central government and local authorities cannot
intervene in the deliberation process of the local assemblies themselves,
they differ from the Venezuelan model in that participants must work with
(and often convince and pressure) local authorities in order to have their
projects implemented and adopted.[12] Typical of the sentiments expressed
are the following statements by a local assembly participant from the
coastal city of Manta, who said that: "We name our own representatives
and the mayor must, according to the law, also name people to act as
broader citizen representatives but he always imposes his own people,
which impedes an authentic process of citizen participation." Local
citizens' assembly participants in San Gabriel expressed similar sentiments,
as exemplified by this comment:

> The problem is that we now have all of these participatory mecha-
> nisms such as the assemblies, which is good, but they aren't taken ser-
> iously by local authorities who still have final decision-making power
> and the resources. So we can all decide on something here but they
> may still say no. What we need is decision-making power, resources
> and the institutionalization of participation so that they can't just
> say no.

Still, of the 46 citizens interviewed, 37 believed that the assemblies allowed
for more inclusiveness than the traditional institutions. A participant in
Manta argued that:

> This (the assembly) is a start. People who never had a voice in any-
> thing—poor people, those without connections—can now at least be
> heard, which is something. The next step is to make sure we are not
> only heard but that they listen, that the powers we are supposed to
> have actually translate into reality, but we now have a place to start.

In Ecuador, most participants are aware that their mechanisms have more
powers on paper than in practice; an anomaly that many of them feel will
be corrected in time.

The research presented here suggests that, as with PB in Porto Alegre,
communal councils and local assemblies have expanded participation to
traditionally disadvantaged groups. State discourse frames inclusiveness as
incorporating the participation of those who previously had no access
points (the poor, the less educated, women, people of African descent,
etc.). The demographic data on participants in these six cases demonstrates
that the vast majority of participants are from 'traditionally excluded'
groups, including high rates of participation from lower socioeconomic
sectors.

In both countries, the participatory mechanisms are also considered to be inclusive by participants themselves, allowing individuals from traditionally unrepresented sectors to have a voice in the local policy process. The vast majority of subjects interviewed emphasized the expanded role of the poor in decision-making under the new institutional framework. Almost all (93%) of individuals interviewed believed that the mechanisms have been successful in terms of engagement of marginalized groups and leverage the experience and abilities of all citizens. Typical of the responses provided, a Caracas participant states:

> It used to be that decisions were made only by a few people in our municipalities. These tended to be people with more money and contacts, projects went to neighborhoods where these people and their friends lived. Now, you don't have to be from one of these families to participate in decisions about your own neighborhood.

Many respondents claimed that the experience of participation made them more confident about engaging in the public sphere. Most point to particular skill sets gained through participation, including experience participating and speaking in public forums. Participants from an assembly in the Calderón parish on the outskirts of Quito stressed the confidence they gained simply by having a forum in which to express themselves. Typical of the comments made, one indigenous participant said:

> Before the assembly, I was too shy to say anything, to express my opinions in front of strangers even though I had strong opinions about what my community needed. Really, I was terrified. But knowing that I have the right to participate, I started to speak and now it is hard to shut me up.

Many in Venezuela point to skills such as developing budgets and proposals, for which communal council members receive training from public agencies. Said one member from Caracas:

> A lot of people around here didn't have much education before. It isn't easy to participate in organizations dominated by people with education when you don't have it; they look down on you. But our communal council received training on things we are required to do ourselves, like develop proposals to put forward to Fundacomunal and manage the money, so we need to make formal budgets.

Still others pointed to increased knowledge and understanding of rights, legislation and government institutions as encouraging them to participate in civil society.

In contrast to Bolivia's OTBs, these "radical" participatory mechanisms have also extended participation to women. In fact, over half of participants

(53%) of the six cases selected were women. Female respondents claimed that representative institutions (national assemblies, municipal councils) are and have always been dominated by men; participatory mechanisms allow women the opportunity to make their voices heard. Also, many women claimed that they feel more comfortable speaking and participating in a group that includes as many or more women than men, indicating that they are more likely to be taken seriously, less likely to have their opinions dismissed, and that participatory mechanisms provide such a forum due to high participation rates among women. Many of the women use the past as a reference point, arguing that they have a far greater role to play in decision-making through these local mechanisms than they did in a recent past dominated by exclusionary institutions. These themes are also reflected in the interviews. Typical of the sentiments expressed is a comment made by a local assembly participant in Quito:

> In the local and neighborhood assemblies, there are a lot of women and many of the leaders are women, the more formal representative institutions are always dominated by men who treat us like children. Maybe because women care more about local issues, but now I participate with my friends and even bring my daughters; we all feel we have a voice in these places because we can speak our minds without being treated like children.

"Radical" Participatory Mechanisms and Cooptation: Controlled Inclusion and Parameters around Civil Society

The "radical" participatory mechanisms in Venezuela and Ecuador are in some ways more ambitious than their liberal equivalents throughout the region. We have seen that they possess a number of characteristics that have the potential to strengthen civil society and to encourage citizenship as agency. Unfortunately, they also manifest many of the weaknesses that have plagued other participatory initiatives, such as Bolivia's OTBs, and these factors introduce the dangers of co-optation and controlled inclusion.

First, while these mechanisms have had considerable success in extending participation to formerly marginalized sectors, their politicized nature means that groups not affiliated with the dominant political agenda may be (or at least feel) excluded. While participants are clearly drawn from the popular sectors (which is the stated intention of the government's participatory democracy agenda), they also tend to be individuals who are inclined to support the government.[13] The majority of participants identify as dedicated *chavistas* or *correistas* and many have participated in other initiatives launched by these governments, such as the various missions that provide social services and educational opportunities in Venezuela. Most individuals interviewed who identified as opposition supporters expressed concern about exclusion based on political allegiance. Exclusion (whether intentional or not) from mechanisms intended to foster inter-action between civil society and the state may force organizations to decide between cooptation and being excluded from the policymaking process. Politicization appears to be a reality that carries the risk of endangering many of the qualities that make these participatory mechanisms successful (such as inclusiveness). Furthermore, as with other initiatives throughout the region, participation among young people remains low. This is reflected in the case studies reported here; across the six cases, over 80% of partici-pants were over the age of 40.

Autonomy is another area of concern. Critics charge that unlike the grassroots neighborhood councils that emerged during the *caracazo* period, the communal councils are state-generated institutions that seek to central-ize and incorporate citizen and civil society participation into sanctioned fora (McCarthy, 2012; García-Guadilla, 2008). The argument that partici-pants are manipulated should not be overstated as it devalues these indi-viduals' capacity to think critically and deprives them of agency. Respondents were very familiar with the powers of communal councils that allow for the devolution of decision-making and extremely vigilant about the possibility of any outside authority intervening in the process. The extent to which the state penetrates and controls communal councils may therefore be exaggerated. Nevertheless, the fact that most participants do support the ruling parties and subscribe to the state's ideology of 21st-century socialism does mean that the framework through which they view politics is highly influenced by the central government. This may limit and shape the range of options they consider, offering the government an indi-rect influence in the affairs of communal councils even when state agents do not directly intervene. This factor may also have an impact on the quality of deliberation, which on the surface appears to be open and pro-ductive but may be constrained by the shared ideological convictions of the majority of participants.

Furthermore, these institutions create certain parameters around parti-cipation, which must be channeled through designated mechanisms to be effective and 'legitimate.' Just as participation under Bolivia's LPP was limited to OTBs, the "radical" participatory programs in Venezuela and Ecuador strongly encourage civil society to engage with these state-sponsored mechanisms in order to play a role in the decision-making process. As Chávez himself stated (a position reproduced in a training manual for communal council participants): "Once elected by the com-munity, the communal council ... becomes the site of participation, articu-lation and integration of the diverse set of community organizations."[14] While the communal councils and local assemblies do have a degree of autonomy (in that state officials cannot intervene in the decision-making process), this limits the scope of organizations through which individuals and groups may effectively engage with the state. It also has the potential to exclude other organizations, including some of these countries' most historically dynamic organizations, including indigenous social movement groups (in the case of Ecuador) and middle-class organizations in Venezuela (García-Guadilla, 2008).

Another important and related consideration is the scope of participation that is deemed relevant and 'available' for public participation. The sphere in which councils can participate is focused on local needs such as improved infrastructure and social development. While these mechanisms do have the power to engage in decisions beyond local infrastructure and public works projects, the cases studied here have not exercised such prerogatives and in any case, their influence can rarely extend beyond the community. Thus far, questions of national importance remain outside the purview of participatory mechanisms. A number of respondents, both supporters and non-supporters, also expressed a broader view about the focus of communal councils on overly practical and technical affairs to the detriment of political matters. These individuals tended to point out that the stated intention of these mechanisms is to provide citizens with both a greater role in everyday decisions that affect their lives and to expand political participation (broadly defined) to 'the people' yet there is consensus that while the former has been achieved, the latter goal lags behind. Many individuals, for example, lamented the inability of citizens to engage in the political arena around matters such as fiscal policy or 'moral' issues such as abortion. A militant from Caracas expressed these sentiments this way:

> Power has certainly been transferred to us when it comes to these things (local projects and services) and that is good because these things affect our daily lives. But participatory democracy—and communal councils are supposed to be the mechanisms through which we exercise this—is about more than that. Some of us worry that people will be satisfied with the achievements we have made and that the councils will just be a way of transferring resources to the people for projects we decide on, but no, we want them to be more; we want to use them to create a new, more equal and democratic society and this means expanding what they do and the issues they deal with to the entire political spectrum.

There is, therefore, the danger that these institutions will become mere instruments for transferring funds to community and civil society groups, a development that downplays the important function of deepening democracy and ultimately weakens the capacity of civil society to engage in high-level issues.

Conclusions and Prospects

The radical democracy model and its related institutions has been either praised as empowering marginalized communities or criticized as an instrument of cooptation. The question is an important one; in countries such as

Venezuela and Ecuador, these institutions have a significant impact on civil society and on citizenship. The reality is more complex than the binary conceptions that are sometimes presented in the literature. These institutions demonstrate elements of both agency and cooptation, which reflects the extremely delicate balance between incorporating civil society into the decision-making process and civil society autonomy; a difficult balance to achieve. This in turn may produce results that both expand yet contain civil society engagement.

These mechanisms provide advantages to strengthen the capacity of civil society (particularly those elements that had long been ignored by traditional liberal representative institutions). These sectors have new opportunities to participate in decisions that affect their lives and the well-being of their communities. In Venezuela and Ecuador, participants themselves demonstrate a strong alignment with a conception premised on active, social, and collective citizenship that places primacy on direct participation in decision-making (at the local level). This can been read as a positive development for both civil society and for the expansion of citizenship as agency. Furthermore, these are spaces where civil society and community have the potential not only to complement each other but to foster the creation of a better 'human situation' by empowering local communities to engage with the state in an institutionalized setting. In order for this to happen, these spaces much encourage inclusiveness, communication, and agency.

However, the design of participatory mechanisms also creates problematic parameters that may weaken civil society (and the communities involved) in the long run. While proponents of participatory democracy in Venezuela and Ecuador claim to be addressing this balance through the creation of participatory mechanisms that remain autonomous from the state, they have been only partially successful. This "radical" active citizenship must be exercised according to certain parameters with respect to both acceptable forms of participation and the mechanisms through which engagement should ideally be exercised. 'Legitimate' civil society is conceived of as being organized into a defined set of participatory institutions and as participating in a collective endeavor. Civil society organizations or political activities that fall outside of the state's participatory 'system' may be framed as illegitimate. In this way, "radical" participatory democracy may encourage participation and inclusion yet demobilize civil society by channeling demands through these approved institutions. Similar to Oxhorn's (this volume) assessment of Bolivia's LPP and its related OTBs, this suggests that Venezuela and Ecuador are attempting to foster citizenship as agency through institutions that generate citizenship as cooptation, or controlled inclusion.

Notes

1 ALBA is an alliance formed between leftist governments generally described as more "radical" by conservative observers such as Castañeda (2006), Corrales

(2006) and Petkoff (2005). They include the administrations of Hugo Chávez (Venezuela), Evo Morales (Bolivia), Rafael Correa (Ecuador), and Daniel Ortega (Nicaragua).

2 For a thorough treatment of the varieties of democratic thought, see David Held, *Models of democracy* (Cambridge, UK; Malden, MA: Polity, 2006).

3 Interviews with two Planning Officials, Corporación de los Andes, Consejo federal de gobierno (Mérida, November 21, 2012) and a Coordinador, Taquilla Unica, Fundacomunal (Mérida, November 13, 2012).

4 Interviews with four "participation specialists", CPCCS (Quito, October 19 and 22, 2012; January 8 and 21, 2013).

5 The diverse case study method seeks to achieve a certain level of variation on a number of important dimensions including regional/cultural differences, ethnic representation, political cleavages, socioeconomic factors, and the urban vs. rural divide (Seawright & Gerring, 2008; Altschuler & Corrales, 2012).

6 $318USD in Ecuador and 2,973 Bs.F in Venezuela. This amounts to about $472USD at the official government exchange rate (which is inaccessible to most Venezuelans) but much less at the market rate.

7 Texts are understood here in a broad sense, as written documents and websites of governments, as well as interviews and meeting transcripts (Fairclough, 2010).

8 In Venezuela, this included texts produced by the Ministry of Popular Power for the Communes and Social Protection (MPComunas), Fundacomunal, the *Consejo Federal de Gobierno, Servicio Autónomo Fondo Nacional de los Consejos Comunales* (SAFONACC), *Escuela Fortalecimiento del Poder Popular, Fondo Intergubernamental para la Descentralización (FIDES), Fundación escuela de gerencia social, Universidad Bolivariana de Venezuela* and departments charged with popular participation in the states of Mérida and Carabobo and the municipalities of Libertador (Caracas) and Mérida. In Ecuador, texts were collected and analyzed from the *Secretaría Nacional de Gestión de la Política, Consejo de participación ciudadana y control social* (CPCCS), Secretaría *Nacional de Planificación y Desarrollo* (SENPLADES) and municipalities of Manta and Montúfar.

9 This information was compiled through interviews with 46 local citizens' assembly participants from the three communal councils.

10 Unless otherwise noted, national numbers in the following section are taken from Latinobarómetro data for 2011, the most recent data available through the online analysis tool at www.latinobarometro.org/latino/LATAnalize.jsp.

11 Latinobarometro 2008 was the last year for which data is available.

12 This information was compiled through interviews with 46 local citizens' assembly participants from the three citizens' assemblies (Canderón, Manta, Montúfar) and with a number of state officials from: Secretaría Nacional de Pueblos, Movimientos Sociales y Participación Ciudadana, Quito, 11 October 2012; Coordinación Nacional de Participación Ciudadana, SENPLADES, Quito, 25 September 2012; Consejo de participación ciudadana y control social (CPCCS), Quito, 19 October 2012; Asociación de municipalidades ecuatorianas, Quito, 4 October 2012; CPCCS, Quito, 22 October, 2012; CPCCS, Guayaquil, 21 February 2013.

13 Of Venezuelan participants, a strong majority (81%, $n = 152$) identified themselves as supporters of the ruling Partido Socialista Unido de Venezuela (PSUV) founded by former president Hugo Chávez (1999–2013). A majority of Ecuadorian respondents (67%, $n = 105$), professed support for the ruling Alianza País party of President Rafael Correa (2007–present).

14 Hugo Chávez, Aló Presidente No 244, 15.

References

Arnstein, Sherry R. 1969. "A Ladder of Citizen Participation," *Journal of the American Institute of Planners*, 35(4), 216–224.

Avritzer, Leonardo. 2009. *Participatory institutions in democratic Brazil*. Washington, DC; Baltimore: Woodrow Wilson Center Press: Johns Hopkins University Press.

Baiocchi, Gianpaolo. 2003. "The Porto Alegre Experiment." In *Deepening democracy: institutional innovations in empowered participatory governance*. London; New York: Verso.

Barber, Benjamin R. 1984. *Strong democracy: participatory politics for a new age*. Berkeley: University of California Press.

Berman, Sheri. 1997. "Civil Society and the Collapse of the Weimar Republic." *World Politics* 49(3).

Booth, John A. & Patricia Bayer Richard. 1998. "Civil Society, Political Capital, and Democratization in Central America." *The Journal of Politics*, 60(3), 780–800.

Cameron, Maxwell, Eric Hershberg & Kenneth Sharpe (Eds.). 2012. *New institutions for participatory democracy in Latin America: voice and consequence*. New York: Palgrave MacMillan.

Castañeda, Jorge. 2006. Latin America's Left Turn. *Foreign Affairs*, May/June.

Castañeda, Jorge & Marco Morales (Eds.). 2008. *Leftovers: tales of the Latin American left*. New York: Routledge.

Chambers, S. & Kopstein, J. 2001. "Bad Civil Society." *Political Theory* 29(6), 837–865.

Cohen, Joshua & Andrew Arato 1992. *Civil society and political theory*. Cambridge, MA: MIT Press.

Cohen, Joshua, Joel Rogers, Erik Olin Wright, & Paul Q. Hirst. 1995. *Associations and democracy*. London; New York: Verso.

Consejo de Participación Ciudadana y Control Social (CPCCS), *Las Asambleas Locales Ciudadanas*. Quito: CPCCS.

Crozier, Michel, & Samuel P. Huntington. 1975. *Crisis of democracy: Report on the governability of democracies to the trilateral commission*. New York: New York University Press.

de Sousa Santos, Boaventura & Leonardo Avritzer. 2005. "Opening up the Canon of Democracy" in *Democratizing democracy: beyond the liberal democratic canon*. London; New York: Verso.

Diamond, Larry. 1992. "Introduction: Civil society and the Struggle for Democracy." In L. Diamond (Ed.). *The democratic revolution: struggles for freedom and democracy in the developing world*. New York: Freedom House.

Diamond, Larry. 1999. *Developing democracy: toward consolidation*. Baltimore: Johns Hopkins University Press.

Dryzek, John S. 1996. "Political Institution and the Dynamics of Democratization." *The American Political Science Review* 90, 475–487.

Ecuador, Republica del. 2010. *Participación Ciudadana*. www.participacionycontrolsocial.gov.ec/web/guest/promocion.

Ecuador, Republica del. 2010b. *Ley Orgánica de Participación Ciudadana*.

Ellner, Steve. 2010. "Hugo Chavez's first decade in office: Breakthroughs and shortcomings." *Latin American Perspectives* 37 (1) (January), 77–96.

Ellner, Steve. 2012. "The Distinguishing Features of Latin America's New Left in

Power: The Chávez, Morales and Correa Governments." *Latin American Perspectives* 38 (1), 96–114.

Foley, M.W. & Edwards, B. 1996. "The paradox of civil society." *Journal of Democracy* 7(3), 38–52.

Fung, Archon. 2007. Democratic theory and political science: A pragmatic method of constructive engagement. *American Political Science Review* 101 (03), 443.

Fung, Archon. 2011. Reinventing Democracy in Latin America. *Perspectives on Politics* 9(4).

García-Guadilla, María Pilar. 2008. "La praxis de los consejos comunales en Venezuela: ¿Poder popular o instancia clientelar?" *Revista Venezolana de Economía y Ciencias Sociales*, 14 (1), 125–151.

Germani, Gino. 1978. *Authoritarianism, fascism and national populism.* New Brunswick, NJ: Transaction Books.

Goldfrank, Benjamin. 2011. *Deepening local democracy in Latin America: participation, decentralization, and the left.* University Park, PA: Pennsylvania State University Press.

Hausmann, Ricardo. 2013. "The legacy of Hugo Chávez: Low Growth, High Inflation, Intimidation." *Guardian.* 25 February.

Held, David. 2006. *Models of democracy.* Stanford: Stanford University Press.

Huntington, Samuel P. 2006. *Political order in changing societies.* New Haven, CT; London: Yale University Press.

IAP2. 2007. *IAP2 Spectrum of Public Participation.* Thornton, CO: International Association for Public Participation.

Kornhauser, William. 1959. *Politics of mass society.* Glencoe, IL: Free Press of Glencoe.

Laserna, Roberto. 2011. "Mire, la democracia boliviana en los hechos." *Latin American Research Review.* 45.

McCarthy, Michael. 2012. "The Possibilities and Limits of Politicized Participation" In Cameron, Hershberg & Sharpe (Eds.). *New institutions for participatory democracy in Latin America: voice and consequence.* New York: Palgrave MacMillan.

Macpherson, C.B. 1977. *Life and times of liberal democracy.* Oxford: Oxford University Press.

Ministerio del Poder Popular para las Comunas y los Movimientos Sociales (MPComunas). *Guía de formulación de proyectos.* Caracas: MPComunas.

Motta, Sara. 2009. "Venezuela: Reinventing Social Democracy from Below?" In Lievesley, Geraldine & Steve Ludlam (Eds.). *Reclaiming Latin America: experiments in radical social democracy.* London; New York: Zed.

Nabatchi, Tina. 2012. *A manager's guide to evaluating citizen participation.* Washington, DC: IMB Center for the Business of Government.

Nylen, William. 2011. "Participatory Institutions in Latin America: The Next Generation of Scholarship." *Comparative Politics* 40 (4), 479–497.

Pateman, Carole. 1974. *Participation and democratic theory.* Cambridge: Cambridge University Press.

Petkoff, Teodoro. 2005. Las dos izquierdas. *Nueva Sociedad* 197.

Piven, Frances Fox, & Richard A. Cloward. 1977. *Poor people's movements: why they succeed, how they fail.* NewYork: Vintage Books.

Ponniah, Thomas, & Jonathan Eastwood. 2011. *The revolution in Venezuela: social and political change under Chávez.* Cambridge, MA: David Rockefeller Center for Latin American Studies.

Postero, Nancy. 2007. *Now we are citizens: indigenous politics in postmulticultural Bolivia*. Stanford, CA: Stanford University Press.

Rodríguez, Francisco. 2008. "An Empty Revolution." *Foreign Affairs* 87(2).

Rueschemeyer, Dietrich, Evelyne Huber Stephens, & John D. Stephens. 1992. *Capitalist development and democracy*. Chicago: University of Chicago Press.

Schumpeter, Joseph. 1950. *Capitalism, socialism, and democracy*. New York: Harper.

Smilde, David, & Daniel Hellinger. 2011. *Venezuela's Bolivarian democracy: participation, politics, and culture under Chávez*. Durham, NC: Duke University Press.

Smith, Graham. 2009. *Democratic innovations: designing institutions for citizen participation*. Theories of Institutional Design. Cambridge, UK; New York: Cambridge University Press.

Universidad Bolivariana de Venezuela (UBV). 2007. *Formación de los consejos comunales*. Caracas: Universidad Bolivariana de Venezuela.

Venezuela, República bolivariana de. 2006. *Ley de los Consejos Comunales*. Available at: http://gp.cnti.ve/site/minpades.gob.ve/view/documentoShow.php?id=24.

Venezuela, República bolivariana de. 2009. *Proyecto de Ley de Reforma de la Ley de los Consejos Comunales*. Available at: www.alcaldiagirardot.gob.ve/consejos-comunales/reforma_ley_consejos.pdf.

Weyland, Kurt. 2003. "Economic Voting Reconsidered: Crisis and Charisma in the Election of Hugo Chávez." *Comparative Political Studies* 36(7), 822–848.

Part IV
Conclusions

13 Towards Civic Community
Conclusions

Gordana Yovanovich and Roberta Rice

There is no doubt that a dialogue has been established between community and civil society in Latin America and the Caribbean. Particularly since the 1980s, communities have served as the basis for the establishment of civil societies, providing them not only with numbers but with traditional wisdom, with a sense of solidarity, and with primordial energy, which have been oriented by civil societies towards goals, supplemented by logistics, and informed and supported by outside organizations. Consequently, various transformations have taken place in the political, social, and cultural outcomes. We have seen national liberation fronts, such as the FSLN or Frente Nacional de Liberación Nacional (Sandinistas) of Nicaragua and the FMLN or Frente Farabundo Martí para la Liberación Nacional of El Salvador, transform themselves into civil society organizations after more than a decade of struggle, while the neo-Zapatistas of Chiapas, Mexico became a civil society organization almost immediately (Eckstein, 1989; McClintock, 1998; Nash, 2001). Indigenous communities have gone through the most noticeable transformation and have achieved the greatest results, but women's groups and racial and other minorities have also benefited from the work of local and global civil societies in Latin America. In general, the normative outlook has been changed, giving more weight to heterogeneity over singularity. This period has shown numerous limitations of traditional patriarchal society, and has worked against these limitations by introducing new ways of seeing the present and the past. Changes have been brought about by coming to accept the idea of collaboration as the modus operandi.

It is difficult to evaluate the changes, and given Latin American history, it is healthy to preserve a dose of skepticism. The period of "NGOization," as Sonia Alvarez (2009) calls it, which has brought so many nongovernmental organizations to Latin America, has been financed mostly by international corporations which are making sure that that there is no "single cultural climate," as Gramsci (1971) would say, which could mobilize the masses. Social forces of the 1960s and 1970s tried to bring about change by organizing a united mass movement but succeeded only to a certain extent. Ironically, the main outcome of the preceding period was that it opened a door for small-scale changes, like the ones discussed in this book.

As the Mexican intellectual, Carlos Monsiváis has argued in *Entrada libre: crónica de la sociedad que se organiza* (1987), external NGOs have had a "free entrance" because state budgets for social and cultural programs have been cut. Society has been left to organize itself, or 'self-organize' as Monsiváis says in Spanish. The subsequent working together of collective memories, newly established governments, free markets, and local and international civil societies has not produced outstanding results, but it has brought more democracy, more peace, and more awareness in the struggle for gaining individual agency.

There is no doubt that different civil societies will have different agendas, and that the new ideology of *difference* is inherently divisive. Nonetheless, community theorists such as Tony Blackshaw (2010), Will Kymlicka (1996), Emitai Etzioni (2004), Michael Taylor (1982), and Piotr Kropotkin (2009) believe in communitarian ideas in which the group is held together by the ideal of a common good. It is also encouraging to read Venezuelan psychology scholar, Maritza Montero's view that in a community members cooperate and show solidarity for the sake of the general good (1998). The cases studied here show that positive attitude has not been lost, and that the desire or the need to engage with fellow humans is alive. As Pablo Ramirez, Maca Suazo and Lisa Bellstedt show in their studies in this volume, the collective memory of survival and good will have not been lost. Hence, one has to trust that local communities will continue to use their popular wisdom in dealing with new situations and to provide shelter and a place of belonging to those who are shaken by global insecurities. The evidence in this volume shows that communities and civil societies are mutually strengthening one another, and that their collaboration has been embraced and analyzed by artists and theorists alike.

The writers studied here, Gabriel García Márquez, Vargas Llosa, Laura Restrepo, and Yxta Maya Murray, together with Nicaraguan composer and singer, Carlos Mejía Godoy and Liberation Theology priest and poet, Ernesto Cardenal, as well as the Cuban group of film directors headed by Alejandro Brugués, show problems of traditional community such as internal rivalry and conflicts, social inequality, and oppression of the individual but they are not concerned with the "crisis of community," the "death of community" (Clements, 2008), "spiritual sickness" (Philips, 2005), or by the problem of "bowling alone" (Putnam, 2000); their communities are alive and on their way to becoming civic communities. The process of *conscientization* and Freire's (1993) educational effort are at work as well. The reader and the spectator are moved emotionally, but rational and civic participation is also required.

It is important to note that while Latin America is struggling to build its rational and civic side, it is necessary to keep a balance between spontaneity and control. In his discussion of a new "participatory paradigm," Dave Clements points out in his article "Faking Civil Society" (2008) that "Whitehall-led missions" in England have led to "coercive participation" (16). He writes that:

We need to rediscover the potential of politics and ideas to transform communities for the better, but this can only be achieved by cultivating a sense of ourselves as robust and truly active citizens able to work together to that end.

(22)

Such a conclusion is echoed by Alastair Donald who also argues against ever greater amounts of regulation. He states that, "In order to build communities successfully, human beings must be seen as central positive actors" (35), putting emphasis on human beings as social agents, not on political and philosophical concepts such as democracy and humanity.

Literature and arts play an important role in keeping human beings as "central positive actors." In his article "Latin American Intellectuals in a Post-Hegemonic Era," George Yúdice shows that since the 1980s and 1990s we have witnessed much talk about the agency of social movements and civil society organizations and "little about the role of intellectuals" (658). In this volume this gap has been addressed, as arguments have been provided as to why literature and arts have a role in the building of civic community: it portrays characters and keeps emphasis on the importance of human actors. In his *Chronicle of a Death Foretold/Crónica de una muerte anunciada*, Gabriel García Márquez does not seek to replace the Hispanic honor system with a more democratic system, nor does he write his novel from the point of view of a political or philosophical position, but approaches it from one significant moment in the life of a young woman which shows the reader that even the most marginalized human beings have the potential to make life more meaningful. The more educated Chicana in Maya Murray's *The Conquest* finds the collective memory passed down to her by her uneducated mother empowering enough to help in the reconstruction of the archive and (official) history. Laura Restrepo's *The Dark Bride/La novia oscura*, similarly shows that even a community of prostitutes, united with workers, can create a period of solidarity and human togetherness, even if it cannot advance the struggle of the proletariat and stand up to large corporations such as the Tropical Oil Company. Similarly, Caroline Hossein's work on the role of informal banks led by entrepreneurial women in the slums of Kingston, Jamaica and Georgetown, Guyana illustrates how in real life marginalized communities can overcome high levels of group division and low levels of interpersonal trust. Nicaraguan peasants, similarly, constitute not only a community which serves as the basis for political development but are a group of human beings who improve their daily lives by playing music and spending their time together in discussion and human exchange, be it through song or preparation of a simple meal. In all of these cases, women played an important role, mainly in the '*toma de la conciencia*' or in the awareness that change is positive and necessary.

A feeling for community also awakens Juan in the film *Juan of the Dead* from his Cuban zombie-like state, because, as Antonio Benitez Rojo (1989) has argued in *The Repeating Island/La isla que se repite*, people on the island live "in one of those ways" and are resilient and almost indifferent to hardship. The "chaos," as Benitez Rojo calls the long life of turbulence and uncertainties on the island, has creative powers, as in the Bible, and maintains individuals and communities alike, always moving because there is no other choice. With their history of difficult experiences and improvisation they also seem to be coping better than those living in societies organized and controlled by reason. Benitez Rojo writes how in Chicago a marginalized person may give in to despair and drugs and die, while a person in Havana goes on, "fucked but happy" (Benitez Rojo, 10). The comparison between the attitudes serves to show that there are qualities acquired throughout history in Latin America and the Caribbean which give reassurance for the survival of communities. The faith-based communities, as in Solentiname, Nicaragua, which have gone through emancipatory processes with new interpretations of the Bible have acquired a new (political) consciousness from inside out and thus have continued in their strong spirit. Neighborhood communities across the continent defined by tradition and culture which values and expects exchange and communication are not in a situation where they are "bowling alone." Their forms of interaction, such as music and sports, are group activities which require involvement and promote improvisation.

As Pascal Lupien shows, their spontaneous communication is now complemented by training provided by civil society and government actors, as in Venezuela and Ecuador, for example, and as a result community members are gaining a consciousness of citizenship. As Lupien states, "they are gaining belief in their own capacity to exercise agency." The nature and aims of civil society organizations are not always trustworthy nor are communities always united and innocent, but in general, associations are undertaking a new practice which is layered and more complex. The complexity of the interaction between different players such as community, civil society, government, and transnational movements, is a new phenomenon which is not entirely vertically structured and as such promises different results. It is positive that indigenous communities have been open to transnational civil society actors and that NGOs have helped in health care, education, gender equality, and community-building. Candace Johnson's article provides a convincing argument that although transnational civil societies can have a neo-liberal flavor, indigenous communities in countries such as Bolivia, Brazil, and Guatemala are benefiting from the marriage or partnership between communities and civil societies.

The relationship between ethnic/racial, religious or artistic communities and the government in Latin American and Caribbean countries is particularly significant. In the Cuban case, the making of the film *Juan of the Dead* involves the Cuban artistic community, international production assistance, and agreement from the Cuban government regardless of the fact that the film is critical of the present political situation in the country. Similarly, local citizens' assemblies in Ecuador, indigenous autonomies in

Bolivia, and communal councils in Venezuela are working together with their respective governments in the promotion of solidarity and citizen involvement in the decision-making process. Bolivia, especially, reflects the powerful synergy between social movements, the governing party, and the state that is a positive model for democratic reform. In such cases, new spaces of citizen engagement are being constructed to enhance governmental performance and improve the quality of life in local communities.

In his seminal work, Robert Putnam (1993) defined a civic community as one that exhibits civic virtues. There are four key features commonly said to be shared by such communities: civic engagement; political equality; solidarity, trust, and tolerance; and civic associations (Putnam, 1993, 86–91). Our contributors have found that civic-mindedness, social solidarity, and the push for positive social change can grow from even the most desperate situations, and from the actions of the most marginalized actors. In fact, as Oxhorn (Chapter 2) notes, the capacity of such disadvantaged groups to organize and mobilize in defense of their collective interests and priorities is what constitutes the basis for a strong civil society. Thus, groups or communities which often have been portrayed in the literature as 'obstacles' to modernization and development, have proven themselves to be at the forefront of democratization efforts. In challenging some of the basic tenets of the literature on community and civil society, our contributors open up the possibility for new and potentially fruitful dialogues on this increasingly important subject.

Community, Civil Society, and the Discipline: A Final Note

Latin American and Caribbean communities and civil societies are undergoing a rapid process of transformation. Instead of pervasive social atomization, political apathy, and hollowed-out democracies, which is the norm in some parts of the world, this region is witnessing an emerging collaboration between community, civil society, and government that is revitalizing democracy. The findings of our contributors suggest that the way in which communities and civil societies work together for the social good is a key factor. Several conclusions can be drawn from this collection of essays. First, there is no set recipe for the emergence of a civic community and a strong and vibrant civil society. Civic attitudes and behaviors can be learned and nurtured from within communities by way of grassroots associations and activists, or from without by way of state-sanctioned channels and international actors. Second, agency matters to the way in which communities and civil society interact. Individual and collective actors made a key difference to most of the outcomes examined here. Finally, our volume has found that communities strengthen civil society when there is an opportunity and space for community members to organize and mobilize and therefore broaden their appeal.

A unique contribution of our work is the space for dialogue it creates between the social sciences and the humanities. Our insights into the community–civil society nexus are derived from diverse methodologies and sources. Collectively, we have analyzed five novels and films and conducted personal interviews in nine countries of the region. Pairing the studies on literature/film with those based on field research methods provides significant added value to our analyses. For instance, Roberta Rice's study of the decolonization and depatriarchalization of the state in contemporary Bolivia is augmented by an understanding of the personal tragedy of the main character in García Márquez's novel, as analyzed by Gordana Yovanovich. If read together, the chapters reveal both the urgent need to reform power structures in the region and the heavy weight of history in preserving the status quo. This collaborative project was conceived in such connection. Scholars seeking a deeper understanding of society need to consider alternative sources of knowledge and new forms of inquiry. In the words of Canada Research Chair in Communication, Culture, and Civil Society, Michael Keren (2015, 15), "[v]iewing empirical research as the only representation of reality bears the danger of taking the political system as defined by those who lead and control it as given, not as an object open to change." The dual purpose of our collection has been to examine the interrelationship between community and civil society while attempting to show how the arts add to our understanding of politics and society.

References

Alvarez, Sonia E. 2009. "Beyond NGO-ization? Reflections from Latin America." *Development and Change*. 52(2), 175–184.

Benítez Rojo, Antonio. 1989. *La isla que se repite: el Caribe y la perspectiva posmoderna*. Hanover, NH: Ediciones del Norte.

Blackshaw, Tony. 2010. *Key concepts in community studies*. London: Sage Publications.

Clements, Dave. 2008. "Faking Civil Society." In D. Clements, A. Donald, M. Earnshaw, & A. Williams (Eds.). *The future of community: reports of a death greatly exaggerated*. London: Pluto Press.

Donald, Alastair. 2008. "The Green Unpleasant Land." In D. Clements, A. Donald, M. Earnshaw, & A. Williams (Eds.). *The future of community: reports of a death greatly exaggerated*. London: Pluto Press.

Eckstein, Susan (Ed.). 1989. *Power and popular protest: Latin American social movements*. Berkeley: University of California Press, 1989.

Etzioni, Amitai. 2004. *The common good*. Cambridge, UK: Polity Press.

Freire, Paolo. 1993. *Pedagogy of the oppressed*. New York: Continuum.

García Márquez, Gabriel. 1981/2009. *Crónica de una muerte anunciada*. Mexico: Random House Mondadori, Debolsillo.

Gramsci, Antonio. 1971. *Selections from the prison notebooks*. Quintin Hoare & Geoffrey Nowell Smith (Eds., Trans.). New York: International Publisher.

Keren, Michael. 2015. *Politics and literature at the turn of the millennium*. Calgary: University of Calgary Press.

Kropotkin, Piotr. 2009. *La selección natural y el apoyo mutuo*. Madrid: Consejo Superior de Investigaciones Científicas.

Lewis, Penny. 2008. "Solving by Brick? The Life and Death of British Communities." In D. Clements, A. Donald, M. Earnshaw, & A. Williams (Eds.). *The future of community: reports of a death greatly exaggerated.* London: Pluto Press.

McClintock, Cynthia. 1998. *Revolutionary movements in Latin America: El Salvador's FMLN and Peru's Shining Path.* Washington, DC: United States Institute of Peace.

Monsiváis, Carlos. 1987. *Crónica de la sociedad que se organiza.* Mexico, DF: Ediciones Era.

Montero, Maritza. 1998. "La Comunidad como objetivo y sujeto de la Acción Social." In Antonio Martín González (Ed.). *Psicología comunitaria: fundamentos y aplicaciones* (211–222). Madrid: Síntesis Editorial.

Murray, Yxta Maya. 2002. *The conquest.* New York: Rayo.

Nash, June C. 2001. *Mayan visions: the quest for autonomy in an age of globalization.* New York: Routledge.

Putnam, Robert D. 1993. *Making democracy work: civic traditions in modern Italy.* Princeton: Princeton University Press.

Putnam, Robert D. 2000. *Bowling alone: the collapse and revival of American community.* New York: Simon & Schuster.

Restrepo, Laura. 1999. *La novia oscura.* Colombia: Editorial Norma.

Taylor, Michael. 1982. *Community, anarchy and liberty.* Cambridge: Cambridge University Press.

Williams, Austin. 2008. "Introduction." In D. Clements, A. Donald, M. Earnshaw, & A. Williams (Eds.). *The future of community: reports of a death greatly exaggerated.* London: Pluto Press.

Williams, Austin. 2008. "The New Urbanism." In D. Clements, A. Donald, M. Earnshaw, & A. Williams (Eds.). *The future of community: reports of a death greatly exaggerated.* London: Pluto Press.

Yúdice, George. 2004. "Latin American Intellectuals in a Post-Hegemonic Era." In A. Del Sarto, A. Ríos, & A. Trigo (Eds.). *The Latin American cultural studies reader.* Durham, NC: Duke University Press.

Contributors

Lisa Bellstedt received a Master of Arts in Latin American and Caribbean Studies from the University of Guelph, Canada. She also completed her undergraduate degree at the University of Guelph, where she decided to take a Spanish elective for fun. She quickly fell in love with the language and with Latin American literature. Her research focuses on the writings of Julio Cortázar and Roberto Bolaño. Lisa has lived abroad in Buenos Aires, Argentina and studied abroad in Antigua, Guatemala. She currently resides in Toronto.

Patrick X. Horrigan received a Master of Arts in Latin American and Caribbean Studies from the University of Guelph, Canada. His research focuses on various aspects of music, film, and literature and their relation to structures of community and identity. He has a background in performance and composition, studying the connection between audiences and performers, politics within music, the influences of supportive structures and institutions, and the impact of music within regional, national, and international communities. He is actively pursuing a career in performance and studies in ethnomusicology as a means to foster awareness towards on-going international conflicts, encouraging individual and collective action.

Caroline Shenaz Hossein received a Ph.D. in Political Science and Gender from the University of Toronto; a MPA from Cornell University; a LL.B from the University of Kent at Canterbury, U.K.; and a B.A. from Saint Mary's University, Halifax. She is Assistant Professor of Business and Society in the Department of Social Science at York University, Toronto. Dr. Hossein's research examines the disbursement of financial resources to racially marginalized communities. Previously, she was a U.S. Fulbright Fellow at the Caribbean Policy and Research Institute and the University of the West Indies-Mona in Jamaica. In addition to her academic work, she has more than a decade of experience as an economic development practitioner in global non-profits, including managing a community bank in Niger.

Candace Johnson received a Ph.D. and a Master's in Political Science from Dalhousie University. She is Associate Professor of Political Science at the University of Guelph, Canada. She is the author of *Maternal Transition:*

A North–South Politics of Pregnancy and Childbirth (Routledge, 2014) and *Care, Entitlement and Citizenship* (University of Toronto Press, 2002) and the recipient of the 2009 Jill Vickers Prize, awarded by the Canadian Political Science Association for her work on Gender and Politics. Her current research projects include an examination of the ways in which women's organizations in Latin America use international human rights documents to pressure their governments for change, especially concerning reproductive rights and maternal health.

Pascal Lupien is Adjunct Professor of Latin American and Caribbean Studies at the University of Guelph, Canada, from where he received a Ph.D. in Political Science and a Master's in Latin American and Caribbean Studies. His doctoral research considers the factors that enhance or diminish the capacity of participatory mechanisms in Latin America to produce positive outcomes. Lupien's research has appeared in peer-reviewed journals such as *Political Science Quarterly*; *Citizenship Studies*; *Democratization*; *Latin American Perspectives*; and *Espacio Abierto*.

Miharu M. Miyasaka received her Ph.D. in Hispanic Studies from The University of Western Ontario, Canada and her B.A. in History of Art from the University of Havana, Cuba. She is an Independent Scholar who has worked as a film programmer and producer at ICAIC, and who is currently working with the Japanese Cuban community *Cubano Nikkei*. She has published articles in the following: *Scope: An Online Journal of Film & TV Studies*; *L'indépendance de l'Amérique andine et l'Europe (1767–1840)*; *La Gaceta de Cuba*; *Revista Anales del Caribe*; *La Jiribilla*; and *Los zombis en el mundo iberoamericano*.

Olga Nedvyga received her M.A. from Kyiv National Linguistic University and is currently a doctoral student in the Department of Spanish and Portuguese at the University of Toronto. In the Ukraine she published two essays on Roberto Bolaño. Her ongoing Ph.D. dissertation deals with Hispanic Caribbean literatures of the late 19th and early 20th centuries. In particular, she studies the ways in which rhetorical tropes of drugs and pharmaceuticals participated in the shaping of emancipatory and nation-building discourses in the region.

Philip Oxhorn received his Ph.D. in Political Science from Harvard University. He is Professor of Political Science and the Founding Director of the Institute for the Study of International Development at McGill University, Canada. He is also the Editor-in-Chief of the *Latin American Research Review*. His research interests include theories of civil society, democracy, and citizenship in Latin America. He is the author of numerous books and articles, including: *Sustaining Civil Society: Economic Change, Democracy and the Social Construction of Citizenship in Latin America* (Pennsylvania State University Press, 2011) and *Organizing Civil Society: The Popular Sectors and the Struggle for Democracy in Chile* (Pennsylvania State University Press, 1995).

Mery Perez is a Ph.D. student in the Rural Studies Program, School of Environmental Design and Rural Development at the University of Guelph, Canada. Funded by the University of Guelph during her M.A. program in Latin American and Caribbean Studies, most of her research was conducted in Nicaragua. Her interviews with Nicaraguan peasants, Nicaraguan poet and past minister of culture, Ernesto Cardenal and renowned Nicaraguan musician, Carlos Mejía Godoy inform her work here and her Ph.D. thesis.

Pablo Ramirez received his Ph.D. in American Culture from the University of Michigan and is presently an associate professor in the School of English and Theatre Studies at the University of Guelph, Canada. He has published articles in *ESQ: A Journal of the American Renaissance*; *Arizona Quarterly: A Journal of American Literature, Culture and Theory*; *the Canadian Review of American Studies*; and *Aztlán: A Journal of Chicano Studies*.

Roberta Rice received her Ph.D. in Political Science from the University of New Mexico. She holds both a Bachelor's and a Master's in Environmental Studies from York University, Canada. She is Assistant Professor of Indigenous Politics in the Department of Political Science at the University of Calgary, Canada. Her book *The New Politics of Protest: Indigenous Mobilization in Latin America's Neoliberal Era* (Tucson: University of Arizona Press, 2012) was nominated for the 2014 Comparative Politics prize by the Canadian Political Science Association. Her work has appeared in the *Canadian Journal of Latin American and Caribbean Studies*; *Latin America Research Review*; *Comparative Political Studies*; and *Party Politics*. She is currently working on a comparative project on indigenous rights and representation in Canada and Latin America funded by the Social Sciences and Humanities Research Council of Canada.

Maca Suazo is a Canadian visual artist born in Chile. She received her Master of Arts in Latin American and Caribbean Studies from the University of Guelph, Canada. She teaches Spanish language and culture at Conestoga College and works as a professional painter, exploring literature and poetry through color and form.

Gordana Yovanovich received her Ph.D. in Latin American Literature from the University of Toronto and is a professor and graduate coordinator for the Latin American and Caribbean Studies Program at the University of Guelph. She is the author of *Julio Cortázar's Character Mosaic* (University of Toronto Press, 1991) and *Play and the Picaresque* (University of Toronto Press, 1999) and editor of *The New World Order: Corporate Agenda and Parallel Reality* (McGill Queen's University Press, 2003) and *Latin American Identities After 1980* (Wilfrid Laurier University Press, 2010). She has published articles in scholarly journals such as *Hispanic Review*; *Hispanófila*; *Revista Canadiense de Estudios Hispánicos*; *Studies in Short Fiction*; and *La Libellula*.

Index

Page numbers in **bold** denote figures.

Taylor & Francis eBooks

Helping you to choose the right eBooks for your Library

Add Routledge titles to your library's digital collection today. Taylor and Francis ebooks contains over 50,000 titles in the Humanities, Social Sciences, Behavioural Sciences, Built Environment and Law.

Choose from a range of subject packages or create your own!

Benefits for you

» Free MARC records
» COUNTER-compliant usage statistics
» Flexible purchase and pricing options
» All titles DRM-free.

REQUEST YOUR FREE INSTITUTIONAL TRIAL TODAY

Free Trials Available
We offer free trials to qualifying academic, corporate and government customers.

Benefits for your user

» Off-site, anytime access via Athens or referring URL
» Print or copy pages or chapters
» Full content search
» Bookmark, highlight and annotate text
» Access to thousands of pages of quality research at the click of a button.

eCollections – Choose from over 30 subject eCollections, including:

Archaeology	Language Learning
Architecture	Law
Asian Studies	Literature
Business & Management	Media & Communication
Classical Studies	Middle East Studies
Construction	Music
Creative & Media Arts	Philosophy
Criminology & Criminal Justice	Planning
Economics	Politics
Education	Psychology & Mental Health
Energy	Religion
Engineering	Security
English Language & Linguistics	Social Work
Environment & Sustainability	Sociology
Geography	Sport
Health Studies	Theatre & Performance
History	Tourism, Hospitality & Events

For more information, pricing enquiries or to order a free trial, please contact your local sales team:
www.tandfebooks.com/page/sales